KABBALISTIC ASTROLOGY

KABBALISTIC ASTROLOGY

THE SACRED TRADITION OF THE HEBREW SAGES

RABBI JOEL C. DOBIN, D.D.

Inner Traditions International
Rochester, Vermont

Inner Traditions International
One Park Street
Rochester, Vermont 05767
www.InnerTraditions.com

Library of Congress Cataloging-in-Publication Data

Dobin, Joel C., 1926–
    [To rule both day and night]
    Kabbalistic astrology : the sacred tradition of the Hebrew sages / by Joel C. Dobin.
        p.   cm.
    Previously published under titles: To rule both day and night; The astrological secrets of the Hebrew sages.
    ISBN 0-89281-763-1 (alk. paper)
    1. Jewish astrology.   2. Bible and astrology.   I. Title.
BF1714.J4D6 1999
133.5'946—dc21   99-18547
                                                                                    CIP

Printed and bound in the United States by Capital City Press

10 9 8 7 6 5 4 3 2

CONTENTS

PREFACE TO THE SECOND EDITION

I recently visited my daughter in North Carolina. She lives in a co-housing community; her next-door neighbor's car bore a bumper sticker that read Be Practical—Expect Miracles.

How times have changed since I wrote the original introduction to this book in the seventies. Alternative medicine is now an accepted practice; acupuncture is being used as a therapy by "real" doctors; science fiction has become an accepted literary genre for study in our universities; paranormal abilities are also being seriously studied; and the existence of planets orbiting other stars has become a proven reality. Theaters show movies depicting the demise of life on Earth caused by asteroid collisions, and the scientific world is taking such scenarios seriously.

These ideas—which had to fight for recognition and news space when this book was first published—are now accepted at face value, and we have now moved on to other, more intriguing areas of speculation. Angels have made their way onto prime-time television and into the serious contemplation not only of religious mystics but also into the minds and belief systems of the average American. All of these emergent phenomena give evidence of the search for meaning outside the normal evidences of the senses and logic. For more and more thinking, feeling, relating, and loving people the words of Hamlet become more and more germane: "There are more things in heaven and earth, Horatio, than are dreamed of in your philosophy."

The study of Kabbalah is presently enjoying a surge of interest, and many are finding within it the path to inner peace, wisdom, contemplation, and unity. Because Kabbalah is a discipline that has developed over the course of more than 2000 years, there are found within it myriad paths to travel to become one with one's fellow human beings, with one's universe, and with one's God. One of the principal paths toward an understanding of divine wholeness—a path that places the person at the center of a totally perceived universal process—is Astrology, and the first book of mysticism compiled in ancient times from sources still more ancient is the Sefer Yetzirah, which links the Divine Creative Process, the Creation, and humanity through a deep understanding of Astrology.

I have prepared some chapters of this ancient text as an appendix to this new edition, to introduce the reader, briefly, to the concepts of creation, communication, contemplation, and connection, in the hope that such an introduction will be rewarding to your spiritual process.

PART I: INTRODUCTION

1

IN SEARCH OF VALIDITY

The universe of Astrology is in a state of excited confusion. The excitement stems from the immense growth of popularity that Astrology has enjoyed in recent decades. There have been more public lectures on Astrology, more enthusiastically received by the average person than have ever been given for the public's consumption, education, entertainment, and titillation. For millions Astrology has become respectable, acceptable, and a legitimate source of guidance for their lives.

The validity of Astrology is based on the philosophy which first turned man's eye towards the Heavens in search of his earthly directions. The basic philosophy of the astrologer is religious, regardless of the religious direction from which he seeks the truth. The basic philosophical thrust of Astrology derives from the conviction that the human being, God, and the universe are in some way a unity; that man and universe, if you will, both swim in the sea of space-time whose substrate is God. This is not a pantheistic doctrine. I do not maintain that God is the sum total of the universe and all it contains. Rather, God is the Creator of all: man, universe, space, and time; that God is greater than all combined, is responsible

3

for all combined, has a direction in the Divine Mind for all combined, and is responsive to all combined. That all-in-existence is subject to God's will is an essential beginning for the astrologer: "One Creator, One Creation" should be the mantra for every astrologer! For, combining this latest statement with its forerunner—that man, God, and universe are an essential unity—allows the astrologer to seek in the Heavens for the evidence of God's will for mankind, which will help the individual person as well as the community realize and act on the most basic religious statement: "Make Thy will, my will."

I write this book to inform all those who read it that although Astrology proved itself tragically truthful in my own life, at the same time it became the force that turned me back to my God, and revealed to me His order and His beauty, and His place for me in the Divine balance that links God, man, and universe into One Balanced Process which never ends in this life or on other planes of awareness of life. This disciplined awareness of harmony and balance has made me a better human being and therefore a better Rabbi in serving my congregants with more sensitivity and more awareness of their needs and of their strengths. Therefore, I write this book as witness to God's work in this universe, to confirm man's ability to be in harmony with God and with His work, to testify to the truth that Astrology helps man to understand God's will and to put himself in balance with Divine and universal forces, thus enriching his life and experience.

I write as a Rabbi. I want my fellow Jews to abandon their knee-jerk opposition to all phenomena which have not been approved by meter readings and test-tube reactions in sterile laboratories. Life is not lived in sterile laboratories, love cannot be meter-measured, nor can compassion turn litmus solutions blue or red. I want my coreligionists to reread their Bible in the light of the information in this book, so that they will realize that Astrology was so much part of Jewish life and experience and so well respected in our tradition and law that the abandonment of Astrology to follow the chimera of scientific linearality was one of the greatest religious tragedies that ever befell our people. For in so doing, we abandoned as well the mystical realities of our faith, our abilities to balance our lives and attain Unity, and we have created of our synagogues and temples arenas of contention for power and concern for financial sufficiency. When was the last time you heard God mentioned at a board meeting, except as a deleted expletive?

I write as an astrologer, seeking to turn all those whose various faiths have seemed to abandon them back to *their own faith*. Perhaps the Grand Design into which each person fits will become more clear to you, through reading this book, and through rereading the works of your own religious heritage. This is not a book of polemics, nor is it a book of apologetics. I do not seek converts to Judaism, such is not our way. I *do* seek converts to God; I *do* seek to help Christians attain a new awareness of the value of their faith to help them turn back to their churches in renewed faith and balanced soul.

I also write for my fellow astrologers. I hope that they may find ancient insights in this book which will aid them in their profession of helping man to attain balance: in this universe, in himself, and in God. This book will show astrologers of all faiths some of the ancient sources of their common astrological practices, and make them more secure in their use of some of those astrological techniques which they may use, but may secretly question, wondering why they work as well as they do!

Finally, I write as a person with personal goals. Can I communicate my concerns to my fellow? Can I convince my fellow of the truths I hold? Did I write a valid and interesting book? Will my life be changed by this effort? I am not so old that I no longer seek adventure: the search for truth, its exposition to others, the community one finds in communication ... these comprise the highest adventure of all.

So I invite you to read on; and hope you will enjoy the experience, and have the experience work for your happiness and fulfillment. Join me!

2

BIBLE, MIDRASH, TALMUD

The history of the Jewish people has been the history of a search. The search has taken us over the largest span of space and time experienced by any people existing as a viable and recognizable religious or social group. The search began with Abraham in the delta of the Tigris-Euphrates river system over four thousand years ago. The search has carried us throughout the continents of the world, but has always had at its geographical center a land known variously in different times as Canaan, Israel, Judah, Judea, and Palestine—a land now known by its ancient name once again, Israel. The search still continues in all lands in which there are Jewish communities. Simply defined, the search is for God, for the truth of His operating in the universe, and for man's relationship to God and to the creative process God initiated.

THE BIBLE

The Bible is but one part of the story of that search. It is the oldest part, to be sure, but its canonization in the year 70 C.E. (common era) closed its era in human time as a description of the search. Other documents have had a crucial part in the continuing story.

It is necessary at this time to define my terminology. When I speak of the Bible, I refer to what the Western world generally knows as the Old Testament. I cannot use this term, however, since as a

Rabbi I do not recognize the validity for my religious community of a New Testament. To me, the Bible begins with Genesis and ends with Chronicles II. As you can see, even the order of books is different. Therefore, when I use the word Bible, I mean those books which my non-Jewish readers would call the Old Testament.

I do not believe that it is necessary to enumerate the narrative history of the Bible. It is sufficient to say that it represents the story of a unique search for humanity's relationship to a Creator God. A surface reading of the Bible will prove beyond any doubt that the search was an on-going, maturing, and exciting process. The God of Abraham was not perceived as being identical to the God of Isaac, nor did Jacob perceive his God as identical to the God of either patriarch; similarly God made Divinity manifest differently to each of the succeeding generations. The God of Joseph and the God of Moses and the God of Joshua were each perceived differently in each generation. We see the growth of the search as we read the continuing relationships of individual people to the God each sought. Yet, each individual's search, and each generation's search, was rooted in the understandings that went before. The insight of Moses was more complex and mature than that of Abraham, and the insight of Isaiah was as far beyond that of Moses as Moses' was beyond Abraham's. But all were linked since each experience of God was built on the experience previously gained. The coming generation knew that God could be reached because the previous generation had reached—and touched. And through it all, the truths of Astrology run as an ever-present awareness.

THE MIDRASH

The Midrash is a unique collection of moral and ethical commentaries on the Bible, dating from the sixth century B.C.E. (before common era). The method of commenting was in itself unique. The commentator would follow one of two methods. With the first method after quoting the verse of the Bible on which he would like to comment, he might offer a parable describing man's activities on earth and offering a comparison between those activities, and the manner in which God would act.

For example, in Genesis 38:1 we read of Judah's leaving his brethren, searching out a Canaanite friend, meeting there a young woman by whom he has two sons, Er and Onan, who bring him to grief in later years, with reference to the story of Tamar, Judah's daughter-in-law. And yet, despite Judah's personal tragedy, he is promised that "the sceptre shall never depart" from his progeny!

How to explain this, in the light of his history? This introductory verse becomes the focus of a parable told in the Midrash Ha-Gadol:

A man of flesh and blood, has a vessel (container); as long as the vessel is whole, he is happy with it. If it is broken, he no longer desires it. But not so the Holy One, Blessed Be He! As long as the vessel is whole, He does not wish to see it; broken, He desires it! And what is the favorite vessel of the Holy One, Blessed Be He? The heart of man! If the Holy One, Blessed Be He, sees a proud heart, He does not wish it; as it is said: *Everyone that is proud in heart is an abomination to the Lord.* [Prov. 16:5] If He sees a broken heart, He says: "This is Mine!" as it is said: *The Lord is nigh unto them that are of a broken heart.* [Ps. 34:18]

Thus, the Midrash interprets Judah's personal tragedy as a lesson in humility, to humble his proud heart, so that he would be worthy of fathering the decendants of his line—King David and the coming Messiah. Please note that the quotations from Psalms directly bear on the lesson being taught in the Midrash.

Using the second method, he might quote a different biblical verse which seems to have nothing to do with the biblical verse in question. But, through an interpretation of the second verse which does not use a parable, but rather some other explanation or allegory, light is shed on the original verse in question. For example, what is the meaning of the first words in the Bible, "In the beginning. . ."? We have the following comment in the Midrash Rabbah on Genesis 9:2:

In the beginning, God created the Heavens and the Earth. Rabbi Tanhuma opened his discussion, thusly: *He has made everything beautiful in its time. . . .* [Eccles. 3:11] In its due time was the word created: the world was not fit to be created before then. Rabbi Abahu said: "From this we learn that the Holy One, Blessed Be He, kept creating worlds and destroying them, creating worlds and destroying them, until He created these worlds of heavens and earth. Then He said: 'These please Me; those did not please Me!'"

THE TALMUD

The Talmud is a collection of writings constituting Jewish civil and religious law. It, too, began before the sixth century B.C.E., and its development proliferated into two vast bodies of legal knowledge: the Mishnah and Gemara. Both began in Judea, but one had its completion in Jerusalem, the other in Babylonia.

The Talmud began as a commentary on the Bible. This body of oral legal traditions, called the *Mishnah*, having its origins in the scribes who accompanied Ezra to rebuild the Temple in 517 B.C.E., was finally collated and written down by Rabbi Jehudah Ha-Nasi, Rabbi Judah the Prince, in approximately 185 C.E. Organized into six sections, this work was a compilation of the laws dialectically decided on by the Sanhedrin during its years as the highest court in the land.

The development of the legal tradition in Judaism by no means ended with the work of Judah the Prince in 185. The oral exposition of Jewish law continued; this time as decisions based on the Mishnah compiled by Judah. This further dialectical development continued in two different streams in two different areas of the world. One development took place in Judea under Roman rule, continuing until the dissolution of the Jewish community as a viable entity in the land. With the dispersion of the Jewish people throughout the Roman Empire in the year 370 C.E., the legal development in the land of our fathers came to an end. This codification became known as the *Jerusalem Gemara*, the word *Gemara* meaning "completion."

The other dialectical development took place in Babylonia, and continued until the Jewish community of Babylonia was no longer viable. These discussion and determinations of Jewish law, based on discussions inspired by the very same Mishnah of Rabbi Judah, continued until its completion in 530 C.E. It became known as the *Babylonian Gemara*. The Talmud, as traditionally published, is therefore two similar and yet different sets of volumes, known either as the *Talmud Bavli* (the Babylonian Talmud) or the *Talmud Jerushalmi* (the Jerusalem Talmud). The latter is much the smaller of the two, and the Talmud Bavli is the work to which one usually refers when making general statements about the Talmud.

There are two reasons for the preeminence of the Babylonian over the Jerusalem Talmud. First, the Babylonian Talmud is approximately nine times longer than the Jerusalem Talmud. Therefore, it covers a great deal more law and custom, especially since its development continued 160 years beyond that of the Jerusalem Talmud. Secondly, life in Babylonia was in essence more akin to life as it has developed in the centuries since the Dispersion of 370 C.E. After 370 C.E. and until 1948, Jewish life has been lived outside our own land and within non-Jewish political and religious systems, similar to the conditions of Jewish life in Babylonia from 587 B.C.E. to 530 C.E. Thus, the Diaspora legal system as developed in Babylonia and reflected in the decisions recorded in the Babylonian Talmud was more applicable to the needs of Diaspora Judaism than the legal system of the Jerusalem Talmud, which was more concerned with the applications and development of Jewish law as it referred to life in our own land.

The literary form of both the Talmud Bavli and the Talmud Jerushalmi is identical. Each Talmud is organized into six "orders," that is, main divisions, or books. Each "order" is then subdivided into a number of "tractates," or volumes. Each "tractate" is then divided into chapters, and each chapter is divided into sections. Each of these sections begins with the quotation of the relevant Mishnah, the section from the compilation of Rabbi Judah the Prince, and then the Gemara discussion of that particular issue is appended to it. In other words, on looking at a page of either Talmud, you will see the Mishnah quotation of the section, followed by the Gemara discussion of the issue.

The six divisions of the Mishnah from which the Gemara and therefore the Talmud take their organization are delineated as follows:

1. *Zera'im*, "Seeds": This order deals with agricultural law. It also deals with prayer since prayer is a recognition of God's goodness and providence without which the agricultural process is futile.
2. *Mo'ed*, "Seasons": This order deals with the religious festivals of the year.
3. *Nashim*, "Women": This order deals with laws of marriage and divorce, family purity, and other family matters.
4. *Nezikin*, "Damages": This order deals with civil and criminal law.
5. *Kodashim*, "Holy Things": This order deals with the Temple cult, sacrifices, and Kashrut (that which is or is not Kosher).
6. *Toharot*, "Purifications": This order deals with laws of ritual purity and cleanliness.

However, the development of both Jewish law and Jewish moral and ethical teachings did not disappear with the end of the Judean community in 370 c.e. nor with the end of the Babylonian community in 530 c.e. This development continued through the centuries and in every land of the Diaspora, and continues to this very day. Why, then, this long exposition of the Bible, Talmud, and Midrash?

Because Jewish life has been a continuum for over four thousand years, we have a human community as well as a community of writings which reflect both man's reaching for God and man's attempt to solidify the insights of the positive results of this reaching into a body of law. The basic law of Judaism is the Bible, Pentateuch (Torah), Prophets (Nevi'im), and Hagiogrypha (K'tuvim). All consequent development of Jewish law and ethics is derived from the interpretation of that Bible. Thus, the Midrash, the Mishnah, and the Gemara are *not* independent and unique developments of disconnected individuals having nothing to do with each other or with the past. The Midrash, the Mishnah, and the Gemara are all connected to the Bible because they are commentaries on the Bible! They are the logical and spiritual continuations of the search for the reality of God in man's life as initiated in the Bible; and the legal developments of that search are the attempts to provide the insights of the Divine Touch to the entire community of Israel. In Judaism, religious law is an attempt to solidify the Divine insight of the prophet in a manner that will make that insight available to the lowliest of men as well as to the highest of men. Thus, the entire legal tradition of the Jewish people is an attempt to create the means whereby the entire society can reach and touch God by means of a religious discipline. The legal tradition of the Jewish people is an attempt to fulfill the wish of Moses: "... would that all the Lord's people were prophets, that the Lord would put His spirit upon them!" [Num. 11:29]

In Jewish life, this entire process of legal development and of moral instruction is subsumed under the Hebrew word *Halachah*, "the way to go." As you can see, Halachah, the Way, is a blueprint for living, but it is a very unique blueprint. Halachah is not an iron-bound set of fiat laws, but rather it is a blueprint for the progressive development of a way of life, and from this progressive development the law for each generation is deduced. Thus, Abraham, Isaac, and Jacob could establish temporary altars for worship wherever their journeys lead them. Moses could have built a traveling Tabernacle toward which all worship is directed. Solomon could build a Temple in Jerusalem which would freeze the center of worship in space. The prophets could substitute "the words of our lips" for the sacrificial cult, and thereby provide for the continuation of the faith in Exile. Ezra and Nehemiah could lead the Return and the rebuilding of the Temple, and provide the beginnings of the institution of the Rabbinate in their establishment of the Scribes. And the Rabbis in 70 C.E. could substitute the table in each Jewish home for the destroyed Altar in the devastated Temple. With each change in Jewish law, a degree of freedom to interpret the workings of Halachah is established, but the Halachah, the Direction and the Way, remains a constant search for the unity of God, man, and universe.

If this is a true picture of the development of Jewish life and law, then we can see that, with the passage of time, life and the legal basis for judging the worth of life proliferates. Thus, the Mishnah is more complex than the Bible, and the Gemara is many times more complex and all-embracing than the Mishnah. And this progressive proliferation did not end in the sixth century. Jewish life continues to this very day, and the interpretation of Halachah is as vigorously pursued today as it was then.

How does all this relate to Astrology? If Astrology is indeed an integral part of the Jewish experience, if Astrology has any validity in the life of the Jewish community, if there is any validity within the history of the Jews and of Judaism for the truths of the Divine Science, then Astrology, too, must partake of the developmental nature of the Halachah. In other words, if Astrology has been a part of the normative Jewish experience and the religious search for unity, then we should find a development within the history of Jewish experience for Astrology, parallel to the development of Jewish law. Thus, we should find that Astrology has a development parallel to the Halachah. If Astrology, however, is only a unique point-in-time aberration in Jewish life, then we should find only sparse mention of it in some of the earliest documents of Jewish life after which it should not appear again in any positive form. Therefore, the religious historian will look for the evidences of Astrology throughout Jewish tradition. If the historian finds that the influence of Astrology grows with the growing maturity of Jewish law (Halachah) and ethics (as viewed in the Aggada), then he or she will conclude that Astrology is indeed a growing and effective agent in the life of our people. Arguing from the viewpoint of a religious historian, I shall show in the following chapters that the evidence of this progressive development of Astrology in both Halachah and Aggada (Midrash) is specific, multitudinous, and overwhelming. If I were to argue from my own viewpoint as Rabbi and astrologer, I would have to add that Astrology has an integrating and wholesome effect on the lives of humanity to this very day. This latter personal viewpoint is the actual motivating factor in outlining the arguments of this entire book, as I have already stated in my first chapters.

Thus far, I have said very little about the third body of Jewish literature within the purview of this book—the Midrash. If we can say that the Talmud feeds the material needs of Jewish life, then the Midrash like music, poetry, and the arts feeds its soul. If the Talmud points to the Way, then the Midrash points to the Why. If the Talmud delineates the manner in which the daily search for unity is to be manifested, then the Midrash delineates the beauty that lies within the attainment of the goal. For people have souls, as well as bodies, and the soul's speech is often more vitally important than the body's well-being. In fact, if the soul has no goal, the body has no life. Therefore, if Astrology does indeed speak to the soul of the Jew as well as to the body, then we must also discover Astrology's place in the Midrash. Once again, the evidence is specific, multitudinous, and overwhelming.

And now, having expounded on the importance of Bible, Midrash, and Talmud in the history of our people, we could very easily ask, so what? What if Astrology proves to be an increasingly important element in these documents of Jewish life? Who can say that these documents themselves have any validity in modern times? Why should non-Jews be concerned with them, or with the advancing status of Astrology within them?

The answers cannot be found within the documents, and not even within the nature of the people who produced the documents. The answers can be found in the development of an integrating concept of man and God in the universe. If, of course, the reader wishes to deny the validity of such a concept, either by denying the existence of God or by denying a concept of order in the universe, or by denying the ability of man to relate to either God or universe, then all discussion is futile and must cease. We would not even be operating in the same universe of conception. However, if the reader has a mind open to the reasoned analyses of others, then our discussion may continue.

The only experience man has in this life is the experience of his senses, which he shares with all other living creatures; everything alive in some way senses its environment and relates to it. Man also shares another area of living with other animals, the area of perception. Both man and animals are endowed with an innate group of reactions to stimuli which enable them to overcome the dangers of their environments, and to profit from its amenities. Both man and most animals also have in common the possession of short-term memory. This enables both man and animal to learn from immediate, life experiences, to avoid dangers experienced before, and to anticipate pleasures known from the immediate past. However, there is one area of activity which man shares with nothing else on earth of which we are presently aware. That activity is the recording of memory, the maintaining of chronicles, the ability to transfer short-term memory to long-term memory and thus to learn from the passage of time beyond the immediacy of one lifetime. In other words, man is the only living creature to experience history, for man's ability to record memory, and to transmit memory from generation to generation, creates history.

It is this ability to record memory and create history which has enabled man to develop the concept of growth toward goals. Without history there can be no goals. If one generation cannot pass its experience to another, there can be no progress. As Santayana said: "He who refuses to learn from history is doomed to repeat it." If there is no memory or no way to pass that memory to a new generation then there is no history. In such a case, we can never talk in terms of the experience of 100 years of history; we would be dealing with one year of experience, repeated 100 times!

But, as soon as man developed the ability to pass memory from generation to generation, history was born. And as soon as history was born, man was able to grope toward maturity in many different areas of experience. Hunting was improved, agriculture was invented, social groups were created, families were sanctified, nations were organized, curiosities were developed and satisfied which led to new curiosities. The more man remembered, the more there was to learn, the wider the horizons appeared, the deeper were the thoughts of the mind, the more searching the yearnings of the soul.

Mankind treated itself to the vast spectacles of the burgeoning agricultural societies of the river deltas—Ur of the Chaldees at the confluence of the Tigris and Euphrates Rivers, the Dynasties of Egypt along the Nile, the Vedic civilization along the Ganges and the Jumna. And yet, of all these great civilizations, none provided an integrating unity for man, universe, and God until Abraham appeared on the scene at approximately the end of the third millenium B.C.E. Buddha appeared in the middle of the sixth century B.C.E. to lead the Vedic civilization in its yearning quest for unity. Abraham's lead was directed toward an understanding of the unity of man and universe with reference to the availability (immanence) of a Creator-God. Buddha's lead was directed toward an understanding of the unity of man with a universe in a nondeistic interrelationship which based its morality on karma and nirvana. *Other than these two great yearning directions*, no other solutions to the searching of the soul were ever developed which were not in some way rooted in and derived from Judaism or Buddhism, or both.

For this reason our ongoing discussion of the relationship of Astrology to the Bible and other historicolegal and historicoethical sources of Judaism takes on its importance. For when we speak of Jewish law, of Halachah which literally means "the way to go," we must ask ourselves, "the way to go where?" What is it that we seek, and why do we seek it?

What we seek, "the way we go," the way to search out, the goal of our yearning is also the source of our being. In Judaism, as also in its daughter religions Christianity and Islam, our end is to find our beginning. We search for no less than unity with God. That is the goal we seek, on the path we tread. In Judaism, we call it *Ichud*—"Unity"—and express it in terms such as those in Leviticus 19:2. ". . . You shall be Holy, for I, the Lord your God, am Holy." Christians express the concept as *Immitatio Dei*, "Imitation of God," and *Immitatio Christi*, "Imitation of Christ." The Buddhist, in seeking his merging with the Universal All, labels it *Nirvana*. But under any and all labels, the path leads to identical goals; balance within life, loving concern for mankind, loving respect for the universe in which we live, and a life whose meaning and value does not end with the grave, but continues on planes unknown to ourselves, but sometimes available to the most balanced and attuned among us.

As a Rabbi and astrologer, I am competent to trace the growth of Astrology through the history of my own people's spiritual heritage and development. This is what I shall try to accomplish in these next chapters. But, in passing, it is not uninteresting to note that the two greatest expressions of man's common yearning—Judaism and Buddhism—are the very two religions in which Astrology plays a major role.

PART II:
ASTROLOGY
OF
ANCIENT
ISRAEL

3

GENERAL PRINCIPLES

As we read the Bible, we must be impressed by the amount of astrological material it contains. Not only are there direct references to astrological interpretations of natural events but also there are astrological allegories, as well as three types of astrologers described in the Book of Isaiah. Therefore, we must seek the answer to the following question: How did the ancient Hebrews practice Astrology? Did they have the same constellations? The same planets? How many planets did they see? What were the bases of their astrological interpretations? Let us begin to answer these questions using the same source for our insights as they did for theirs—the Bible.

The key to understanding the astrological process in ancient Israel is contained in a biblical statement in Deuteronomy 32:8:

When the Most High gave to the nations their inheritances,
When He separated the children of men,
He set the borders of the peoples
According to the number of the Children of Israel.

Israel (Jacob) had 12 sons—one for each constellation. Thus, the early Israelites used the personalities of these 12 sons, as those personalities are enumerated in Holy Scripture, as the key to understanding the powers inherent in the constellations of the Zodiac. This was clearly understood by later generations of Rabbis, who quote this verse in

19

proof of their calculation that the world rests on 12 pillars.* Later mystical writings (*Zohar* Vay'hi: *Sefer Raziel* 52a) and apocalyptic writings (*Book of Enoch: Testament of the Twelve Patritarchs*, Levi) all assume this correspondence between the sons of Jacob and the constellations of the Zodiac to be the normative rule in Astrology. There are too many Midrashic and Talmudic references to this correspondence either to be enumerated here or to be ignored by anyone. Perhaps, the finest compilation of the legends of the Jews, L. Ginzberg's *The Legends of the Jews*†, illustrates this correspondence most dramatically in Volume II and thoroughly documents it in notes 67-70 of Volume V, Joseph:

> Jacob was thus the only one among Joseph's closest kinsmen who remained in ignorance of his son's real fortunes, and he was the one of them all who had the greatest reason for regretting his death. He spoke: "The covenant that God made with me regarding the twelve tribes is null and void now. I did strive in vain to establish the twelve tribes, seeing that now the death of Joseph hath destroyed the covenant. All the works of God were made to correspond to the numbers of the tribes—twelve are the signs of the Zodiac, twelve the months, twelve hours hath the day, twelve the night, and twelve stones are set in Aaron's breastplate—and now that Joseph hath departed, the covenant of the tribes is set at naught."

When we see that the Prophet Isaiah considered the dividing of the heavens into constellations of the Zodiac, a legitimate astrological practice, we can understand that the astrological use of the twelve sons of Jacob as delineators of the forces of the constellations was a natural development.

If we consider that the lives of the twelve sons of Jacob and fathers of the Tribes of the Children of Israel represent an historicoreligious vector of the beginnings of Astrology in Judaism, we can then delineate two other vectors of input into the earliest astrological considerations. One we may call the *religionatural vector*, the other we may call the *theological vector*, for want of a better word.

The religionatural vector of input into astrological interpretation is that body of experience which the Hebrews had as desert nomads at first, and then as members of an agricultural-urban social complex in their later history. In both aspects of their communal

---

* See Rabbi Jose in the Babylonian Talmud, Hagigah, p. 12b.
† Jewish Publication Society of America, Vols. II and V, Philadelphia, 1946.

development, the heavens were vital to their very survival. In the desert "... an empty, howling waste...." (Deut. 32:10) the stars in their constellations provided the signposts to their wanderings. They steered by the stars in the desert of sand as well as on the deserts of water we call the seas and oceans of the world. Nomads had to be good rule-of-thumb celestial navigators in order to survive. Likewise, the lambing and the calving of the flocks and the herds were recognized quite early as having to do with the cycle of the years. When the social pattern changed from nomadic-herdsman to farmer-sedentary, life became even more attuned to the cycles of the years; and these cycles were already related to the heavens and constellations of their earlier experience. Since all natural phenomena were ascribed by our Israelite ancestors to the providence of a good God, all these natural phenomena were religious events, as well. Today, this is still reflected in the religious calendar of Judaism.

Finally, the theological vector was exceedingly simple. All phenomena occurred at the will of God. Wealth or poverty, health or sickness, war or peace, life or death—all occurred either as God's beneficent reward or as His stern punishment. Since our Israelite ancestors believed this to be true, and since both their religiohistorical and their religionatural experiences were intimately linked with the heavens, a natural extension of these experiences into the theological realm was to consider the heavens as being the messengers of God. Thus Astrology became in ancient Israelite minds the Divine Science, that body of knowledge which informed man of God's will and of His intentions for man. Thus, man was given the opportunity to respond to this knowledge of God's will by correcting his own life in accordance with Divine will. Thus, Astrology became the science of balance: the balance between God and His universe of created matter, and God and His created partner, humanity.

In summary, the three input vectors through which the Astrology of the ancient Hebrews may be understood are the theological (God's will for humanity in His universe) which demands *balance*, the religiohistorical (Sons of Jacob corresponding to the twelve constellations of the Zodiac), and the religionatural (experience of the constellations of the Zodiac through life-experience as nomad and farmer). We are now ready to discuss Astrology, linking the concepts of time, space, and man in a *dynamic balance of forces* all responsive to the will of God.

THE CONSTELLATIONS OF THE ZODIAC

The Zodiac is an imaginary belt of space in the heavens. Its center line is known as the *Ecliptic,* an imaginary line in space parallel to the equator of the Earth. The band of the Zodiac is the imaginary band of space defined by two imaginary lines, each 17° north and south of the Ecliptic, respectively, and parallel to it. Within this band of space the planets, with the exception of Pluto, transit in their orbits around the Sun; and within this band of the Zodiac the 12 constellations of the Zodiac are located. Thus, as each planet circumnavigates its orbit, it will pass beneath each of the signs of the Zodiac. The Earth completes its orbit around the Sun in 1 year: the Earth transits each constellation of the Zodiac in 1 month, and transits all 12 constellations in one calendar year. This transit of the Earth through its orbit is referred to as a person's Sun Sign.

When someone says: "I am a Leo," that person means that he or she was born during the monthly period when the Sun is visible in the Heavens against the constellation Leo. The Moon travels around the Earth in 1 month, and therefore is visible, from the Earth, against any particular constellation for about 2.5 days (360° ÷ 30 days = approximately 12° per day: a constellation covers 30° of the sky; therefore, the Moon transits one constellation in approximately 2.5 days, and all 12 constellations in one month).

The ancient astrologers used the actual observance of the planets as the planets transited the constellations of the Heavens at the time of birth as seen from the place of birth. They were also able to calculate the Moon cycles and future planetary positions for the purposes of making predictions. They worked with constellations not with "signs."

Orbital speeds are relative to the Sun; therefore, transit times for each planet, as viewed from the Earth, will vary with the speed and place of the Earth in its own orbit, as well as with the orbital speed of the planet being seen. In any event, it is immediately obvious that the planets will assume different relationships to each other every single day. These relationships of the planets to each other are measured in terms of the number of degrees in the angles between them, and are called *Aspects.*

There are two other measurements used in casting a horoscope: the Ascendant and the Midheaven. These two points in a chart are determined by the time of birth because they are defined by the Earth's rotation on its axis each day, rather than by the Earth's position in orbit around the Sun. Imagine that you are spending 24 hours on a beach facing East: if you continually looked eastward at the horizon, then every two hours you would see one constellation of the Zodiac rising out of the sea. Since there are 30° in a constellation and 120 minutes in each 2-hour period, we can say that the Ascendant rises at a rate of one full degree of the Zodiac every 4 minutes. At approximately 6:00 A.M., the Ascendant degree would correspond to the Sun Sign degree (at sunrise).

The Midheaven point in a horoscope is the point of noon which would correspond to the observed or calculated Ascendant position. Thus, since noon will vary about 2 hours away from an average of 6 hours from sunrise, depending on the time of the year, we should expect the Midheaven point to vary about 30° or so either way from a distance of 90° from the Ascendant. Although this is true, even larger differences than 30° between Ascendant and Midheaven can occur since the observance of the constellation rising on the horizon is affected by both the latitude and longitude of the place, whereas the Midheaven depends only on the longitude.

Two other astrological positions must be explained, and then we shall know as much as the ancient Hebrews did about casting a horoscope. These two points are the North and South Nodes of the Moon, known in ancient times as the *Head* and *Tail of the Dragon*, respectively. Because of the motion of the Moon and the path of its orbit in relation to the ecliptic, we may draw a line through the north and south poles of the Moon which will intersect with the ecliptical path of the constellations of the Zodiac. The points of that intersection are called the *Nodes of the Moon*. It takes 18 years for the Nodes to return to their original position; this is called the *Saros Cycle*. Now we are ready to cast a horoscope the way our ancestors did.

A horoscope is usually defined as a "Map of the Heavens, for the date and time of one's birth, as viewed from the place of one's birth." To this definition of the horoscope, our Israelite ancestors would add the following words: "... which will reveal the will of God for the person, and the place of the person in the balance of man, God, and universe." For the horoscope was used in ancient times to direct the course of men and nations in the path of God's will. To cast the horoscope, one would view the Heavens at the time of birth from the place of birth, to determine the correct positions of the seven planets, the North and South Nodes of the Moon, and the Ascendant and Midheaven.

These points are then charted on a horoscope (graph) from which the astrologer can then delineate and discuss the significance of the planets in their positions in the constellations and in their aspects (angular relationships) to each other, the Ascendant, Midheaven, and Nodes. In ancient times, they were charted within a rectangular figure, the "corners" of the rectangle representing the "Cardinal points" of the Zodiac. Today, the points are charted on a

circular form, with the Midheaven at the top of the form and the
Ascendant to its left and close to perpendicular to it.

It is important to know what the "houses" of a horoscope are.
There are 24 hours in a day, and since there are 12 constellations on
the Ecliptic, it is obvious that an important point will rise above the
horizon every 2 hours. The 6:00 A.M. point is called the *Ascendant*,
and the noon point is called the *Midheaven*, as already mentioned.
The 6:00 P.M. point is called the *Descendant* and the midnight point
in Latin is called the *Imum Coeli* or "below Heaven." The Ascendant
begins the person's "life-day," and becomes the Cusp of his 1st
House. Its opposite is the cusp of the 7th House. The Midheaven is
the "high point" of one's life and is placed at the 10th house Cusp; its
opposite, the *Imum Coeli*, or *Nadir*, is placed at the 4th house Cusp.
The other house Cusp pairs, 2nd to 8th, 3rd to 9th, 5th to 11th, and 6th
to 12th, all rise at 2-hour intervals. Thus the horoscope chart is
divided into 12 sections. However, the "width" of the houses, that is,
the number of degrees more or less than the 30° norm depends on the
latitude of the place of the observer: the farther north or south of the
Equator, the greater will be the deviation from 30° for each twelfth of
the circle of 360° of the Zodiac. Later, I will interpret the houses of the
horoscope in relation to different areas of a person's life. The reader
shall see that these delineations are logically derived from the concept
of the "life-day" of the person.

With this personally observed information, the ancients would
then cast the horoscope chart, placing the constellations in their
proper degrees on their respective house Cusps, placing the planets in
their proper positions in the houses according to their positions
beneath the constellations, placing the Midheaven, Ascendant, and
Nodes in their proper places, and noting the angular relationships
(aspects) among the elements of the horoscope. Now, how did our
ancestors "delineate," or interpret the chart? They used a basic system
of seven indicators to interpret the strength of the planets in the chart,
and the meanings to be assigned to them. These seven general
indicators were

1. Cardinal, Fixed, and Mutable (quadruplicities)
2. Fire, Earth, Air, and Water (triplicities)
3. The 12 Sons of Jacob
4. Rulership of the planets
5. Solar—lunar directions
6. Masculine—feminine influences
7. Ascending or descending; elevated or depressed planets

CARDINAL, FIXED, OR MUTABLE CONSTELLATIONS

Of the seven indicators just mentioned, the first six deal with attributes assigned to the constellations; the seventh deals with the position of the planets with relation to the Ascendant-Descendant and Midheaven-Nadir axes. The first of these indicators deals with the constellations and the seasons of the year. The Bible states that the month in which Passover falls shall be the first month of the year:

> And the Lord spoke to Moses and Aaron in the land of Egypt, saying: "This month shall be unto you the beginning of the months; it shall be the first month of the year to you."
>
> [Exodus 12:1-2]

This month, known in the Bible as *Abib*, is the month which begins spring, the Vernal Equinox, or zero° Aries.

Cardinal Constellations begin the seasons; they are natural phenomena. Spring begins when the Sun crosses the Equator from south to north: this point in time is known as the *Vernal Equinox*, and corresponds to the Sun transiting the cusp, or zero° of Aries. Six months later, the Sun will cross the Equator from north to south. This point in time which marks the beginning of autumn is knows as the *Autumnal Equinox*, and corresponds to the Sun transiting zero° Libra. After spring comes, the Sun will reach its zenith around June 21 when it has reached its northernmost point. This point in time is known as the *Summer Solstice*, and corresponds to zero° Cancer. Six months later, the Sun will reach its Nadir, its southernmost point, around December 21. This point in time is known as the *Winter Solstice*, and corresponds to zero° Capricorn. Therefore, these four constellations which today mark the beginning of the seasons Aries, the spring; Cancer, the summer; Libra, the autumn; and Capricorn, the winter, are known as the *Cardinal Constellations*.

The four constellations that end each season, providing the transition periods from one season to the next, are known as the *Mutable Constellations*. They are now Gemini, the end of spring; Virgo, the end of summer; Sagittarius, the end of autumn; and Pisces, the end of winter.

The four constellations which are solidly in the middle of each season are known as the *Fixed Constellations*. They are today Taurus, the middle of spring; Leo, the middle of summer; Scorpio, the middle of autumn, and Aquarius, the middle of winter.

In interpreting the chart, the astrologer looked to see which group of constellations was occupied by the greatest number of planets, the Ascendant, and the Midheaven. If most were in Cardinal Constellations, then the person was most probably a leader, just as Cardinal Constellations "lead" the seasons of the year. If most were in Fixed Constellations, then the person might be very security oriented, needing a "fixed" home base, a "fixed" income, a "fixed" social status. If most of the planets and other indicators were in Mutable Constellations, the person might be always on the go, a traveler, since these constellations provide the road which "travels" from season to season. The person might also be communicative since these constellations "communicate" between seasons, and might also be "adaptable" since these constellations "adapt" the seasons to one another.

FIRE, EARTH, AIR, WATER (TRIPLICITIES) CONSTELLA-TIONS

Although most astrologers are aware that the triplicities are in some way connected to the ancient concept of the "building blocks" of matter, many are not aware of the origin of the *order* in which they are related to the constellations of the Zodiac. The order is found in the very first verses in the Bible and concerns the order of creation. In the relevant biblical passage quoted from Genesis 1:2-3, the number in parentheses following each element indicates the order in which the elements appear in Scripture:

> Now the earth (1) was unformed and void, and darkness was upon the face of the deep, and the Spirit of God (2) hovered over the face of the waters (3). And God said: "Let there be light," (4); and there was light.

In this quote (1) represents the element Earth; (2) represents the element Air (In newer translations, this phrase is translated as ".... the wind of God....."); (3) represents Water; (4) represents Fire. These elements are repeated in this order three times in the Zodiac; thus, we have a biblical order.

Some astute observers, and most astrologers, will demur at this point: the Zodiac starts with Aries which is a Fire sign. The order should be Fire, Earth, Air, Water and not Earth, Air, Water, Fire. The answer to this lies in the concept of Zodiacal Ages. According to Jewish astrologers, a Zodiacal Age (which they called a *Prophetic Age*) is 2,160 years. According to Jewish tradition, at the beginning of each Great Year the positions of the planets in their constellations are identical to their positions at Creation. The Prophetic Ages precess through the 12 constellations of the Zodiac, and the Great Year is equal to 12 times 2,160 years, or 25,920 years.

Let us trace the origin of the figures for the Great Year and Prophetic Age. Jewish astrologers were very observant of the actual positions of the Heavens and of the transits of the planets in their constellations. They noted that Jupiter-Saturn conjunctions took place approximately every 20 years. They linked this observation to the biblical injunction that every young man of 20 years and over was responsible for the collective good of the community (Exod. 28:36, Numb. 1:3). The number 20 also appears many times in the descriptions of the building of the Tabernacle (see Numbers, many places). Since Saturn is such a slow-moving planet, and the farthest planet visible without instruments, the ancients considered Saturn to be the transmitter of mysteries, the Divine Messenger. And since the Jupiter-Saturn conjunction was a 20-year occurrence, the idea developed that God passed on the message of His Divine Will at every Jupiter-Saturn conjunction. Jupiter then passed the message on to every planet in the Heavens during the year following the conjunction since the planets sunward of Jupiter make at least one conjunction with Jupiter each year. (A conjunction of two planets occurs when they are both located in the same degree, in the same constellation of the Zodiac, at the same time.) Thus, the astrological rationale for the necessity of reaching the age of 20 to be counted as a responsible member of the community was that at least one Jupiter-Saturn conjunction would have occurred before the twentieth birthday—and the young man could know God's will for him by consulting his astrologer.

Astrologers also noticed that such conjunctions occurred at least three or four times in the same triplicity, and that the change from one triplicity to the other heralded a major change in the manifestation of God's will. For example, the last four Jupiter-Saturn conjunctions occurred at the following times:

September 8, 1921	at 26°	Virgo	(Earth triplicity)
February 15, 1941	at 9°	Taurus	(Earth triplicity)
February 19, 1961	at 28°	Capricorn	(Earth triplicity)
December 31, 1980	at 9°	Libra	(Air triplicity)

The next conjunction of Jupiter and Saturn will take place on the date of May 28, 2001, and will be at 23° Gemini, an Air triplicity in the Mutables. Notice that the conjunctions before 1901, which began approximately 1821, were in the Water Signs (Cancer, Scorpio, Pisces). Please note that, historically, the years from 1821 to 1901 involved expansion of trade routes through the sea lanes, and that the wars during those years were overseas expansionist wars. Since 1901, the two great world wars were fought mainly on land (Earth triplicity) for the control of geopolitical land masses. This period was also the period of the greatest exploitation of the natural resources both on and under the land masses of our Earth. Also note that the exploration of the air as a means of travel began in earnest in the latter part of the Earth-triplicity period and that the new conjunctions will begin in the Air triplicity. The key to the next 80-year period will probably lie in the solution to problems of communications, air pollution, and space exploration. There are no coincidences: the Jupiter-Saturn conjunction following the one in 1980, is calculated to take place in the year 2001, in Aquarius, and we may very well be involved in some type of space odyssey. Can it possibly be that Stanley Kubrick knew of the upcoming Jupiter-Saturn conjunction, and named his famous picture for it?

In investigating the biblical origins of the triplicities, and trying to answer the objection to having the order begin with Earth, rather than with Fire, we began our argument with a delineation of the 25,920 years of the Great Year, and the 2,160 years of the Prophetic Age, and the 20 years of the Jupiter-Saturn conjunction cycle, which occurs four times in each triplicity and then moves to another triplicity. However, there is another pattern to the cycle of these conjunctions. Note that they precess through the Zodiac Constellations within each triplicity and that they precess through the quadruplicities, as well. If we were to set up an arbitrary set of dates beginning with 1981 and continuing into the future, we would see that the conjunction not only move backward through the triplicities but also forward through the quadruplicities. (These are all hypothetical dates after December 31, 1980—Table 3.1 is for illustrative purposes only.)

As you read down the date order in each column, you discover that each sign in the triplicity is followed in time by the sign which preceeds it in the Zodiac. Note, however, that when all four triplicities have been completed in the Cardinal cycle (i.e., the constellation that begins each triplicity pattern is a Cardinal Constellation), the pattern repeats itself through all four triplicities, but each starting in a Fixed Constellation.

In Table 3.1, note that the time-span of one complete pattern (1981 to 2701) is 720 years: When the cycle has been completed three times, 2,160 years will have passed, and a new Prophetic Age will

Table 3.1 Cycle of Conjunctions through Triplicities and Quadruplicities

Sign	Cardinal	Fixed	Mutable	Cardinal
Earth		2161—Taurus	2401—Virgo	2641—Capricorn
		2181—Capricorn	2421—Taurus	2661—Virgo
		2201—Virgo	2441—Capricorn	2681—Taurus
Air	1981—Libra	221—Aquarius	2461—Gemini	2701—Libra
	2001—Gemini	2241—Libra	2481—Aquarius	
	2021—Aquarius	2261—Gemini	2501—Libra	
Water	2041—Cancer	2281—Scorpio	2521—Pisces	
	2061—Pisces	2301—Cancer	2541—Scorpio	
	2081—Scorpio	2321—Pisces	2561—Cancer	
Fire	2101—Aries	2341—Leo	2581—Sagittarius	
	2121—Sagittarius	2361—Aries	2601—Leo	
	2141—Leo	2381—Sagittarius	2621—Aries	

begin. This is the kind of beautiful pattern of balance that was glorified by Astrology in Biblical times for it showed the Divine Pattern of Creation repeated in the Heavens. However, after a few centuries of experience astrologers observed that the period of time between conjunctions was not exactly 20 years, but closer to 19 years and approximately 290 days. Thus, in each 720 year cycle, there was approximately one-third of a conjunction period left over; in the three cycles making up one complete Prophetic Age, there will be one full conjunction left over. Thus, we have a situation in which the pattern holds true if we add one extra conjunction for each 2,160 years. Over the period of the Great Year, that is, a cycle of 12 Prophetic Ages, or 25,920 years, there will be 12 such extra conjunctions, one in each Constellation, and one extra Conjunction. At the beginning of a new Great Year, we shall know its beginning because there will be five consecutive Jupiter-Saturn conjunctions in the Fire triplicity, the first, third, and fifth conjunctions being in Aries. The first Aries conjunction because we shall begin the Cardinal series with the conjunction at the Vernal Equinox (According to tradition, this was the position at the Creation!), the second Aries conjunction to indicate that this is the beginning of a new Prophetic Age, and the third Aries conjunction to mark the beginning of a New Great Year. These various conjunctions of Jupiter and Saturn had particular names. The normal conjunction within its triplicity was called the *Normal Conjunction*. The conjunction that marked the change of triplicities every 60 years was known as the *Great Conjunction*. The conjunction that occurred once every 2,160 years and marked the beginning of a Prophetic Age was known as the *Magnificent Conjunction*, and the conjunction which occurred every 25,920 years to mark the beginning of a new Great Year was known as the *Divine Conjunction* or the *Conjunction of Power*.

We have still not answered the question of why the biblical order of triplicities begins with Earth, rather than Fire. The answer lies in the concept of the Prophetic Ages, or what we now call the Zodiacal Ages. We are all familiar with the concept of the "Age of Aquarius" which implies that we are entering a new Prophetic Age, and that we are leaving the Age of Pisces (the ages precess through the Zodiac). The Prophetic Age before the Age of Pisces was the Age of Aries, and the age before that was the Age of Taurus. We know that, at present, in the Age of Pisces, the Cardinal house on the Ascendant is Aries. The Talmud tells us that before the common era the Cardinal house on the Ascendant was ruled by Taurus. (Today known as a Fixed Constellation of the Earth Triplicity!) During the Age of Taurus, the Ascendant Cardinal house was ruled by Gemini. Thus, the appearance of the order Earth, Air, Water, and Fire as the order of triplicities is now explained. At the time the Bible was being formulated, Taurus of the Earth Triplicity *was* the 1st house Cardinal Ruler.

Permit me two more digressions. First, there is a great concern over the exact date which will begin the Age of Aquarius. If our ancestors were correct, it is very easy to determine that date. Remember that there is one extra Jupiter-Saturn conjunction that heralds the beginning of every new Prophetic Age. That conjunction, a Magnificent Conjunction, occurred on February 19, 1961 at 28° Capricorn, marking the fourth Conjunction in the Earth Triplicity and the *end of the Age of Pisces.* The new conjunction in 1981 on New Year's Day almost at midnight of New Year's Eve, will be a Great Conjunction in Libra, marking both a change in triplicities and the arrival of the Age of Aquarius. Second, an analysis of what we know about history and a comparison of that knowledge with what we know about Astrology will give ample proof that the Cardinal Ascendant Houses do indeed precess along with the Prophetic Age. Let us begin with the Age of Gemini.

The Age of Gemini existed 26,000 years before the emergence of the dynasties of Egypt and the ziggurats of Sumer. People worshipped the heavenly twins, the Sun and Moon, and the Moon Cult of mother-earth worship and the beginnings of fertility cult worship began here. This is astrologically to be expected, since the Ascendant Cardinal house would have been Cancer, Moon-ruled, and devoted to the home, and fertility. This was an age in which the mysteries of the female estrus cycle were worshipped, and the priestess was the ruler of the society.

The Age of Taurus, an Earth Triplicity, followed, and the first national groups dependent on areas of the earth arose. We had the dynasties of Egypt, the Mittani, Hurrian, Sumerian, Akkadian, Assyrian, and Babylonian Empires developing, growing and dying, as the fortunes of war governed the control of land areas. During this time, Gemini was the Ascendant Cardinal house, and we have this twin influence reflected in the entire Egyptian experience. The name of the land in Hebrew, *Mitzra'im*, is a plural, meaning the "two Egypts." Upper Egypt and Lower Egypt were distinctly different parts of the Empire; they had, in fact, been separate states originally. The Pharaoh wore a twin mitre, or crown, recognizing the two Egypts. The Pharaoh married his sister—once again an indication of Gemini, as were the dualistic animal-human gods of Egypt.

The Age of Aries is the Age of the Nomad, the age which heralds the decline of the Egyptian dynasties. Aries is the Ram, impetuous, driving, prolific. It is the age in which Israel is born, in which Abraham is told to wander with his flocks. It is the age of the wandering of the patriarchs in search of pasture for their herds. We should expect this astrologically, since during this age, Taurus is the Ascendant Cardinal House. We see the importance of the calf, the bull, and other cattle during this time. When Israel sins, it is through the worship of a Golden Calf. The Bible refers often to the Bull of Bashan, and cattle is the major animal accepted as an offering on the altar of God. In addition, the bull becomes the symbol of the might of Assyria and Babylonia.

The Age of Pisces is now almost concluded. We see its influence as a symbol in Christianity; Jesus, who is called the "Fisher of Men," has a strong following among the fishermen of Galilee, and performs miracles on the water. The leader of Christianity in its earliest stages is known as the *Pontifex Maximus,* "the Great Bridgebuilder," implying that there are waters to be crossed. However, the First House is ruled now by Aries on the Ascendant, and the Lamb of God now rules in the world. Christianity takes all of the lamb-ram symbolism of Judaism and the Passover and political freedom and uses it to spread its gospel of resurrection and freedom from sin.

What happens now, in 1981, when we enter the Age of Aquarius? Pisces will become the Ascendant House Constellation. Christianity (originated in the Age of Pisces) will now either become more attuned to the inner occult needs of the human spirit or it will wash away! Judaism will find that its earthiness (Taurus Ascendant House in Age of Aries) will be fructified by the 1st house waters of Pisces in sext (60° apart) to it, and a new development of its spiritual heritage will mature. It will be a fascinating age in which to live. Incidentally, we shall begin, in the Age of Aquarius, under the influence of Pisces as the Ascendant House, to begin to pipe air into the sea, to begin to live in the seas as fish do, and to take more of our energy and sustenance needs from the sea itself!

4

THE TWELVE SONS
OF JACOB

Since our ancestors considered Astrology to be the hand of God written boldly across the Heavens, it was natural for them to assign spiritual rulerships to the constellations which corresponded to the actions of God in the history of Israel: The first of those confrontations between God and history in Judaism arose in response to the necessity for continuity. Both Abraham and Isaac had only one son who carried on the tradition of the father. However, Jacob, son of Isaac and grandson of Abraham, had twelve sons, thus ensuring the continuity of the nation. This was considered to be an act of Divine intervention and approval, and was reflected in the Astrology of Judaism by having each son of Jacob (called Israel) assigned the spiritual rulership of the constellations. How was this done? By what means were the sons of Jacob assigned to the particular constellations as rulers? After all, an astrologer who knew Bible well could easily make arbitrary assignments of sons to constellations and then declare them divine! Were such a priori assignments indeed the case? The answer is a resounding *no*!

The most logical and balanced method of assigning rulerships to the constellations would be in the order of birth. That is, Jacob's firstborn son, Reuben, should logically be assigned spiritual ruler of the Ascendant House Constellation. The secondborn son, Simon, should be assigned to the next constellation in order, the thirdborn, Levi, to the third constellation in order, and so forth. This is exactly the method used. Reuben, the firstborn of Jacob, is assigned the

33

Ascendant House Constellation. But remember, during the time of the development of Scripture, the Ascendant House Constellation was Taurus, and Reuben is therefore assigned spiritual ruler of Taurus. The following is a list of constellations and their rulers beginning with Taurus as the Ascendant House Ruler in the Age of Aries, when this took place:

Constellation	Ruler	Constellation	Ruler
Taurus:	Reuben	Scorpio:	Dan
Gemini:	Simon	Sagittarius:	Gad
Cancer:	Levi	Capricorn:	Asher
Leo:	Judah	Aquarius:	Naphtali
Virgo:	Zebulun	Pisces:	Joseph
Libra:	Issachar	Aries:	Benjamin

This order of constellations is the zodiacal order; and this order of the sons of Israel is in the order of their birth, and therefore the order of their blessing by Israel at his deathbed, as reported in Genesis 29:1-27. It would be indicative of the manner in which these spiritual rulerships were used for interpretation to investigate the personalities of these sons of Israel, and to relate them to the constellations and what we know about them. We may even discover that some of the ancient interpretations were closer to the truth than some of our modern readings.

Reuben, spiritual ruler of Taurus, was a man who took his earthly pleasures where he found them, regardless of whether or not he was entitled to them. We read in Genesis 35:22 the following short message:

> And it came to pass, while Israel dwelt in that land, that Reuben went and lay with Bilhah his father's concubine; and Israel heard of it.

Reuben's father, Jacob known as Israel, had a long memory. When he parcels out the blessings on his deathbed, he says of Reuben:

> Reuben, thou art my firstborn
> My might, and the first-fruits of my strength;
> The excellence of dignity and the excellence of power.
> Unstable as water, have thou not the excellency;
> Because thou wentest up to thy father's bed;
> Then defiledst thou it—my couch he mounted!
> [Genesis 49:2-4]

However, we know that Reuben felt responsible enough to argue against killing Joseph and hoped to return him safely to his father (Gen. 37:21-22) and was quite distraught when he discovered Joseph to be missing from the pit in which he was placed (Gen. 37:29-30).

Taurans were thus thought of in ancient times as persons who waste their dignity and strength because of their animal appetites. They will be impulsive only in the pursuit of physical beauty of all types—but especially of sexual beauty, and this tendency can be their downfall. Otherwise, Taurans are quite sensitive to the needs of others; they are slow to anger and seek to keep things peaceful and placid around them.

Simon rules Gemini, and Levi rules Cancer: In the Bible they are linked together as "brothers in violence." The two brothers acted together to take horrible vengeance on the king, prince, and people of Shechem (see Gen. 34) in the matter of the rape of their sister Dinah, and it took a miracle to extricate Jacob and his tribe from the situation (Gen. 35:5). Therefore, Jacob's remembrance of them is summed up on his deathbed, as follows:

> Simeon and Levi are brethren.
> Weapons of violence their kinship.
> Let my soul not come into their council;
> Unto their assembly let my glory not be united;
> For in their anger they slew men,
> And in their self-will they hewed oxen.
> Cursed be their anger, for it was fierce,
> And their wrath, for it was cruel;
> I will divide them in Jacob, and scatter them in Israel.
> [Genesis 49:5-7]

This certainly does not square with the modern picture we have of Geminis and Cancerians. We never really think of them as violent people. We think of Geminis as intellectuals and of Cancerians as emotional and fickle. What else does the Bible say of them?

There is another set of blessings in the Bible...this one for the tribes, given by Moses, is in Deuteronomy: 33. In this list, one tribe is missing; Simon. Levi is blessed by Moses as the tribe that separates itself from the rest of the community to act as priests and servants of God. We also find that Levi is named by his mother at birth as the son who will be the cause of his father Jacob's delight in his mother, and will "cleave unto" her (Gen. 29:34).

Simon's name derives from his mother's belief that God "heard" her plight and answered her with a son (Gen. 29:33). Simon is also the son who is imprisoned and then released by Joseph (Gen. 42:24 and 43:23).

How did the ancients think of Gemini and Cancer? As two sides of one coin: Gemini the communicative, but locked into the communicative pattern; Cancer the one who separates from others for holy purposes, living as the "mother-symbol" of the rest of the tribes. Both were considered to be violent; Geminis are intellectually violent, and Cancerians are emotionally violent. Geminis, when angered, will attack verbally until reputations lie in shambles; Cancerians will pile guilt upon guilt on the poor victim of their wrath, until egos lie in shambles!

Judah rules Leo, and Leo is a Fire-Cardinal in olden times. Judah is the brother whose leadership gets them out of trouble. Judah is the tribe from which King David, and thus the Messiah, arises. The Bible is full of the activities of Judah, and his father's fullsome blessings (Gen. 49:8-12) include the statement:

> The sceptre shall not depart from Judah,
> Nor the ruler's staff from between his feet,
> As long as men come to Shiloh;
> And unto him shall the obedience of the peoples be.
> [Genesis 49:10]

Leos were thought of as kings, and so they consider themselves to be kings. The typical Leo must always be on top. Friends are treated magnanimously, as befit friends of royalty. But should one fall from grace, watch out! The Leo will wreak royal vengeance, grinding the face of the enemy into the dust, until apologies are made and amends accepted. Then the Leo will lift up the former friend, and set him or her back on the former pedestal, but always lower than the one on which the Leo stands.

Virgo is ruled by Zebulun, of whom very little is known except that the origin of his name comes from the word meaning "to dwell" (see Gen. 30:20). Jacob blessed Zebulun as one who would be engaged in overseas commerce (Gen. 49:13), and Moses blesses the tribe of Zebulun, linking them with the tribe of Issachar:

> Rejoice, Zebulun in thy going out, and Issachar in thy tents.
> They shall call peoples unto the mountain;
> There shall they offer sacrifices of righteousness;
> For they shall suck the abundance of the seas,
> And the hidden treasures of the sand.
> [Deuteronomy 33:18-19]

Zebulun is always linked with Issachar, and the Talmud indicates that they were like two brothers joined in one life; they complimented each other well. Zebulun was the overseas merchant; Issachar was the overland merchant, and the maker of glass from the sand. Just as Zebulun carried his wares overseas, always seeking new markets and new connections, so does the Virgo constantly seek new experiences.

The modern interpretation of Virgo is falsely colored by the Christian concept of the Virgin Mary. Remember that Astrology originated in the Near East—in Asia, not Europe—and in a society far different from that of the Christianity which eventually formulated its romanticized concepts of the Virgin. In the Near East, virgins were locked up in harems because their fathers and/or husbands, or both, believed that they were so anxious to experience new delights that they were incapable of controlling their natures. Thus, the Virgo of Jewish Astrology is not the prim, prissy, overorganized, undersexed (or at least uncommunicatively sexed) rather introverted person depicted in most superficial Sun sign lists in the Western world. In Jewish Astrology, Virgos were always on the look out for new experiences: physical, intellectual, commercial, or psychological. Virgos will try anything once, and then keep very concise records of their experiences about the things they try. This combination of drive for experience and penchant for analysis is the combination that makes the Virgo a prime candidate for the sciences.

Issachar, Zebulun's alter ego, rules Libra, which in those days was a Mutable Air Triplicity. Recall how Issachar's blessing by Moses was included in the same breath as that of Zebulun. The whole tale of Issachar's birth is itself a fascinating one, and bears on his rulership of Libra. The name *Issachar* stems from the Hebrew word meaning "payment," and that is exactly what Issachar was. The story of his birth is told in Genesis 30:14-18.

Reuben, eldest son of Jacob and Leah, found mandrakes in the field. Mandrakes were shaped like a man with a very large male organ, and were considered to be aphrodisiacs and potent aids to conception. Rachel, Jacob's other wife and most beloved by him [He worked seven years for her, and got Leah through the deceit of their father Laban (Gen. 29:16-30)] was barren, and purchased the mandrakes from Leah. The purchase price was the right to sleep with Jacob that night. In biblical times, women had the legal right to insist on sharing equally in the sexual vigor of their mutual husband; and such rights could be bought and sold (Gen. 30:16). Leah conceives again and bears a son, naming him Issachar, meaning that he was the issue of her "purchased night" with Jacob. Jacob, in blessing Issachar, says:

Issachar is a large-boned ass,
Bent low beneath his burdens.
He saw a resting-place, that it was good
And the Land that it was pleasant;
And he bowed his shoulder to the burden
And became a hired servant.

[Genesis 49:14-15]

Astrologically, people always seem to look on Librans as judicious, even-handed people, always weighing the results of an action in their minds before committing themselves. One would expect most judges to be Librans, but they are not: most judges are Scorpios; most generals are Librans. If we recall the biblical origin of Issachar in a purchase-sale of nuptial rights, and if we understand the meaning of Jacob's blessing, then we shall understand the astrological meaning in Jewish terms. Having been the result of a hastily arranged bargain, Issachar was wary of making any decisions. He became the worker and supplier to Zebulun, working at assigned tasks under another person's direction because he hated to make decisions. In this same manner, modern Librans seem judicious because Libra has become a *Cardinal Air Triplicity* in our Age of Pisces, and so the Libran can talk a terrific game. When presented with a problem, the Libran no longer demurs from making decisions, at least not verbally. When Libra was a *Mutable Air Triplicity*, Librans were not unhappy to let the world know that they would rather have others make the decisions. However, as a *Cardinal Air Triplicity*, Librans began to feel that they ought to take leadership positions; and so they did, but without losing their distaste for decision making. Now, instead of openly admitting that they do not like to make choices, Librans talk all problems to death, round and round, until the problem is solved by *Time*. At this point, the Libran says: "Remember, I said that!" And everyone does indeed remember, and the Libran gets the reputation of a judicious person. The non-Librans always forget that the Libran, in talking the problem to death, also mentioned every conceivable possibility, in the process.

Dan comes from the Hebrew word meaning "to judge," and his mother thus named him because she felt that God had judged her favorably in giving her another son. Dan rules Scorpio, which in biblical days was a *Cardinal Water Triplicity*. Jacob's blessing of Dan was as follows:

Dan shall judge his people as one of the tribes of Israel.

Dan shall be a serpent in the way, a horned snake in the path
That biteth the horses heels so that his rider falleth backwards.
[Genesis 49:16-17]

Let us add to this, the blessing of Moses (Deut. 33:22):

And of Dan he said: "Dan is a lion's whelp
That leapeth forth from Bashan."

How can one constellation seem to produce two such different
types in one person? In ancient times, Scorpios were depicted as either
eagles or snakes. This reminds me of the nursery rhyme of the little
girl who had...

...a little curl, right in the middle of her forehead.
When she was good, she was very, very good,
But when she was bad, she was horrid.

Remember that, in ancient times, Scorpio was a *Cardinal Water
Triplicity,* and therefore bound to act forcefully in emotional matters.
Other factors, which I shall describe further, rulership by Mars, a solar
constellation, (see Chap. 5) feminine in nature, all indicate that when
emotions were under control, Scorpios would channel their drive into
judgemental areas. When their emotions were not under control,
Scorpios would become vindictive, sly, and prone to seek their ends
through violent means.

Gad rules Sagittarius, and the fascinating story of Gad and its
link to Sagittarius through Jupiter, through archery, and through the
Babylonian God of Good Fortune of the same name, is well-
documented in Chapter 18. Here, let me just say, the word itself means
"good fortune," and thus was he named by his mother (Gen. 30:11).
The blessing of Jacob is horribly mistranslated in the English, and
this, too, is elucidated. However, the blessing of Moses is very
interesting for it shows us some of the meanings that can be applied to
a delineation of those fortunate Sagittarians:

Blessed be he that enlargeth Gad;
He dwelleth as a lioness, and teareth the arm,
Yea, the crown of the head.
And he chose a first part for himself,
For there a portion of a ruler was reserved;
And there came the heads of the people,

> He executed the righteousness of the Lord,
> And His ordinances with Israel.
> [Deuteronomy 33:20-21]

Sagittarians are most fortunate people, even their misfortunes seem to be mitigated and lead to better things. Sagittarians are as direct as an arrow's flight, and thus they are quick to spot a bargain or an opportunity, and to appropriate it to themselves, to "... chose the first part for himself...." Sagittarians have most of their problems when they are too expansive, too trusting of their natural good fortune. Sagittarians have the ability to consider a problem and intuit the proper solution: In a committee meeting at which Librans would talk the problem to death, the Sagittarian would declare the proper solution, and leave.

Asher rules Capricorn, and Asher means "wealth." The word really means "fortunate," in the material sense, in having your work provide your sustenance, and more. Remember that Capricorn was a *Mutable Earth Triplicity* when these rulerships were assigned—and the Capricornian will move heaven and earth for creature comforts and material security. Jacob's blessing of Asher was short and to the point:

> As for Asher, his bread shall be fat,
> And he shall yield royal dainties.
> [Genesis 49:20]

Moses' blessing is no less promising:

> Blessed be Asher above sons,
> Let him be the favored of his brethren,
> And let him dip his foot in oil.
> Iron and brass shall be thy bars;
> And as thy days, so shall thy strength be.
> [Deuteronomy 33:24-25]

All indications are that Capricorns never have to worry about which side their bread is buttered ("oiled") on: they seem to always have enough to eat, clothing to wear, and a place to sleep. They work very hard for their success: "... Iron and brass shall be thy bars ..." and life carries them on its flow for a long time, and their strength seems to grow, the older they get. As a matter of fact, we see revealed in the blessing of Moses the astrological addage that Capricorns are old in their youth, and young in their old age.

Naphtali rules Aquarius, in those days a *Cardinal Air Triplicity* Constellation. Naphtali's name derives from the Hebrew word meaning "to wrestle," and the blessing of Jacob and of Moses are very revealing:

> Naphtali is a hind let loose:
> He giveth goodly words.
>   [Genesis 49:21]

> O Naphtali, satisfied with favor,
> And full with the blessing of the Lord:
> Possess thou the sea and the South.
>   [Deuteronomy 33:23]

One would certainly expect a *Cardinal Air Triplicity* to give goodly words... communication is its forte. Swift as a free deer, Naphtali roams the sea and the South, both deserts. Naphtali is full of the blessing of the Lord, and although assigned both sea and sand, is satisfied with his lot. Perhaps we can expect the coming Age of Aquarius to initiate a period wherein man will be satisfied with his lot, and competition will diminish in the war against the Earth's bounty.

Joseph rules Pisces, and this alone is enough to explain the strange ways of Pisceans. In Western Astrology, Pisces has become the garbage dump of the Zodiac. It seems that astrologers got tired of parcelling out attributes, so when they came to Pisces, they dumped in everything that was left over, and Pisceans were described as poor, confused people. Pisceans are indeed sometimes confusing, but rarely confused... they march to a different drum. In ancient times, Pisces was ruled by Jupiter—and how could that be all bad?

Let us begin with Joseph's rulership of Pisces. We immediately discover that Joseph was not the name of a tribe. And we also discover that two of the named tribes were not sons of Jacob, they were the adopted sons of Joseph, whom Jacob took as his own and assigned them a major portion of the land he had conquered. Therefore, although the attributes of all the other brothers were manifested openly through their stewardship of tribal lands and affairs, the attributes of Joseph were hidden, being revealed only in the reflection of his two sons, whose stewardships were openly manifested. We all know how difficult it is to arrive at the personality of a person if all we have is the observed activity of that person's children.

But this is not all: the natures of the two sons, Ephraim and Manasseh, were further confused because their grandfather Jacob, in the blindness of his old age, gave the older son the blessing of the younger, and gave the younger son the blessing reserved for the older brother. When Joseph pointed out this error to his father, Jacob insisted on carrying out the blessing as he began, insisting that, in the future, all Israelite fathers would bless their sons with the words "....God make thee as Ephraim and as Manasseh." To this day, these are the words of blessing which fathers give to their sons on the Sabbath Eve. (In case you are wondering, fathers bless their daughters with the words, "God make thee as Sarah, Rebecca, Rachel, and Leah.") The entire fascinating story is contained in Genesis: 48.

To review: Pisces is ruled by Joseph. Joseph's influence is seen only through its manifestation in the works of his two sons Ephraim and Manasseh, whose blessings were reversed by their grandfather Jacob. And yet, we know that Joseph was no slouch of a man. He overcame all kinds of early troubles, caused mostly by the combination of his own occult abilities and his big mouth, and became second-in-command to Pharaoh, a position he received through his occult abilities, and because he had learned humility. Because the blessing of Joseph by his father Jacob (Gen. 49:22-26) and the blessing by Moses (Deut. 33:13-17) are very long, I will quote to give you an idea of the kind of fulsomeness with which Joseph was blessed:

> But his bow abode firm, and the arms of his hands were made supple...,
> By the hands of the Mighty One of Jacob...,
> And by the Almighty, who shall bless thee
> With blessings of heaven above,
> Blessings of the deep that coucheth beneath,
> Blessings of the breasts and of the womb.
> [Genesis 49:24-5]

> Blessed of the Lord be his land,
> For the precious things of heaven, for the dew...,
> And for the precious things of the fruits of the sun,
> And for the precious things of the yields of the moons...,
> And for the precious things of the earth and the fullness thereof....
> [Deuteronomy 33:13-16]

What has happened to our interpretations of Piscean? Where can we have gone wrong? Well, first we look on Pisces as a *Mutable Water Triplicity* today, whereas in Bible times it was a *Fixed Water*

Triplicity. Whereas they saw Pisces as having emotional security, we see Pisces today as needing emotional security, so naturally, our interpretations would all be a little off. Besides, the recognized occult abilities of Pisceans were in those days respected and rewarded and sought out, whereas in the Age of Pisces these abilities were denigrated and ridiculed and forced to remain hidden. However, in the Age of Aquarius, Pisces is becoming a *Cardinal Water Triplicity*, and the talents of the Pisceans in occult and parapsychological matters have begun once again to be sought out, and in demand.

Finally, we come to Aries, ruled by the youngest son, Benjamin. The word means "son of my right hand," or "favorite son," and after the trumped-up pseudodeath of Joseph, Benjamin did indeed become his favorite son; after all, he was the only child remaining of Jacob's love-union with Rachel, who died in childbirth in bringing Benjamin into the world. It also seems that Benjamin was treated much better by his brothers, who knew of his value to their father Jacob. We know, from Benjamin's actions and words in confrontation with the as-yet-unrevealed-brother Joseph, that Benjamin was impulsive and intensely loyal. Jacob's blessing of Benjamin indicates this hastiness and impulsiveness, and a little of his selfishness:

> Benjamin is a wolf that raveneth; In the morning he
> Devoureth the prey, and at even he divideth the spoil.
> [Genesis 49:27]

The blessing of Moses is equally brief:

> The beloved of the Lord shall dwell in safety by Him;
> He covereth him all the day, and He dwelleth between his
> shoulders.
> [Deuteronomy 33:12]

From this it seems obvious where Arians get their supreme self-confidence, their belief that nothing can go wrong, their intense loyalties, and their ruling impulsiveness.

5

THE OTHER INDICATORS

It was clear to those who studied the Heavens in the biblical period that the Sun and the Moon were the largest bodies in the sky. The Sun gave both heat and light, and ruled either as a benevolent or tyrranical despot over the agricultural cycle of the year. They knew of the equinoxes and the solstices, and considered the Sun to be king of the revealed heavens, and thus assigned the Sun to rulership over the Constellation Leo, ruled by Judah, from whom "... the scepter shall never depart...." In like manner, the Moon was the beautiful Queen of the Heavens, a fit consort to the Sun; the various names of the Moon in Hebrew refer to the monthly cycle, the "White One." Since a nation needs only one king and one queen, who are enthroned side by side, the Moon was assigned to the rulership of Cancer. However, many courtiers are needed, who must divide their attentions between king and queen. Therefore, the five remaining planets were assigned to the king and queen in a very rational order: in the order of their distance from the Sun and the Moon. Thus the planet beyond Earth, yet next in order in the Solar System is Mercury. It is assigned to the Constellations immediately next to Cancer and Leo, namely Gemini and Virgo. The next two constellations equidistant from Cancer and Leo are Taurus and Libra, and Venus, the next planet in order, is assigned to them. The next two equidistant constellations are Aries and Scorpio, and the next further planet, Mars, is assigned to their rulership. The next two equidistant constellations are Pisces and

Sagittarius, thus Jupiter rules them. The final two constellations, the opposite constellations to the Sun and the Moon, are Capricorn and Aquarius, respectively, and they are ruled by the last planet which could be seen, Saturn. Therefore, the logic of distance in the Heaven was kept, and the balance of the universe was preserved in the concept of planetary rulerships of the constellations.

SOLAR AND LUNAR DIRECTIONS

In keeping with the Bible narrative of Creation, we are told that

God made the two great lights: the greater light to rule the day, and the lesser light to rule the night and the stars.
[Genesis 1:16]

Thus, a difference in the nature of the day and the night was indicated. Solar or day-matters were handled differently from nocturnal or night-matters. Therefore constellations which were in the Moon-ruled half of the Zodiac manifested their true powers in a more hidden, more subtle way than those which were located in the Sun-ruled half of the Zodiac. The ancients divided the constellations into Lunar and Solar Constellations—Moon and Sun Constellations. If a constellation was located between Cancer and Aquarius, it was called a *Lunar Constellation;* if it was located between Leo and Capricorn, it was called a *Solar Constellation.* Note now that each planet ruled one Solar and one Lunar Constellation; its powers were therefore modulated through that particular constellation in that particular way.

MASCULINE AND FEMININE INFLUENCES

The Sun was considered to be masculine in its essence, and the Moon was considered to be the controlling force of essential feminity. Therefore, each alternate constellation was considered to be either masculine or feminine in nature, and thus to extend its influences. Starting with Leo, the Masculine Constellations continued with Libra, Sagittarius, Aquarius, Aries, and Gemini. Starting with Cancer, the Feminine Constellations were Virgo, Scorpio, Capricorn, Pisces and Taurus. Note that the Constellations of Fruitfullness and Receptivity, the Earth and Water Triplicities, are Feminine; the Constellations of Force and Movement, the Fire and Air Triplicities, are Masculine.

ASCENDANT OR DESCENDANT, ELEVATION OR DEPRESSION

The terms, *Ascendant* or *Descendant* and *Elevation* or *Depression*, were most important in the astrological analyses of biblical times, for they dealt with the emergent and the revealed, the repressed and the hidden. The explanation is to construct a simple diagram.

Draw a circle and then draw two diameters through it: one horizontal or parallel to the Earth, the other perpendicular to the first diameter. You will now have a circle with a large plus sign through the center of it. Think of the horizontal side-to-side arms of the plus sign as dividing day from night. Nighttime will be below the line, and daytime above the line. (This has *nothing* to do with Solar or Lunar Constellations, which deal with spacial position on the ecliptic in the Zodiac. I am now speaking of the 24-hour motion of the Earth itself.) Let us assess the plus sign in the circle with the following direction-values: The top of the plus sign as North: Noon; the bottom of the plus sign as South: Midnight; the left arm of the plus sign as East: 6 A.M.; and the right arm of the plus sign as West: 6 P.M.

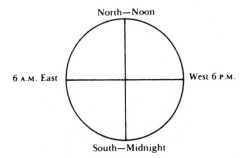

North—Noon

6 A.M. East   West 6 P.M.

South—Midnight

As the Earth turns on its axis, it will take each constellation 2 hours to pass a given point. Since 6 A.M. is approximately dawn, a constellation which is seen on the eastern horizon is said to be rising, or in its Ascendance. Its opposing constellation will be disappearing below the horizon, and is said to be descending. It will take the constellation on the Ascendant 6 hours to reach the Noon position. Therefore, the constellation which rose 6 hours earlier will be at the

Noon position, the highest position and most open spot in the sky—
at its *Elevation*. Its opposite constellation will be at its lowest, most
hidden position, called in its *Depression*, or at its Nadir. In like
manner, planets that are within 7 degrees of these key reference points
are also called the Ascendant or the Descendant, Elevated or
Depressed. These positions are essential in interpreting a chart. For
example, a person having Mars in Aries on the Ascendant will act
much differently from one whose Aries and Mars are hidden from
view at the Nadir.

    If we now number the four quadrants in our diagram, starting
in the lower left-hand quadrant, we will be able to understand the
development of the house positions and the meanings of the divisions
of the houses.

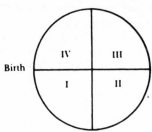

If we think of the developmental history of the native from birth
through death, we can recognize four phases of that growth.

Phase I.   Survival as a person
Phase II.   Survival in the family; expanding to close "others"
Phase III.   Relationships with strange "others"
Phase IV.   Relationships with groups of others plus self

    In each of these quadrants, we shall find three constellations.
However, their positions in the quadrants will be determined by
which constellation, in which degree of the constellation, is on the
Ascendant. Thus if Pisces is on the Ascendant, the constellation
immediately below it, that is, the constellation that rises after Pisces,
is Aries, to be followed by the others in order around the Zodiac. The
determination of the degree of the constellation on the Ascendant is
determined by the time of birth, and the Latitude and Longitude of
the place of birth.

    Since there are 360° in any circle, including the circle of the
Zodiac on the ecliptic, and since there are 12 constellations, there are
30° in each constellation. Therefore, in each 90° quadrant in our

diagram, there are three Constellations. However, since we do not know where each constellation falls within the quadrant, we cannot arbitrarily assign the divisions of the constellations in each quadrant: that is determined by the birthplace and birthtime. However, we do have our developmental history of each person's life expressed in generalities in each quadrant. We may now divide each quadrant into three "houses," each of which will delineate, in a logical order, a more precise definition of the lifecycle of the native. We usually number these "houses" from 1 through 12, beginning with the Ascendant.

Phase I.   Survival as a person:
House 1.   The "I" and its immediate needs of identity
House 2.   The "I" and its physical, material support
House 3.   The "I" and its intellect

Phase II.   Survival in the family; expanding to close "others"
House 4.   The immediacy of family; the mother
House 5.   The materialism of family; the father, speculation, creativity
House 6.   The intelligence of the family; health, work, service.

Phase III.   Relationships with strange "others"
House 7.   The "I" and its identification with other "I's"; thus, marriages, partnerships, and so on
House 8.   The relationship of the "I" to the materialism of others. Thus, inheritances which involve the death of others, handling financial affairs of others, and so on
House 9.   The relationship of the "I" to the intellect of others. Thus philosophy and religion, travel to foreign lands

Phase IV.   Relationships of groups of others to the self
House 10.   The "I" and its relationship to the expectations of others; thus, status, profession, and so on
House 11.   The "I and its relationships to organized groups of others; thus, societies for creative activities, social activities, and so on
House 12.   The "I" and its relationship to the work and service, health, and intellect of the group; thus, schools, hospitals, and jails, and so on.

I have now presented the major elements which were available to the ancient Hebrews in the interpretation of the natal chart. Naturally, each of these elements was taken into consideration in determining the life pattern of the native, both as a means of guiding the person into God's path, and of rectifying the person's behavior if they discover that the native had taken the improper path in his or her life. In Table 5.1 there is a list of these elements, constellation by constellation, according to the quadruplicities of the present Age of Pisces.

There is one more important astrological pattern that the ancients used extensively in chart interpretation. The aspects, or angular distances, between planets and the Nodes of the Moon, Ascendant and Midheaven. These aspects themselves developed out of a rational understanding of the properties of plane geometry. These properties were known, if only through physical observation and trial-and-error tinkering, since the times of the Egyptian dynasties. These properties have been taken over by numerology as part of its understanding of the rhythms of nature. They are the properties based on the concepts of balance. To understand them as they were understood by our ancestors, no advanced geometric theories are necessary: all we need is a circle of 360° and three or four different points on that circle.

First from practical engineering applications, the ancients knew that the smallest number of points on which a flat surface could be balanced, was three. That number therefore came to represent the concept of balance. They also knew that a flat surface could be supported on four points, at the corners. However, they soon discovered that this kind of support system, under stress, would break down into four three-point systems. The fourth, unsupported point, if pressure were applied to it, would result in the breaking of the flat surface along a line between the two points adjacent to it. Thus, the number 4 was linked to the concept of stress.

With these practical experiences of balance and stress at hand, the concepts of the balance of forces among the planets developed.

1. Take three points and distribute them equidistantly around the circumference of a circle. When the points are connected, you will have an equilateral triangle, each point being 120° from the other.
   This is considered the symbol of perfect balance in Astrology, and is called the *Grand Trine*. Any two planets which are 120° apart are thus said to be in trine to each other. This is usually considered to be a favorable aspect, and is linked in its effects to the effects of the Greater Benefic

planet, Jupiter. (Incidentally, two Grand Trines that are interlocked with one point indicating Heaven and the other point indicating Earth, is known in Hebrew as a *Magen David*, or shield of David. It is also called a *Jewish Star*, but that is an error: it just looks like a star. Its meaning is the perfect balance sought by man in his relationship with himself, Heaven, and Earth. And where is man? In the middle of the Magen David. The word *Magen* is also a technical term in Hebrew, meaning "horoscope." Since King David was our finest leader, from him the Messiah must prove descent, the position of the stars in his chart were considered to be in the position of that Magen David.)

2. Divide these 120° by 2, so that the three points now form a triangle having two points 120° apart, with the third point equidistant from them at 60° from each end. This 60° aspect is known as a *sext,* and is considered to have the same influence as the planet Venus, the Lesser Benefic. Note that this point of 60° is opposite the original Grand Trine point.

3. Mark four points equidistant from each other on the circle. These points will describe a square when they are connected seriatim, and within that square the opposite points will describe a cross. This is known as the *Grand Cross,* and is considered to be a "make or break" aspect; it is very rare in a natal chart. The four points in the Grand Cross are 90°

apart, and this aspect is considered to be a tense aspect, having the same influence as Saturn, the Greater Malefic.

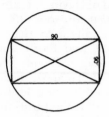

4. Now find three points on the chart, two of which are 90° apart in square aspect, and the other is halfway between them and 45° from each. This aspect is called a *semisquare*, and is said to have the same influence as does Mars, the Lesser Malefic.

5. There is another point that can be equidistant from the two points that are 90° apart. This point is opposite the semisquare point at a distance of 135° from each end of the square aspect. This is known as the *sesqui-quadrate:* it is the sum of a square and a semisquare, and it is a very tense aspect, the problems it portends in the life of the native are resolved with great difficulty over long periods of time, if ever.

6. There is another long aspect, and another short aspect, both of which revolve around the 60° sext aspect. These two points located on opposite sides of the circle are equidistant from the points which are 60° apart. One is at 30°, and is called a *semisext;* the other is 150° away, and is called a

Quinqunx. These are really communicative aspects, and have influences similar to those of Mercury. Since Mercury is the messenger who carries all kinds of news, these aspects can be either beneficial or inimical. However, when the native has in his natal chart two quinqunx aspects from the same planet to two other planets which are therefore in sext to each other, it is known as a *Yod,* and is a very powerful aspect, indicating hidden talents which must surface so that the native can become a blessing to both self and society.

7. Two other aspects are the *conjunction* and the *opposition.* Planets are in conjunction when they are within 10° of each other forming, or 6° separating. The same orbs (allowable distances within which planets may be said to be in aspect to each other) apply to oppositions. Conjunctions are said to have the same influence as the Sun, and oppositions the same influence as the Moon.

Finally, we must know about *allowable distances,* or orbs, of the aspects, and how much distance is usually allowed between forming and separating aspects. The inner planets obviously move faster than the outer planets; the farther from the Sun, the slower the orbital speed. Therefore, if two planets are in aspect to each other, the faster planet is said to be making the aspect to the slower planet. The Ascendant and the Midheaven move at the same speed as the Sun, so that all aspects among the three are considered to be forming aspects. For the sake of clarity, a list follows of the planets and their orbital periods, that is, the amount of time taken to complete one circuit of the Sun. For astrological purposes, the orbital period of the Sun, Ascendant, and Midheaven is assumed to be 1 year, the period of the Earth's orbit. They are in the order of the fastest to the slowest planets.

* See Chapter 7 for our description of the influences of the Sun and Moon.

Moon	28 days	Mars	1 yr 322 days
Mercury	88 days	Jupiter	11 yrs 315 days
Venus	224 days	Nodes of the Moon	18 yrs
Ascendant	1 yr		
Sun	1 yr	Saturn	28 yrs
Midheaven	1 yr		

Thus, if Mars stood at 15° Scorpio, the Sun at 8° Scorpio, Jupiter at 20° Scorpio, and Saturn at 5° Scorpio, what could we say about their possible mutual conjunctions?

1. The Sun, faster than all the planets mentioned, is separating from Saturn by 3° and is within orb: it is approaching Mars and Jupiter; it is within a forming orb of Mars, but not yet within orb of Jupiter. Therefore, the Sun is conjunct Mars and Saturn.
2. Mars is beyond Saturn and outside of a separating orb of 6°. Mars is approaching Jupiter and is within a forming orb of 10°. Mars is therefore also conjunct Jupiter.
3. Jupiter is beyond both a separating orb with Saturn and a forming orb with the Sun.

You now have the basic information that our ancestors possessed as they studied the heavens for evidence of God's will for mankind. They interpreted their natal charts in much the same way modern Astrologers interpret charts today. However, the one principle that they possessed which has been lost in modern Astrology is the principle of balance. As you have read in this chapter, the concept of balance in the universe, balance among man, God, and universe was uppermost in their minds. They built their house system logically, and to balance each other's elements. Every thing that they conceived had to contribute to the perfection of balance in the life of humanity. When they cast horoscopes, they sought out the needed balance in each natal chart to complement the Divine attributes already present in the person, to guide the native in the paths of God—that which in Hebrew we call Halachah, "the way to go." Although this Halachah was usually conceived in legal and ritualistic dimensions, its spiritual dimension was reflected in the Astrology of the day. As a practicing astrologer, in casting horoscopes I still seek balance for the native: the way he or she ought to go—the move towards wholeness.

Table 5.1 Elements for Determining Life Pattern in Age of Pisces Today

Constellation	Quadru-plicity	Tripli-city	Son of Jacob	Planet Ruler	Solar Lunar	Gender
Aries	Cardinal	Fire	Benjamin	Mars	Lunar	Masculine
Taurus	Fixed	Earth	Reuben	Venus	Lunar	Feminine
Gemini	Mutable	Air	Simon	Mercury	Lunar	Masculine
Cancer	Cardinal	Water	Levi	Moon	Lunar	Feminine
Leo	Fixed	Fire	Judah	Sun	Solar	Masculine
Virgo	Mutable	Earth	Zebulun	Mercury	Solar	Feminine
Libra	Cardinal	Air	Issachar	Venus	Solar	Masculine
Scorpio	Fixed	Water	Dan	Mars	Solar	Feminine
Sagitarius	Mutable	Fire	Gad	Jupiter	Solar	Masculine
Capricorn	Cardinal	Earth	Asher	Saturn	Solar	Feminine
Aquarius	Fixed	Air	Naphtali	Saturn	Lunar	Masculine
Pisces	Mutable	Water	Joseph	Jupiter	Lunar	Feminine

6

THE TESTIMONY OF
THE CONSTELLATIONS

Ancient Hebrew astrologers viewed the workings of the planets and the constellations very differently from our modern astrologers. They considered at all times the need to find the balance in the universe, and read the heavens as a key witness to that balance of forces which kept the universe in ethical as well as physical motion. Therefore, they developed the concept of constant forces and changing forces, and of the relationships between them.

To my astrological ancestors, the constellations presented the constant forces in the universe for our use, and the planets represented the changing forces in the universe. The forces of the constellations could be pictured in physical terms as the carrier wave, which was modulated by the play of planetary forces and aspects, presenting their influences to our waiting world.

I am not an advocate of "Sun Sign Astrology." In this type of "Astrology" a person, having declared the totality of personal astrological knowledge in the statement "I'm a Pisces," then proceeds to interpret, direct his life, and predict all good and evil in the universe on the basis of that Sun Sign statement! For that is all the statement "I am a Pisces" really means; the person knows only that the birth was during the Hebrew month of Adar (approximately February 22 to March 21): this cannot really be considered astrological knowledge of any depth. Yet, this is indeed the extent of astrological knowledge and interest held by many people in the world. It seems as if the entire nation wants to know more about its Sun Sign! How did our ancestors in Astrology view the constant forces of the constellations?

First of all, my astrological ancestors viewed each constellation as having the following constant forces operating within it: Triplicity (Fire, Earth, Air, or Water); Spiritual Rulership (a son of Jacob); Planetary Rulership (for example, Sun rules Leo, Moon rules Cancer); Gender (Masculine or Feminine); Solar and Lunar (east of the Sun and west of the Moon). Decanate (Lords of each 10°); Planetary Limits (4 to 8° arcs in each constellation, ruled by each of five planets); Novenas (3-1/3° equal arcs ruled by the five planets and the Two Lights: Sun and Moon); Duods, or Duodecads (2½° arcs ruled by the planets and Lights according to their order in the zodiacal rulerships).

The operations of these constant forces were well documented and based on actual physical observation of the Heavens. In modern Astrology, most of these forces and their influences are not even considered although almost all of our modern Sun Sign delineations depend on their development in ancient times. Because of the familiarity of the ancients with the movements of the heavens as observed, their delineations of the Sun Signs seem to us almost too specific in some senses, and not nearly specific enough in others. For instance, the ancients were very specific in their descriptions of the physical appearance and health indications of the Sun Sign native, but much less specific in terms of the psychological vectors of the native's life. This seems strange to us until we realize that constant forces will manifest themselves in physical constancies which have little ability to change, whereas variable forces will easily affect those areas of life, the psychological, the social, the ethical, and the material dimensions, which are themselves very amenable to change in human life.

The *variable* forces which modified the constant forces of the constellations depended on: the *planet* which transited the constellation: the *aspects* made to that planet by other planets and the Ascendant and Midheaven as well as other *sensitive points* in the constellation itself, such as the *Well of the Stars* (certain degrees within each constellation in which the effects of certain nonzodiacal constellations "drown out" the effects of transiting planets); *Degrees of Honor* (certain degrees within each constellation which are occupied by certain nonzodiacal constellations that enhance the positive qualities of the transiting planets); certain degrees in each constellation which represent the exact points in which the *Dignities* and *Debilities* of specific planets are most strongly shown (exact degrees of *planetary rulerships* or *exaltations, detriments* or *falls* according to the well-known system of these forces); the degrees in the various constellations of the *Aphelions* and *Perihelions*, and the *North* and *South Nodes* of each planet.

It is obvious that any exhaustive treatment of all these *constant* and *variable* points in each constellation would need a new book devoted entirely to their explication. However, I shall explain one constellation, Leo, in the ancient manner, and then list the "Sun Sign" delineations of the other eleven constellations by their constants and decanates. These delineations will most often refer, not to the "Sun Sign" but to the Ascendant (see Chapter 21).

Before explaining the Constellation Leo, however, I am quite sure that one of my sharp-eyed readers who is familiar with Astrology will ask: Why weren't the quadruplicities mentioned (Cardinal, Fixed, and Mutable Constellations)? I should have mentioned those, but I am not sure about their category: Are they *constant* or *variable* forces? You see, every time a Prophetic Age changes, that is, from the Age of Aries to the Age of Pisces to the coming Age of Aquarius—the *quadruplicity value* of the constellations change, and then remain constant for 2,150 years. During the Age of Aries, the *First House Cardinal Constellation* was Taurus; during the now-ending Age of Pisces, the *First House Cardinal Constellation* is Aries: when the Age of Aquarius arrives around 1980, the *First House Cardinal Constellation* will be Pisces! For delineation's sake, however, let us call the power of the quadruplicity a *constant* force (See Table 6.1).

LEO: MASCULINE, DIURNAL (DAY), ORIENTAL (EASTERN), FIRE-TRIPLICITY CONSTELLATION. (In biblical times it was the Fire-Triplicity Cardinal Sign: today it is the Fire-Triplicity Fixed Sign.)

General: Leo will have a fine body on tapering legs, a keen appearance and catlike eyes. Reddish hair will predominate, but hair will always be the Leo's crown of glory. Leo will be educated, clever, generous, and self-reliant in danger. Leo will also tend toward melancholy, preemption in speech, contrariness, sensuous lustfulness, and gluttony. Leo women will tend toward modesty.

First-decan Leo. (born within the first 10°) will keep his or her ruddy hair, be beautiful in body and face, have an erect bearing, but be bleary-eyed. Illness tends to settle in the upper parts of the stomach. Well known among the people, first-decan Leo will be modest only in the presence of those who are recognizably greater than himself!

Table 6.1 DEGREE—RULERSHIPS OF THE CONSTELLATION LEO

Degrees of Leo	Ruler of Leo	Ruler of Triplicity	Ruler of Limits	Ruler of Novenas	Ruler of Duodecads	Gender	Magnitude*
00:01—02:30	Sun	Sun	Jupiter	Mars	Sun	Male	Bright
02:31—03:20	Sun	Sun	Jupiter	Mars	Mercury	Male	Bright
03:21—05:00	Sun	Sun	Jupiter	Venus	Mercury	Male	Bright
05:01—06:00	Sun	Sun	Jupiter	Venus	Venus	Female	Bright
06:01—06:40	Sun	Sun	Venus	Venus	Venus	Female	Bright
06:41—07:00	Sun	Sun	Venus	Mercury	Venus	Female	Bright
07:01—07:30	Sun	Sun	Venus	Mercury	Venus	Male	Neutral
07:31—10:00	Sun	Sun	Venus	Mercury	Mars	Male	Neutral
10:01—12:00	Sun	Jupiter	Venus	Moon	Jupiter	Male	Dark
12:01—12:30	Sun	Jupiter	Mercury	Moon	Jupiter	Male	Dark
12:31—13:00	Sun	Jupiter	Mercury	Moon	Saturn	Male	Dark
13:01—13:20	Sun	Jupiter	Mercury	Moon	Saturn	Female	Dark
13:21—16:00	Sun	Jupiter	Mercury	Sun	Saturn	Female	Dark
16:01—16:40	Sun	Jupiter	Mercury	Sun	Saturn	Female	Blank
16:41—17:30	Sun	Jupiter	Mercury	Mercury	Saturn	Female	Blank
17:31—18:00	Sun	Jupiter	Mercury	Mercury	Jupiter	Female	Blank
18:01—20:00	Sun	Jupiter	Saturn	Mercury	Jupiter	Female	Blank
20:01—21:00	Sun	Mars	Saturn	Venus	Mars	Female	Blank
21:01—22:30	Sun	Mars	Saturn	Venus	Mars	Female	Bright
22:31—23:00	Sun	Mars	Saturn	Venus	Venus	Female	Bright
23:01—23:20	Sun	Mars	Saturn	Venus	Venus	Male	Bright
23:21—24:00	Sun	Mars	Mars	Mars	Venus	Male	Bright
24:01—25:00	Sun	Mars	Mars	Mars	Venus	Male	Bright
25:01—26:40	Sun	Mars	Mars	Mars	Mercury	Male	Bright
26:41—27:30	Sun	Mars	Mars	Jupiter	Mercury	Male	Bright
27:31—30:00	Sun	Mars	Mars	Jupiter	Moon	Male	Bright

* Bright influence of planet strengthened at this degree; dark indicates influence of planet occluded at this degree.

Second-decan Leo (born from 11 to 20°) will have an overpowering physical presence and a beautiful body to match. All this will be placed on small legs. When sickness hits, it is usually in the diaphragm. Second-decan Leo will be magnanimous, and honored by his people.

Third-decan Leo (born from 21 to 30°) will have a short body and blotches on the skin. He will be very fond of women, and have a powerful voice. Third-decan Leo will have many friends and many enemies, and many illnesses!

Leo controls: Chest, heart, cardiac parts of the stomach, the diaphragm, back, loins, ribs, and the nape of the neck.

Illnesses: Same areas of the body as controls. If the planets in Leo are afflicted (have squares or oppositions to them from other planets in the chart, or occupy hazardous degrees), then you can expect the following diseases to manifest themselves:

Jupiter	afflicted in Leo:	diseases of the testicles
Mercury	afflicted in Leo:	diseases of the arms
Saturn	afflicted in Leo:	diseases of the genitalia
Venus	afflicted in Leo:	diseases of the chest
Mars	afflicted in Leo:	diseases of the heart
Moon	afflicted in Leo:	diseases of the neck
Sun	afflicted in Leo:	diseases of the head

Leo is the constellation of the Sun's rulership and the detriment of Saturn (detriment: the constellation opposite a planet's ruling constellation). No planets are in their Exaltation or Fall in Leo. The Aphelion of Mars is in the 12°.

In Chapter 9, I discuss Samson and Delilah, and make the statement that Samson was a typical Leo male. If we look at the delineations of Leo in ancient times and compare them with the character of Samson in the biblical narrative, we can see how true that statement is. Samson's strength was in his hair, a typical Leo preoccupation. Although cheated and duped by his wife, he displayed his magnanimity by forgiving her. His keenness of eye brought to his view the honeycomb in the skull, his preemption of speech issued the riddled challenge which began the tragedy of his life, his self-reliant courage in the face of danger was shown by his bare-handed victory over the lion and his defeat of the Phillistine army using the jawbone of an ass as his only weapon. His lustful sensuality led him into the liason with Delilah, and his cleverness was shown in the way that he evaded giving the truth about his source of strength, three times in a row. He was indeed well known among men, making many friends and even more enemies. And he ended his career in a blaze of destructive glory! The statement that Samson was a typical Leo male is amply documented, both in Astrology and in the Bible.

And now, let me delineate the Decans of the other eleven constellations:*

ARIES: FIRE, MASCULINE, DIURNAL, ORIENTAL

General. An unusual body with a long face and dark eyes, and the habit of looking toward the ground constantly; a thick neck, soft ears, and abundant wavy hair; weak legs, garrulous in speech, weak but pleasant voice; irascible but fond of justice; eats copiously.

First Decan. Little flesh on the body, reddish face; will have numerous friends, and abhor evil.

Second Decan. Strangely formed body; a dark but beautiful complexion; easily aroused to uncontrollable angers; will combine high principles with perfect comprehension and breeding; will have numerous enemies.

Third Decan. Reddish or golden complexion; will be isolated from mankind.

Controls: Head, face, ears, and pupils of the eyes.

Ills: Unexplained problems of balance, sudden unconsciousness, ear trouble, pains in the nostrils, teeth, or eyes.

TAURUS: EARTH, FEMININE, NOCTURNAL, SOUTH

General: Erect posture, a long face with a broad forehead and large eyes, balanced on a thick, short neck; an aquiline nose and a shock of black, curly hair; possibly of deformed limbs; lustful and gluttonous, contrary, incoherent in speech, and deficient in knowledge.

First Decan: Short in stature, with large eyes, thick lips, and a mark on the neck; noble at heart; will have many friends and hedonistically enjoy all delights of the senses.

* Often, the decanant characteristics of a person's rising sign are more accurate than those of his Sun Sign (Ed.).

Second Decan: A round head, broad stomach, and beautiful eyes; will have a generous soul and be intelligent.

Third Decan: Although Taureans will have a beautiful head and body, they will suffer from overwork and have little luck with the opposite sex.

Controls: Neck and throat.

Ills: Diseases of the neck and throat, plus goiter and scrofula.

GEMINI: AIR, MASCULINE, DIURNAL, OCCIDENTAL

General: Gemini will be erect in stature, handsome of form and face, will have a large stomach and broad shoulders; with beautiful eyes, curly hair, and a strong voice; will be magnanimous, truthful, skilled in their work and in all tasks, and are religious moderates. Gemini will be an astronomer, mathematician, writer or sage.

First Decan: A handsome body with a pointed face and beautiful eyes and hair; will have a mark on the head or cheeks; patient but suffering from overwork; they will have little luck with the opposite sex.

Second Decan: Well-built, but short and dark. Well bred and pleasant speech; will associate with the current nobility.

Third Decan: Small face, with small eyes, will be extremely sexual. Tendency to telling lies and using language improperly.

Controls: the "tubes" of the body (blood vessels, lymphatics), the arms, hands and shoulders.

Ills: Diseases of the upper extremities, lymphatics and the blood.

CANCER: WATER, FEMININE, NOCTURNAL, NORTH

General: Thick, heavy limbs, a wide forehead, and teeth spread widely apart; may have hearing and speech problems; a highly respected person and lover of mankind.

First Decan: Physically attractive, with hairline and eyelids close together, long nostrils, and broad shoulders; will be a good soul, having many friends, but when necessary will be an expert in perpetrating fraud.

Second Decan: Short, with reddish face; will be beloved by all creatures.

Third Decan: Fat, short, with broad stomach, and large abdomen, and hairy eyelids; very strong physically, but one who suffers alone, and is subject to heart attacks.

Controls: Breast, mammalia, cardiac region, ribs, spleen, lungs.

Ills: All ills of same regions and organs as controls.

VIRGO: EARTH, FEMININE, NOCTURNAL, SOUTH

General: Virgo will have a good-looking, erect body, straight hair; will be learned and intelligent.

First Decan: A pleasing, powerful voice, a pleasing face and kind soul; there will be the danger of impotency; will be a writer, an expert in mathematics.

Second Decan: Will have small eyes and pretty nostrils; will be charming, well bred, magnanimous, candid, and fond of receiving compliments.

Third Decan: Will be beautiful physically, as well as educated, truly intelligent, humble, and wise.

Controls: the stomach, intestines, and diaphragm.

Ills: Melancholia, plus stomach, intestines and diaphragm.

LIBRA: AIR, MASCULINE, DIURNAL, OCCIDENTAL

General: Libra will have straight limbs, pleasant speech; will be sensible and well bred, with hands capable of plying any trade; Body color will be lighter than the facial color, so that the body will look "cleaner" than the face. Libra will be noble and reliable, a hunter, fond of the opposite sex, probably a musician or composer.

First Decan: Humble, refined, having beauty of facial characteristics. Subject to overwork, head wounds, and smarting pains in hands or feet.

Second Decan: Liberal and friendly, with attractive body, face, and stature; however, eyes may be deformed.

Third Decan: Good-looking body and a winsome smile, but with poor vision; well known and respected.

Controls: The lower bowels (small intestine just above the appendix; the appendix itself, and the large intestine and colon).

Ills: Same as control regions, plus burning urine, hemorrhage, amblyopia.

SCORPIO: WATER, FEMININE, NOCTURNAL, NORTH

General: Scorpio will be dark, hairy, with small but normal eyes in large face with narrow forehead, and a wide shouldered body. Neither the voice nor the enunciation will be particularly pleasant. Scorpio will have many children. "Good" Scorpios ("eagles") will be generous, refined, reliable, and astute; "bad" Scorpios ("snakes") will be destructive, unreliable, deceitful, irascible, calumnators, and prevaricators. Both "eagle" and "snake" Scorpios are subject to melancholy.

First Decan: Rather attractive, with catlike eyes, a wide chest, a mark on the right hand, on the left leg, or on the head; educated, sensible, and glib of speech.

Second Decan: Large head on rather handsome body; well bred and loquacious, may have a mark on the back.

Third Decan: Short in stature, problems with eye focus, fond of both women and men, and food; usually feels dejected.

Controls: Sexual organs.

Ills: Diseases of the sexual organs.

SAGITTARIUS: FIRE, MASCULINE, DIURNAL, ORIENTAL

General: Sagittarius has an erect stature, ruddy complexion, and sharp forehead, large stomach, heavy legs, and sparse hair. Jovial, strong, generous, agile, and fond of horses; Sagittarius has a weak voice, will have few children, and can be sly and inconsistent.

First Decan: Beautiful face and figure, holding self erect,

Sagittarius will associate with the rulers and the magnates, and always uphold the good.

Second Decan: Elegant body, but with golden tinge to face and eyelids that insist on sticking together.

Third Decan: Tall, strong, broad chest, with a charming countenance setting off catlike eyes, Sagittarius will be modest, helpful, and well bred.

Controls: Testicles, larynx, and supernumerary growths.

Ills: Blindness, fever, venoms, falling from heights.

CAPRICORN: EARTH, FEMININE, NOCTURNAL, SOUTH

General: Capricorn will have thick cheeks in a small head on an erect and attractive body; will be well educated but deceitful; austere, irascible, and often destructive; lack of energy will often make his actions futile. Addicted to sexuality, Capricorn's children will be large at birth, and often twins. Capricorn will acquire wealth through the ruling powers of the time and place, but the opposite sex will be Capricorn's downfall.

First Decan: Capricorn will have a wide chest and pleasing body; will be intelligent, modest, refined, and magnanimous.

Second Decan: Capricorn will have large nostrils, handsome eyes, and an imposing manner. But be careful: although ingratiating, Capricorn's intention will be evil and Capricorn will turn irascible.

Third Decan: Will have a beautiful body and a golden complexion which will be irresistible to the opposite sex to which this Capricorn is addicted; is also sociable and refined, and shuns evil.

Controls: External genitalia.

Ills: Scabies, pruritus, leprosy, deaf-mutism, fevers, amblyopia, and hemorrhage.

AQUARIUS: AIR, MASCULINE, DIURNAL, OCCIDENTAL

General: Aquarius will be rather short, having a large head, and feet of different sizes; magnanimous, attractive, and self-laudatory, Aquarius will always drive to increase wealth, and have few children, either through desire or impotence.

First Decan: Refined, gregarious, the possessor of a beautiful body and face.

Second Decan: Aquarius will be tall and ruddy, and will have a life full of grief.

Third Decan: Bearing a short and attractive body, this Aquarian of ruddy complexion will be overfond of the opposite sex.

Controls: Legs.

Ills: The legs, plus depression, black jaundice, hernia.

PISCES: WATER, FEMININE, NOCTURNAL, NORTH

General: Pisces will have a medium-sized but broad-chested body, black eyes, and a serene forehead, a white complexion. Pisces will have a weak voice; will be irritable but not preemptory, polite but deceitful, and indulge freely in food, drink, and sleep.

First Decan: Narrow-chested, but beautifully proportioned shape and facial characteristics.

Second Decan: Short and hirsute, this Piscean will have a preposessing appearance, and will be hostile to all.

Third Decan: Auburn hair and beautiful eyes, this Piscean will have the misfortune to be ill quite often.

Controls: Feet and toes.

Ills: Feet and toes, plus hemiplegy, leprosy, and itching.

Arians provide the world with kings who practice justice; leaders in war, fire, and bloodshed; surgeons, butchers and travelers.
Taureans provide the world with procurers, sensualists, and entertainers.
Geminians provide the world with kings, magnates, heroes, magicians and sorcerers, and delicate craftsmen.
Cancerians provide the world with plebians, wanderers, and those other people find repulsive.
Leonians provide the world with kings, princes, and noblemen; artisans in gold, silver, and gems; and all who exercise any useful trade.
Virgoans provide the world with writers and sages, mathematicians and geometers, and all intermediaries and exponents of mockery.

Librans provide the world with mathematicians, businessmen, merchants, and dealers in food and beverages, judges, and singers.

Scorpios provide the world with judges and all despicable persons.

Sagittarians provide the world with judges and servants of God, philosophers and interpreters of dreams, merchants, philanthropists and all others who are merciful, and archers.

Capricornians provide the world with farmers, sailors, intermediaries, and shepherds.

Aquarians provide the world with sailors and tanners, the downcast and the afflicted.

Pisceans provide the world with fishermen and outcasts.

At the beginning of this chapter I mentioned that Sun Sign Astrology is a very new phenomenon in the history of Astrology. The chapter on Astrology in the Talmud, shows our Talmudic ancestors considered the Ascendant to be the most important indicator in the natal horoscope, and that the planetary hours were also extremely important. They recognized this as valid even into the sixteenth century. Rabbi Abraham ibn Ezra in Spain wrote seven books on Astrology. The first book "The Beginning of Wisdom" has nine chapters, only one of which deals with Sun Signs.

This does not imply any derogation to the importance of the Sun in a natal chart, but rather that the Sun is only 1 of 14 indicators in a modern horoscope (10 planets, Ascendant, Midheaven, North and South Nodes of the Moon) and a native's astrological profile cannot be determined on the basis of Sun Sign alone.

In the chapter on Astrology in the Talmud, you will see that all discussions of the characteristics of man are based on the birth-sign of the Ascendant and of the hourly ruler. When one sage speaks of those born under certain planets, and is indicating that this means the Sun Sign in a Constellation which is ruled by that particular planet or the planetary ruler of that particular day of birth (Rabbi Joshua ben Levi), another Sage insists that this is wrong, and that the hour of birth (Ascendant or hourly planetary ruler) is more important (Rabbi Hanina).

I hope that those who have been introduced to Astrology through a fascination with their Sun Sign will develop their interest along more exacting and exciting lines, and learn the meanings of all the planets in their constellations, in their dignities and debilities, in their aspects to other planets, and in their individual contributions to the overall synthesis of a life as seen through the eyes of a competent astrologer. In this manner they will enrich their experience in Astrology, and through Astrology, they will enrich their lives, as well.

7

THE TESTIMONY
OF THE PLANETS

The first book in Jewish tradition which linked Astrology directly to the mystical vector of our faith was written during Talmudic times, in the third century of the Common Era. It matched the planets, constellations, and elements (Fire, Water, and Air, from which three elements Earth coalesced) to the letters of the Hebrew alphabet, and to the Paths of Wisdom which linked the 10 Divine Emanations (10 Sephirot) into a Tree of Life. This is not the place, nor is there space in this book, to review the correspondencies involved. The work under discussion, *Sefer Yetsirah,* "The Book of Formation," has already been analyzed by others. The reason for mentioning it here is to point out that the 12 constellations were linked to the 12 letters of the Hebrew alphabet which had a constant pronunciation, whereas the 7 planets were linked to the 7 letters of the Hebrew alphabet which had double pronunciations. Astrologers thought each planet had capabilities for both good and evil, whereas they thought of the constellations as having constant forces, which varied only as the planets transitted them, and took on positive and negative vibrations. And since each letter of the Hebrew alphabet represented an esoteric tool used by God in the creation of the Universe, its influence had to extend from Divine will through time, space, and man. This concept explains the influences of the planets on the life of man and on the lives of every growing thing. It also explains the Midrashic statement that there is not one blade of grass that does not have its own planet directing its growth. (See Gen. Rabbah 10:7) In Table 7.1 there is a list of the letters of the planets, the opposite forces in God's will which they represent, and the parts of man's body which they affect.

Whether or not a particular planet had a beneficial or baneful influence on a person depended on its position in the natal chart. Was it strong because it was in the constellation it ruled, or was it weak because it was in the opposite constellation? Was it strong because it was in the house normally ruled by it. (That is, the house in which its constellation normally fell although that house may be ruled by a different constellation. For instance, Mars rules the Constellation Aries, which normally occupies the First House of the natal chart. If Mars is in Leo, but Leo occupies the First House, then Mars in Leo would be in the 1st house, and would gain strength because of its placement there.) Was it rising (near the Ascendant) or falling (near the Descendant)? Was it elevated (near the Midheaven) or depressed (near the Nadir)? There were and still are many factors which indicate the strength or weakness of a planet.

In like manner, the aspects to the planet had to be considered. A planet in the chart having no aspects to any other planets was considered particularly strong. A planet having many tense aspects from other planets (squares, oppositions, and some conjunctions) would shed tense and difficult influences. A planet with many flowing aspects from other planets (sexts, trines, and some conjunctions) would have a beneficial influence on the native. There were many factors to consider in deciding the effect of a planet in a particular chart: whether, in the words of the Kabbalah, God's benign will would manifest itself in mercy, or God's stern will would manifest itself in harsh judgement. As we delineate the various qualities of the seven known planets of ancient times, remember that good is mixed with evil, that the planets represent both possibilities, and that all possibilities flow through them to influence the native in his life.

Sun

The Sun is equally warm and dry. Its human qualities are clearness and sensitivity of soul, knowledge, intelligence, majesty, beauty, and vigor. On the negative side, it denotes vaulting ambition, attachment to wealth, garrulity, and excessive desires. In the natal chart it denotes laws and precepts, the union of society, fathers and half-brothers.

Table 7.1 Opposite Forces in God's Will, Letters of the Planets, Part Affected in Man

God's Will	Wisdom Folly	Wealth Poverty	Victory Defeat	Life Death	Ruler Slave	Peace War	Beauty Ugliness
Letter of Planet	B	G	D	K	P	R	T
Heaven	Sun	Moon	Mars	Mercury	Jupiter	Venus	Saturn
Earth	Height	Depth	East	West	North	South	Center
Day of week	Sunday	Monday	Tuesday	Wednesday	Thursday	Friday	Saturday
Man's affected part	Right eye	Left eye	Right ear	Left ear	Right nostril	Left nostril	Mouth

Note: The extension of the Divine will in the universe has its heavenly vector in the prime directions which enclose a volume, plus its center. Not many people consider the center to be a direction, and yet that concept is basic to the development of Gestalt psychology (that is, that person sits at the center of the perceiving universe). Note also that the parts of man represented by the planets are those parts with which he exercises his sense perceptions of sight, hearing, smell, taste, and touch, the mouth representing the latter two senses. In Jewish mysticism, the five senses are called the "Five Gates of Salvation."

Moon

The Moon is cold and damp, and leads all living things to mold and putrify. Its positive human qualities are skill in magic and a knowledge of stories, plus a love of pleasure and an abundance of food. (The typical Jewish mother—Cancer—eat, eat my child!) On the negative side are excessive introspection, amnesia, phobia, indifference, and meditation in a mind lacking adequate knowledge. In the natal chart it denotes the mother, the mother's sisters, anyone's older sisters, and pregnant women.

Mercury

Mercury is mixed and variable, changing according to the other planets with which it is in aspect, and according to the constellations. (Remember, Mercury is the messenger, who carries information but rarely originates it.) Mercury refers to the soul of man and to man's powers of comprehension. On the positive side it leads to clarity in thought and speech, education, wisdom, Astrology, accuracy of expression, talent for composing poetry, and prophecy. In its negative phase, it leads to excessive argumentation, resorting to trickery and the forging of documents. In the natal chart it denotes any messenger or intermediator.

Venus

Venus is cold and damp, and corresponds to fructification and growth, and the lustful mind. In its beneficial phase, it offers cleanliness, love, laughter, joy, dancing, pleasant conversation and a love for children, as well as a devotion to justice and to worship. Its negative influences include incessant longing for lustful sexual intercourse, drunkenness, gambling, giving of false testimony, and excessive desires for everything. In the natal chart, it represents the mother, daughters and younger sisters.

Mars

Mars is hot and scorchingly dry, corresponding to flames, death, devastation, rebellion, massacre, and war. Its positive elements are strength, victory and power. Negative influences leads to excessive wrath, failure to keep one's promises, larceny, and cruelty to others. In the natal chart, it refers to brothers.

Jupiter

Jupiter is warm and moist and corresponds to life, increase of well-being, productivity and development, and the growing soul. Its positive elements are supporting the rule of law, seeking the good of his fellowmen, serving in the courts of law and the courts of the Lord. Negative elements can lead to talking too much, seeking too much wealth, and seeking too much the approval of his peers. In the natal chart it refers to children and grandchildren.

Saturn

Saturn is cold and dry, denoting death and destruction, weeping and grief, and all ancient things. It does have positive influences: astuteness of mental faculties, the ability to meditate on death and mysteries, a knowledge of secrets, worship of the Lord, and the power to dominate men. Its negative aspects include isolation from man, conquest and pillage of others, overbearing anger, and the betrayal of his fellowman. In a natal chart it denotes fathers, grandfathers, and the deceased.

PART III:
ASTROLOGY
IN THE
BIBLE

8

"... TO RULE BOTH DAY AND NIGHT"

If Jacob was ignorant of Astrology, why did he react so swiftly, and so astrologically, to Joseph's second dream? If Astrology were of little matter to the Children of Israel, why did the prophet Isaiah feel obliged to attack astrologers in very detailed, specific references to their astrological "specialties"? Why are Samson and Delilah astrological personalities? Did the Israelites believe that the planets in their orbits effected the rise and fall of nations on earth? If they did not, then what other meaning can one give to the Song of Deborah?

These biblical events and the biblical answer to these questions make up only a part of the body of direct evidence to verify that Astrology was part of the everyday living concern of the Children of Israel and of their non-Israelite contemporaries. Direct evidence shouts "Sun! Moon! Stars! Relationships!" directly by name in the Bible text.

Both "secondary evidence" and "statistical evidence" that complete the picture of Astrology in biblical times are just as important although more subtle than "direct" evidence that Astrology was of concern in biblical times. "Secondary evidence" arises when the knowledge of Astrology helps previously meaningless or difficult passages in the Bible become clear in their intent and meaning. This type of evidence will be covered in Chapter 13.

Also, the firm foundation for proof of the importance of Astrology to our biblical forbearers rests solidly on a statistical and linguistic analysis of the text of Scripture itself, that is, analysis of the direct and secondary evidence. This anaylsis yields strong statistical and linguistic evidence of the power of Astrology and of astrological uses in biblical times.

As we continue investigating evidence of Astrology in the Bible, we shall deal with the analysis of biblical material in the following order:

1. What the Bible is to me, a Rabbi? How the books of the Bible are categorized.
2. The *key* to understanding Astrology in the Bible: In Genesis 1:16 what is the meaning of the word $M\overline{S}L$, which is usually translated as "rule"?
3. In the Bible what is the significance of the heavens?
4. How are terms used in Scripture, for example, Heavens, Earth, Stars, Sun, Moon? How these terms are used singly, and in conjunction with each other. The importance of these terms in investigating Astrology in Scripture.
5. What is the importance of the concept of "witness" in the Bible to our astrological investigation?
6. What is the difference between the "natural" and "paranatural" use of words in the Bible?
7. Finally, what are the relationships among questions 4, 5 and 6. That is, when we connect the concept of "witness" in the Bible—the need, for example, for at least two witnesses to establish the truth of a situation—with the occurrences of the joint use of "Heaven and Earth" versus the use of "Heaven" alone as witness; with the occurrence of "Sun plus some other heavenly body" versus the use of "Sun" alone: do these uses lead to any change in the numbers of "paranatural" verses over "natural" verses? Is there a strong enough positive relationship between "witness" and multiple use and "paranatural" use in Scripture to indicate that the use is not a mere accident, but deliberate and therefore evidence for the valid conclusion that Astrology was an integral part of the thought-processes of our forefathers?

In Hebrew, the entire Bible is called *ṬNKʃ*. This word is an acronym, composed of the first Hebrew letters of the names of the three traditional divisions of the Bible. These divisions are known in English as the *Pentateuch*, the *Prophets*, and the *Hagiogrypha* or *Writings*. Their Hebrew equivalents are

Pentateuch	*TWRH*	(pronounced Torah)
Prophets	*NBYAYMſ*	(pronounced Nevi'im)
Hagiogrypha	*KTWBYMſ*	(pronounced Ketuvim)

Taking the first Hebrew letter in each word seriatim, and placing the vowel "a" between each of these three consonants yields the acronym *TaNaK;* an English equivalent acronym, using the initial letters of the words Pentateuch, Prophets, Hagiogrypha, and placing the vowel "a" between the consonants yields *PaPaH!*

In the Hebrew Bible, the traditional order of the books within each division is different from the order of the books in Christian translations. Table 8.1 is a list of the order of the biblical books within each division of the *ŦNKſ.*

Table 8.1   Biblical Order in Each Division of the Hebrew Bible

TWRH ("Pentateuch")	*NBYAYMſ* ("Prophets")	*KTWBYMſ* ("Hagiogrypha")
1. Genesis	6. Joshua	27. Psalms
2. Exodus	7. Judges	28. Proverbs
3. Leviticus	8. 1 Samuel	29. Job
4. Numbers	9. 2 Samuel	30. Song of Songs
5. Deuteronomy	10. 1 Kings	31. Ruth
	11. 2 Kings	32. Lamentations
	12. Isaiah	33. Ecclesiastes
	13. Jeremiah	34. Esther
	14. Ezekiel	35. Daniel
	15. Hosea	36. Ezra
	16. Joel	37. Nehemiah
	17. Amos	38. 1 Chronicles
	18. Obadiah	39. 2 Chronicles
	19. Jonah	
	20. Micah	
	21. Nahum	
	22. Habakkuk	
	23. Zephaniah	
	24. Haggai	
	25. Zechariah	
	26. Malachi	

    The books of the Bible can also be divided according to their topical contents: that is, Mosaic, Prophetic, Historical, and Didactic books. The Mosaic books include those books ascribed to Moses. Prophetic books include only those 15 books of prophecy called by the names of their authors. Historical books are those dealing primarily with the narrative history of the Israelite people. Didactic books are those of primarily literary, ethical, polemical, or instructive content. Topical divisions of the books of the Bible are listed in Table 8.2. The Traditional *TNKf*, threefold division, and the topical, fourfold division, become extremely important in the analysis of the astrological material in the Bible especially in relation to the developmental nature of Jewish life, as presented in Chapter 2.

Table 8.2   Four Topical Divisions of Hebrew Bible

Mosaic	Prophetic	Historical	Didactic
Genesis	Isaiah	Deuteronomy	Psalms
Exodus	Jeremiah	Joshua	Proverbs
Leviticus	Ezekiel	Judges	Job
Numbers	Hosea	I Samuel	Song of Songs
	Joel	II Samuel	Ruth
	Amos	I Kings	Lamentations
	Obadiah	II Kings	Ecclesiastes
	Jonah	Daniel	Esther
	Micah	Ezra	
	Nahum	Nehemiah	
	Habakkuk	I Chronicles	
	Zephaniah	II Chronicles	
	Haggai		
	Zechariah		
	Malachi		

    As with any foreign language, if there are two words in the particular language that can both be translated into the same English word, then the English translation cannot reveal the important difference in the nuance of meaning between them, differences that make all the difference in the world when considering our problem. For example, there are two words in Hebrew that are both translated as "rule." For this reason, I am going to begin with a full development of my method of research as applied to the very first astrological indication in the Bible so that you may become familiar with my methodology. The data used for other analyses are in Appendices for your ready reference.

The first astrological indication in Scripture occurs in Genesis 1:16:

> And God made the two great lights, the greater light to rule the day, and the lesser light to rule the night and the stars.

This rulership pattern is repeated in verse 18: ". . . to rule the day and the night. . . ." Notice that nowhere are the two lights identified as the Sun and the Moon. However, this is assumed not only from our knowledge of both the text and nature but also from Psalms 136:8-9:

> The Sun to rule by day, for His mercy endureth forever;
> The Moon and Stars to rule by night, for His mercy endureth forever.

Note that the psalmist understood the verses in Genesis as meaning that the Stars shared rulership of the night with the Moon.

The question is this: What does the word "rule" mean? Does it mean to control or to rule like a king? In English we can come to no conclusion although there are those who insist that the use of the word "rule" in this context is merely a poetic manner of saying "to appear" or "to shine." There are two problems, however, for those who insist on this poetic use only. The first problem is that Hebrew is a most specific language: there are words in Hebrew meaning "to appear" or "to shine." If this meaning was intended, then these words would have been used.

The second problem is that there is very little poetry in the Mosaic books of the Bible; but there is a great deal of poetry in the Prophetic books. In the Prophetic books in which poetry is the style, poetic use reverses the use of the word "rule" in Genesis. What do I mean by "reverse"? In the books of the Prophets, words like "bright," "warmth," and "light" are used poetically to refer to the sun; words like "white" and "new" are used to refer to the Moon. But the reverse is never true: the word for "Sun" is not used to refer to "shining" or to "light," nor is the word for "Moon" used to mean "white."

Since the books of the Prophets are the most poetic in the Bible, we would expect to find the most poetic licence in them and not in the Pentateuch which contains the least amount of poetry in the Bible. In other words, in poetic Hebrew use in the Bible, descriptive adjectives and adverbs are used to substitute for the nouns of nature—never the other way around, as those who insist on poetic translation wish us to believe were used in Genesis.*

What, then, is the key to understanding the meaning of rulership assigned to the Sun, Moon, and Stars in this verse? The key lies in the Hebrew word $M\overline{S}L$ used in this verse to mean "rule."† There are two words in Hebrew which are translated as the verb "rule": $MLKf$ and $M\overline{S}L$. (In Hebrew there are no printed vowels; all letters are consonants. The two words above have three-letter roots, as do over 90 percent of the Hebrew verbs.) The most common form is the root $MLKf$, which is used 2,697 times in Scripture. Compared to this, the use of the root $M\overline{S}L$ 166 times in the Bible is rare. However, more important than the total frequency of their respective uses is the manner in which they are used: what does "rule" really imply in the Hebrew when used as either $MLKf$ or $M\overline{S}L$? Table 8.3 clearly demonstrates the difference between the two words, and the frequency of their respective meanings.

Table 8.3 Comparison of Frequency and Meaning of $MLKf$ and $M\overline{S}L$

No. Times $M\overline{S}L$ Used	Category of Meaning	No. Times $MLKf$ Used
0	As noun: "king"	2,115
0	As noun: "queen"	38
21	As noun: "kingdom"	235
78	As verb: "to rule"	308
0	As verb: "to consult"	1
56	As verb: "to exemplify" or As noun: "to be an example"	0
11	As verb: "to exhibit conscious or self-control"	0

It should be obvious to anyone comparing the usage of these two words, that there are two very different meanings involved here. It is obvious from their use as "king" and "queen," and from the absence of their use in the sense of "exemplify" or "to exhibit

* For Hebrew transliteration, see Appendix 1.
† For biblical analysis of rulerships, see Appendix 2.

conscious or self-control," that the word *MLKf* is used politically; it refers to the governing of men politically, to the hereditary reign of kings, and to all things pertaining to governments and their interrelationships. It is also quite obvious that the word *MSL* means much more than this. Note well that there are no derivative nouns of the root *MSL* which mean *king* or *queen*.

MSL clearly refers to the ethical exercise of authority and the moral use of power; this use implies conscious and intelligent control of both self and subjects as well as leadership by example; the type of leadership which man should expect and desperately craves from his national leaders. It is exactly this root *MSL* that is used in Genesis 1:16 and 1:18 and also in Psalms 136:8-9 to describe the rulership of the Sun, Moon, and Stars. This is precisely the type of rulership that has been ascribed by Astrology to these heavenly bodies.

Some examples of the different uses of *MSL* and *MLKf* will illustrate most clearly the specific emphases these root-words bring to the concept of rulership in the biblical material:

To rule: The God of Israel said, the Rock of Israel spoke to me: "Ruler *(MSL)* over men shall be the righteous, even he that ruleth *(MSL)* in the fear of God." [2 Samuel 23:3]

Kingdom: Thy kingdom *(MLKf)* is a kingdom *(MLKf)* for all ages, and Thy dominion *(MSL)* endureth throughout all generations. [Psalms 145:13]

King: And Ben-Haddad the King *(MLKf)* of Aram gathered all his host together... [1 Kings 20:1]

Example: Unto Thee, O Lord, do I call; my Rock, be Thou not deaf unto me lest, if Thou be silent unto me, I become like *(MSL)* them that go down into the pit. [Psalms 28:1]

Self-Control: He that is slow to anger is better than the mighty; and he that ruleth *(MSL)* his spirit than he that taketh a city. [Proverbs 16.32]

It is even more important to discover which form of the word is used when God's rulership is involved. Since there are no derivatives of the Hebrew *MSL* which mean "king," it is obvious that we cannot compare the number of times in the Bible that God is called "king." But there are derivatives of both roots which mean "to rule." Let us compare the use of each root derivative meaning "to rule," when referring to rule by God (see Table 8.4):

Table 8.4 Comparison of Meaning and Frequency of Use

No. Times $M\overline{S}L$ Used	Category of Use	No. Times $MLKf$ Used
78	As verb: "to rule"	308
11	Used as: "God rules"	12
14.1%	Percentage of uses	3.9%

Note that, although the use of *MLKf* in the Bible as a verb meaning "to rule" is four times more frequent than the use of the form *M̄S̄L*, this latter form is used with a frequency 3.6 times greater than *MLKf* when the rulership of God is involved. Since the use of the root *M̄S̄L* is also used with the greatest frequency when it means the rulership of the heavenly bodies in Scripture, it is quite obvious that rule by God and rule by heavenly bodies are quite closely related. They are so closely related, in fact, that they are inseparable in the biblical material. We shall observe this phenomenon more closely as we continue. (In the Appendix, there is a complete list of all biblical verses in which *M̄S̄L* is used as the Hebrew root translated as "rule.")

Finally, the difference between these two roots is demonstrated in Genesis 37:8 in which both roots are used in the same verse. This verse is in the story of Joseph's dreams and is the statement of the brothers' initial reaction to the first of Joseph's two dreams:

HMLKf TMLKf 'LNW   AMf MSL TMSL BNW....

...will he indeed rule over us? Will he indeed match examples of control with us?

The key to understanding this verse lies in the two words *'LNW* and *BNW*. The word *'LNW* is the combined form of the preposition *'L* meaning "over" or "upon" and the possessive pronoun suffix *NW* meaning "us" or "ours." The word *BNW* is the combined form of the prefix *B* meaning "with" and the same possessive pronoun ending *'NW* meaning "us." From this use, we can see that one must "rule" *(MLKf)* "over" *(LNW)* in the royal, hereditary, political sense, and that one must "match examples" *(M̄S̄L)* "with" *(BNW)* in the true sense of Divine example, leadership, and rulership. It is in this latter sense of "rule" meaning "by example" that the rulership of the heavenly bodies is placed.

9

"THE EVIDENCE OF TWO WITNESSES SHALL ESTABLISH THE MATTER"

Just how involved *is* the Bible with the heavenly bodies? When I try to imply that there is a significant amount of biblical material dealing with the Heavens, am I exaggerating? How much material is there in the Bible to support the existence of Astrology as a discipline of import to understanding the Scriptures?

In the total Hebrew Scripture, there are 23,144 verses. Of these verses, 866, or 3.74 percent, refer to one or more of the following: Heavens, Sun, Moon, Stars, lights, constellations (the word), constellations (by name), Hosts of Heaven, Stars by name, planets by name. In the following analysis, I shall deal only with *numbers of verses* in the Bible, and not with word *repetitions*. For instance in Job 9:9 there are references to Orion, the Pleiades, Ursus, and the three winter constellations of the Zodiac, and one might logically count these as six instances, but I will count this verse only once. As you can see, I am being most conservative.

Of these verses, only 222 refer to these heavenly phenomena as natural phenomena in their natural setting. Fully 74 percent of these verses, 644 in all, refer to these heavenly bodies as being directly involved in making manifest the will of God either as omens, as witness, or as active agents. In other words, 3.74 percent of the total

Bible is devoted to the Heavens and its contents, and 2.78 percent ot the Bible tells us that the Heavens and their contents are the active participants, under God's control, in the lives and the destinies of humanity on Earth.

These percentages may seem quite small, and their significance may become lost because they are small figures. Perhaps two examples using well-known printed material may be sufficient to indicate exactly how important these heavenly bodies and events are: First, the average copy of the daily edition of the *New York Times* is approximately 72 pages. If this newspaper printed the same percentage of news about the heavens as the Bible does, then there would be *two full pages* plus *five and a half columns* of *the third page* devoted to such news. And of this "spread" of Heaven-oriented news, *only three columns* would be devoted to scientific or astronomical news. The other two full pages and two and a half columns would be devoted to news concerning the effect of the Heavens and their bodies on the lives of men and women, acting as active agents of God. In other words, we would have two full pages plus two and a half columns *New York Times daily coverage* of Astrology in a paper that does not even contain one column on popular Astrology.

Second, I have the 1963 edition of the *World Book Encyclopedia:* twenty volumes, containing 11,093 pages of text and pictures. If it printed its information about the Heavens in biblical proportions, there would be at least *one whole volume,* 343 PAGES, on Astrology, and 61 pages on astronomy. In actuality, there are 25 pages on astronomy and one page on Astrology.

At this point it is necessary to establish criteria for listing any particular verse of Scripture as either a "natural" or a "paranatural" use of the Heavens or their contents, or both. I have coined the term "paranatural" to represent verses in which the uses of the heavens or their bodies, or both, have nothing to do with the natural forces in the universe, but indicate that something other than the laws of nature and their expected results are involved. *Natural use* means that which it states: the Heavens or Stars or planets occur in the context of the verse-use, as the natural locus of natural events. *Paranatural use* in the context of the verse and in its meaning implies that the Heavens or the heavenly bodies are the locus of activities which could not be expected to occur in the natural course of events: or these Heavens and their minions are called on to exhibit intelligence or awareness not in consonance with their natural place in the physical universe. Some examples of these differences should be helpful in delineating the difference between natural and paranatural use. These examples are about the *Heavens* and are taken from each of the three traditional divisions of the Bible.

Pentateuch

Natural: And He brought him forth abroad and said: "Look now toward Heaven, and count the Stars." [Genesis 15:5]

Paranatural: Then said the Lord to Moses: "Behold, I will cause to rain bread from Heaven for you." [Exodus 16:4]

Prophets

Natural: I beheld and lo, there was no man, and all the birds of Heaven were fled. [Jeremiah 4:25]

Paranatural: Be astonished, O ye Heavens, at this, and be horribly afraid, be ye exceedingly amazed, saith the Lord. [Jeremiah 2:12]

Hagiogrypha

Natural: Beside them dwell the fowl of the Heaven, from among the branches they sing. [Psalms 104:12]

Paranatural: And the heavens declare His righteousness: For God, He is judge. Selah. [Psalms 50:6]

Note, however, that the distribution of paranatural verses is not equal throughout the Bible. Some books of the Bible have more natural than paranatural types of verses, and vice versa. It is therefore most instructive to analyze the distribution of these verses throughout the Bible to see if our original hypothesis holds; that there is a progression of the uses of paranatural verses as the biblical material becomes more sophisticated or of a later date chronologically, or both. Let us first analyze the occurrence of these verses in two separate groups, by two separate criteria. Let us divide the 866 verses into two groups (Table 9.1); one group will be the 405 verses in which the Hebrew word for "Heavens," *SMYMf*, is used; the other group will be the 461 verses in which the heavenly bodies are mentioned in general or by name. We shall analyze each group by its distribution according to each division of biblical books (the Traditional *TNKf* and the Topical), and within each division, by natural versus paranatural use.

(The *ratio* is the number of paranatural verses divided by the number of natural verses. Thus, in the Torah there are more natural than paranatural verses. However, in the Prophets there are 3.5 times as many paranatural uses of $\overline{SMYMf}$ ("Heavens") as there are natural uses, and 8.8 times as many paranatural uses of various mentions of heavenly bodies as there are natural uses.) It takes only a brief inspection to realize that we have a most interesting distribution of the use of these terms in Scripture. Before we examine this distribution, let us speculate on what might be expected if our hypothesis holds true.

When modern preachers speak of the development of Scripture from an ethically developmental point of view, they visualize an increasing ethical involvement from the Pentateuch through the historical books, culminating in the vision of the prophets. If this is the developmental history of the religious ethic of the Judeo-Christian tradition in its biblical phase, then we ought to expect a similar development pattern to take place with Astrology. In other words, if we find that astrological indicators in Scripture occur most often in the earliest books of the Bible and rarely in the prophetic books, then we would have to state that any astrological indicators in Scripture were of ancient origin; that, as the people and its ethical leadership developed through the centuries, both the people and its leadership saw the error of Astrology and progressively eliminated it from their religious and ethical teaching. On the other hand, if we find that astrological indicators occur only rarely in the earliest Mosaic books of Scripture, but occur in increasingly large numbers through the historical books, culminating in the largest number of uses in the prophetic books, *then we would be forced to conclude* that the basis for Astrology was laid in the earliest books of Scripture, that the people and its leadership discovered Astrology was an increasingly valid guide to proper ethical behavior, and that therefore Astrology was deliberately included in the highest expression of the people's ethic, that the intention was to develop this Divine Science to the greatest possible extent. Now, let us look at the evidence:

A cursory glance at Table 9.1 will show the exciting indication that astrological concerns did develop along with the ethical concerns in scriptural times. Looking only at the use of the word "Heaven" (405 verses), we see that the word itself is used 1.5 times as often in the Prophets as in the Torah according to the traditional division, 1.66 times as often in the Prophetic as in the Mosaic books according to the fourfold division.

If we glance at the use of the heavenly bodies (461 verses) in Scripture, we see an even greater development. These uses are 3.5 times more numerous in the Writings, and almost 12 times more numerous in the Prophets than they are in the Torah. If we glance at the fourfold division for this category of uses, the developmental

Table 9.1 Comparison of Use of Heavens and Heavenly Bodies

	Heavens (405)				Heavenly Bodies (461)			
Ratio	Para-Natural	Natural	%	Book	%	Natural	Para-Natural	Ratio
0.94	43	46	22.0	Torah	6.7	19	12	.62
3.50	102	29	32.3	Prophets	70.3	34	290	8.80
2.60	133	52	45.7	Writings	23.0	42	64	1.50
0.74	23	31	13.3	Mosaic	4.6	12	9	.75
2.20	110	50	39.5	Historic	16.7	35	42	1.20
4.40	71	16	21.5	Prophetic	58.8	8	263	37.60
2.50	74	30	25.7	Didactic	19.9	40	52	1.30

nature of the information is even more pronounced: Historic use is 4.5 times that of the Mosaic; didactic usage is 4.75 times and Prophetic use of this astrological information is 15.5 times the frequency of the Mosaic use.

If we compare the use of these heavenly indications with their use in natural versus paranatural situations, a similar development appears. Considering all verses containing the word "Heaven," the frequency of paranatural situations is only 0.94 times the frequency of natural situations. However, in the Writings the paranatural situations are 2.6 times more frequent than the natural; and in the Prophets the paranatural situations rise to a frequency 3.5 times that of the natural situations. When we use the fourfold division, the differences are even more apparent. Mosaic paranatural verses are only 0.74 times as frequent as natural verses; Historic paranatural verses are 2.2 times more frequent than natural verses; Didactic paranatural verses are 2.5 times more frequent than the natural verses. The greatest difference is found in the Prophetic books of Scripture wherein, for every natural use, there are 4.4 paranatural uses of the word "Heaven."

When we look at the use of the heavenly bodies in Scripture, the difference is even more striking. In the Torah, the paranatural use is only 0.42 times the natural uses, less than half. In the Writings, the paranatural use frequency "triples" that of Torah use; paranatural verses are 1.4 times more frequent than natural verses. However, in the Prophets the frequency of paranatural use verses leaps to 8.6 times the natural use verses—20 times the frequency found in the Torah. When we consider the fourfold division of the Bible, we can appreciate the real magnitude of the change. The Mosaic use of paranatural referents to which heavenly bodies are related is but 0.42 times the frequency of natural referents. Both Historic and Didactic use show a threefold increase over Mosaic use of paranatural over natural verses—1.2 times and 1.1 times the natural uses, respectively. The striking figure is that for the Prophetic uses of paranatural versus natural referents. The Prophets used the heavenly bodies to refer to paranatural events in the universe 36.7 times more often than to refer to natural events; an increase in frequency 87.4 *times greater* than the frequency found in the Mosaic books of Scripture.

Some might now pose the following question: Is not the twenty-fold increase in paranormal use in the Prophets as compared to the Pentateuch explainable in that there is a great deal more poetry in the Books of the Prophets than in the Pentateuch? Are we not dealing with a phenomenon that is a function of poetic license rather than a function of paranormal use as a deliberate and meaningful reflection of Divine will as carried out by and reflected in the heavens and their hosts? To some extent this may be true: but one glance at Table 9.2 will show that this cannot possibly account for the vast differences in use:

Table 9.2 Analysis of Poetic Verses in Scripture

Book	No. of Poetry Verses	% of Poetry Verses	% of Prose Verses	Ratio of Prose Verses	Ratio of Poetic Verses %Prophets/%Pentateuch
Pentateuch	176	3.04	5,621	96.96	⎰
Prophets	2,832	30.48	6,461	69.52	⎱ 10.03
Mosaic	104	2.15	4,740	97.85	⎰
Prophetic	2,709	54.43	2,268	45.57	⎱ 25.32

From Table 9.2 it is obvious that at best only half the paranatural uses, when comparing the Pentateuch to the Prophets, might be attributed to the greater frequency of poetry in the latter than in the former. The paranatural use in the Prophets is 20 times greater than its use in the Pentateuch, but the frequency of poetic verses is only 10 times greater. When we use the fourfold division, less than one-third of the frequency of paranatural use can be attributed to poetic license in the Prophetic Books. For whereas the frequency of paranatural use in the Prophetic Books is 87.4 times greater than in the Mosaic Books, the frequency of poetic verses in the Prophetic Books over that in the Mosaic Books is only 25.32 times greater. This difference accounts for less than one-third of the difference between paranatural verses as attributable to poetic license. Thus, we see clearly that the differential use of poetic license cannot account for the phenomenon.

Surely, now we could jump to the conclusion that we have indeed proved that Astrology is part of the dynamic growth that led to the highest ethical pronouncements of the Prophets. Let us, however, not jump so fast. Although we have supported our hypothesis, there is one other question to be investigated: Why are the paranatural uses of the heavenly bodies 2 to 8 times more prevalent in the Prophets than the use of the word "Heaven"? After all, and especially in the fourfold division of Scripture, to have the Prophetic Book use of paranatural referents 36.7 times more often than the natural referents when the heavenly bodies are used, and then to have the paranatural referents only 4.4 times more frequent than the natural referents when the word "Heaven" is used, is a difference of 8 times the frequency of the former over the latter: Is this not a difference too great to be glossed over? What is the cause of this difference, if there is a cause? Can we find the reason for this discrepancy? The answer is yes. The data on which the reason is based is given in Appendix 3.

Of the 405 uses of the word "Heaven" in the Bible, 185 are used in connection with the word "Earth" (ARŚ). The other 220 uses are not connected to the paired use, "Heaven-and-Earth." Table 9.3 is a chart of these 185 uses that are similar to Table 9.1.

Now we can see from where the differential derives. When we consider the use of "Heaven-and-Earth" as a unit, contrasting it with the use of "Heaven" alone, we see that the combined use makes up for at least half the discrepancy we noted before: that between the total uses of the word "Heaven" and the total uses of the heavenly bodies.

Two more questions must now be answered. Why did I work with the differences between paranatural and natural uses of the words for "Heaven" and heavenly bodies in Scripture? And why did I seek to differentiate between the uses of "Heaven-and-Earth" as a combined use, and the use of "Heaven" singularly? If I can prove there is a significant difference in the use of paranatural referents over natural referents, while comparing their respective uses in both "Heaven-and-Earth" combined verses and in "Heaven" only verses, this significant difference, will point to a unique relationship that the combined form of use bears to the frequency of paranatural phenomena. Indeed, I shall prove that this unique relationship is of deep significance in Jewish history and in our religiolegal development: the relationship of being valid witness to the working of the Divine Will.

If the Heavens are to mean anything in astrological terms, they must in some way be connected to the life of the person. However, there must be more than just a physical connection. The Sun must mean more than its physical involvement in producing light, heat, energy, and sunburn. Its relationship to the universe and to man must say something specific about the person. To have any astrological value then, the Sun must be in some way involved in the process of birth, growth, and death in a nonphysical manner, that is, in some mystic, some psychic, or some Divine manner. In other words, the Sun must reveal to man the workings of a Divine plan, workings which link man to the universe through the Creator and Designer of both. The Sun must also be available to man as an indicator of God's will. If the Sun, or any other heavenly body, or the Heavens themselves reveal God's functioning in the universe, and if this

Table 9.3 Two Witnesses versus Heaven Alone

	Heaven-and-Earth (185)			Books	Heaven Unconnected (220)			
Ratio	Para-natural	natural	Percent		Percent	Natural	Para-natural	Ratio
0.95	21	22	23.3	Torah	20.9	24	22	0.92
8.38	67	8	40.5	Prophets	25.5	21	35	1.67
2.53	48	19	36.2	Writings	53.6	33	85	2.58
0.35	7	20	14.6	Mosaic	12.3	11	16	1.45
3.44	31	9	21.6	Historic	54.5	41	79	1.93
8.57	60	7	36.2	Prophetic	9.1	9	11	1.22
2.92	38	13	27.6	Didactic	24.1	17	36	2.12

information is available to man in terms that man can understand and count on, then indeed we can say the Sun, the other heavenly bodies, and the very heavens themselves have astrological importance and validity. For this reason the data are presented in terms of their use as referents to the natural, physical universe, and to some universal referent not of the recognizable natural physical universe; a referent capable of being recognized as paranatural, paraphysical, representative of the Divine will operating within and on behalf of both the natural universe and man, and linking the two in an understandable and available system.

The separation of "Heaven-and-Earth" verses also partakes of the need to investigate the possible astrological uses of these terms in the Bible. It would seem that the use of these words should manifest itself primarily in descriptions of the natural universe. As demonstrated, the opposite is true; the terms are more often used in some paranatural sense. If, then, the Heavens reveal God's will, they must of themselves have been considered to be more than just physical entities.

Appendix 4 provides a breakdown of the uses of "Heaven" and of "Heaven-and-Earth" into categories. The groups within these categories are given in Table 9.4.

Table 9.4   Groups in the Heaven and Heaven-and-Earth Categories

Groups	No. of Times Heaven Used	No. of Times Heaven-and-Earth Used
(1) Physical place only	78	49
(3) Place of God's Abode	69	0
(3) As a Divine omen	30	0
(3) "God of Heaven"	21	1
(3) Subject to God: owned/ruled	9	35
(2) An active agent of God	2	47
(2) As witness to God's glory	4	26
(2) As witness to God's deeds	7	23
(3) Used for idolatrous worship	1	0
(3) Other astrological indications	4	2
(2) They are intelligent	0	1
(2) God swears by them	0	1
Total	220	185

If we combine the groups in Table 9.4 into three categories, Natural (1), Active and intelligent witness (2), and all others (3), we get the results shown in Table 9.5.

Table 9.5 Groups Combined into Categories of Heaven and Heaven-and-Earth

Category	No. & % of Times "Heaven" Used		No. & % of Times "Heaven-and-Earth" Used	
	No.	%	No.	%
(1) Physical place only	78	35.5	49	26.5
(2) Intelligent, active witness	13	5.9	98	53.0
(3) All others	129	58.6	38	20.5
Total	220	100.0	185	100.0

Note that when used in the combination "Heaven-and-Earth," the Heavens are indicated as active, intelligent witnesses and agents of God more than half the time, nine times as often as when the word "Heavens" is used alone. There is good scriptural reason for this: a scriptural reason that has carried over into Jewish law, and has been further developed in the Talmud as the basis of all court action.

Whoso killeth any person, the murderer shall be slain at the mouth of witnesses; but one witness shall not testify against any person that he die.

[Numbers 35:30]

At the mouth of two witnesses, or of three witnesses, shall he that is to die be put to death; at the mouth of one witness he shall not be put to death.

[Deuteronomy 17:6]

One witness shall not rise up against a man for any iniquity, or for any sin, in any sin that he sinneth; at the mouth of two witnesses, or at the mouth of three witnesses, shall a matter be established.

[Deuteronomy 19:15]

The uniqueness of the "Heaven-and-Earth" combination now becomes obvious. God needs two witnesses in order to have any matter stand up to the scrutiny of an earthly court. Since the entire system of justice in ancient Israel depended not on documents, but on the production in court of at least two witnesses to the event or transaction, it became scripturally necessary to establish two valid witnesses to the glory and the deeds and the promises and the omens of God—witnesses legally acceptable to the minds of those who were to receive the promises and deeds and omens and glory. Therefore, the Bible establishes the two eternal physical entities of the universe immediately available to man, to be constant witnesses to the Divine will and to its operation in the life of mankind—the Heavens-and-Earth.

There are in Jewish law, however, impediments to being a witness. Since the ancient Near East was a patriarchal, male-dominated area of the world, it would stand to reason that men would have the monopoly on court procedure. Only men could act as valid witnesses. Only men of mature age could act as witnesses; minors were not admitted to the witness stand. Only men with all their physical and mental faculties intact could be admitted as witnesses: deaf or mute persons, blind, insane, or castrated persons could not become witnesses. Only men present at the event or transaction could be witnesses: heresay evidence, documents, and the like were not admitted as evidence before the court. Now, how does the Heaven-and-Earth combination conform to these requirements?

1. In Hebrew, "Heaven" (SMYMf) is masculine, as is the combined form (SMYMf VARS) "Heaven-and-Earth." There is no neuter gender in Hebrew, and all combined forms of nouns are masculine.
2. Since the "Heaven-and-Earth" were present at the Creation, and especially at the Creation of man, they are valid witnesses as far as maturity is concerned, and also as far as being present at the event is concerned.
3. Finally and most important, to qualify as witnesses, "Heaven-and-Earth" have to be free of the loss of any faculties. To put it bluntly: "Heaven-and-Earth" must be intelligent, capable of active participation in the life of both man and the universe, and capable of testifying truthfully to events in time and space.

We now see how important this concept of witness becomes to our astrological concerns. For all the criteria just enumerated, which are necessary to being an acceptable witness in a Jewish court of law, are also necessary to the efficacy of Astrology—with the exception of those devolving from the male chauvinist society. If Scripture insists that the "Heavens-and-Earth" are acceptable witnesses to both the glory of God and the deeds of God in the universe, then they most certainly must also be acceptable witnesses to man's relationship to the Divine will. Indeed, Scripture has God Himself taking an oath by the Heavens:

For I lift up My hand to Heaven and say: "As I live forever....!"
[Deuteronomy 32:40]

If I carry my investigative method as developed for the words "Heaven" versus "Heaven-and-Erth" over to the investigation of the uses of the word "Sun" (*SMYMf*) versus "Sun-and-another-body," you will see that the trend continues. The word "Sun" is mentioned in the Bible 137 times: 106 verses mention the "Sun" alone, 31 verses link "Sun" to other heavenly bodies. When I charted these two uses in Scripture against their distribution in natural versus paranatural verses, I discovered the pattern shown in Table 9.6.

Table 9.6   Distribution of Uses of "Sun Alone" and "Sun Plus Another Body"

| Sun Alone | | | Sun Plus Another Body | |
Natural	Para-natural	Book	Para-natural	Natural
19	0	Torah	4	0
34	8	Prophets	16	0
41	4	Writings	11	0
94	12	Total	31	0
12	0	Mosaic	1	0
36	2	Historical	6	0
8	6	Prophetic	13	0
38	4	Didactic	11	0
94	12	Total	31	0

Once again we see the most significant shift in the value of the Sun as an astrological entity, when it is linked to another body of the Heavens as a *witnessing pair*. We also continue to see the increasing importance of the Prophetic over the Mosaic, Historic, and Didactic uses of astrological concepts and activities.

Let me conclude my analysis logically, by treating first the "Remaining astrological bodies," versus the uses of "Hosts" and "Lord of Hosts" (see Appendix 5) in the same manner (see Table 9.7). Next, let me present a total analysis of "Heaven" alone plus "Sun" alone versus "All other uses" of all heavenly bodies in combination (Table 9.8), and then determine whether my original hypothesis can therefore be stated with greater certainty.

Table 9.7   Analysis of Occurrences of Remaining Heavenly bodies versus Hosts and Lord of Hosts

Remaining Heavenly Bodies			Hosts and Lord of Hosts	
Natural	Para-natural	book	Para-natural	Natural
0	4	Torah	3	0
1	7	Prophets	268	0
2	10	Writings	29	0
3	21	Total	300	0
0	4	Mosaic	1	0
0	2	Historic	36	0
1	6	Prophetic	246	0
2	9	Didactic	17	0
3	21	Total	300	0

The overwhelming evidence of the proof of my hypothesis, taken from an analysis of the words of Scripture itself, now lies before us. Whether we consider the threefold traditional division of the books of the Bible or the fourfold topical division, it remains quite clear that there is a definite development of the use of the "Heavens" and heavenly bodies in paranatural meanings and situations, as

Table 9.8 Analysis of Occurrences of Heaven Alone and Sun Alone versus All Other Combined Indicators

Heaven Alone and Sun Alone				Book	All Other Combined Indicators			
Ratio	Natural	Para-natural	Percent		Percent	Para-natural	Natural	Ratio
0.5	43	22	19.9	Torah	10.0	32	22	1.4
0.8	55	43	30.1	Prophets	68.0	358	9	39.8
1.2	74	89	50.0	Writings	22.0	98	21	4.7
(N=326)	172	154	100.0	Total	100.0	488	52	(N=540)
0.7	23	16	12.0	Mosaic	6.1	13	20	0.6
1.1	77	81	48.5	Historic	15.6	75	9	8.3
1.0	17	17	10.4	Prophetic	61.7	325	8	40.6
0.7	55	40	29.1	Didactic	16.6	75	15	5.0
(N=326)	172	154	100.0	Total	100.0	498	52	(N=540)

parallel to the development of the ethical functions of the Bible. This becomes most apparent when we separate the most common possibilities from the most esoteric possibilities. After all, the Heavens and the Sun have the greatest probabilities of being used in strictly natural senses and strictly physical connotations. Even so, they are used in paranatural senses almost half of the time, that is, 47.2 percent of the time. And when we find these elements conjoined with another element—such as Earth with Heaven, or Sun with Moon, for example—in a pair that stands as witness to God's effectiveness in the world, then *nine out of every ten uses* of this combined form are paranatural in content.

However, the truly impressive data are those involving the progression of paranatural use in Scripture. Let us analyze the use of these terms using both the threefold and the fourfold divisions of Scripture, using the data of all combined indicators. Using the threefold division, these indicators appear as paranatural referents three times more often in the Writings than in the Torah, and eleven times more often in the Prophets than in the Torah. Using the fourfold division, both the Historic and the Didactic indicators appear as paranatural referents 5.77 times more often than in the Mosaic books; and paranatural referents appear in the Prophetic books 25 times more often than in the Mosaic books. There is now no possible way to deny the absolute validity of my opening hypothesis.

In summation, this analysis of the Biblical information available proves that

1. A much larger volume of biblical information is involved with the heavens and their contents than has heretofore been suspected.
2. By far the greatest proportion of this information is used in such a manner as to convey meanings that are not apropos to the natural universe; they are used to convey paranatural information.
3. By every biblical statement and implication, the Heavens and their contents play an intelligent, active, quasi-independent role in giving witness to the glory and deeds of God, and in carrying out Divine will.
4. By every measure available to us, we find that there is significant growth and development of the use of paranatural referents in Scripture. This growth and development parallels in every way the literary, ethical, and legal development of Scripture, beginning in the Mosaic, Torah tradition and culiminating scripturally in the profound Prophetic tradition.

We may therefore conclude that this development has kept pace with all Jewish development in the biblical period. This proves the biblical development and legitimacy of Astrology.

However, the story of Astrology in Jewish life does not end with its biblical history. Indeed if it did thus end, all the proof I have so far presented linking Astrology to the developmental history of the Jewish faith and people would immediately be given the lie. Then there would have been no reason for writing this book, except as a study of past times which has no application for us today. However, the Bible has ever been the source book of the Jew: a source of both ethics and law. The ethical vector of the biblical ethic finds its postbiblical development in that body of writings known collectively as Midrash, that is, "Exposition." The legal vector of the biblical law sees its postbiblical continuity in that body of writings known as the *Mishnah*, the "Teaching," and the *Gemarrah* the "Completion," which taken together comprise the *Talmud*, "that which is to be Learned"—and that which covers a span of 10 centuries.

From this brief analysis of biblical material, do not feel that it has in any way been exhausted. There is much more waiting for the scholar who can combine an accurate knowledge of Hebrew and Aramaic with a sound knowledge of Astrology and its history and a firm foundation in the mythology of the ancient Near East. I have written these brief chapters on the Bible only to open the legitimate possibility so that others will be enticed into this field, and also to provide a sound biblical basis for the argument that I make that Astrology has been an evergrowing part of Jewish tradition, that its development parallels the highest development of the Jewish ethical and legal traditions, and that to this very day, the Divine Science is still one religiously, ethically, and legally legitimate area of concern and scholarship for the Jewish people, specifically, and for all those who derive from the Judeo-Christian and the Judeo-Islamic traditions, generally.

In Part IV, Astrology in the Midrash keep in mind the next two points which have been developed in these biblical chapters:

1. When you read about the Midrash-ethical vector, keep in mind the astrological concommitants of the "Day of the Lord" for they will be involved in a fascinating Midrashic development of the history of the universe.
2. When you read about the Talmudic-legal vector, keep in mind the concept—also developed in the discussion of the "Day of the Lord"—of the validity of astrological indications as they apply to Israel or other nations, or both; and of the concept of the return of the "Righteous Remnant of Israel."

10

JOSEPH,
THE PISCEAN DREAMER

Let me begin this chapter with dramatic direct evidence of the importance of Astrology in the Bible by quoting the well-known story of the sale of Joseph into slavery, in Egypt:

> Now Israel loved Joseph more than all his children, because he was the son of his old age; and he made him a coat of many colors. And when his brethren saw that their father loved him more than all his brethren, they hated him, and could not speak peaceably unto him. And Joseph dreamed a dream, and he told it to his brethren; and they hated him all the more. And he said unto them: "Hear, I pray you, this dream which I have dreamed: for behold, we were binding sheaves in the field and lo, my sheaf arose and also stood upright; and behold, your sheaves came round about and bowed down to my sheaf." And his brethren said to him: "Shalt thou indeed reign *(MLKf)* over us?" And they hated him yet the more for his dreams, and for his words. And he dreamed yet another dream, and told it to his brethren, and said: "Behold I have dreamed yet a dream: and behold, the sun and moon and eleven stars bowed down unto me." And he told it to his father and to his brethren; and his father rebuked him, and said unto him: "What is this dream that thou hast dreamed? Shall I and thy mother and thy brethren come to bow down to thee to the earth?" And his brethren envied him; but his father kept the saying in mind.

Genesis 37:3-11

103

As we read this biblical tale, its surface meaning is familiar in that it seems to relay the age-old story of sibling rivalry brought about by the love of an old parent for the last issue of his masculinity. The youngest born is pampered, does less labor, is best dressed; in short, he is spoiled. Not only is he spoiled, but he also talks too much, is a dreamer, harbors delusions of grandeur—all in all, not the kind of kid brother that hard-working older brothers like to have around.

To understand the deeper meaning it is most important to know what the coat of many colors symbolized. The coat of many colors—better translated in the new translation as "an ornamented tunic"—symbolized the leadership of the tribe. What Joseph flaunted before his brothers was that he had already been chosen by their father to lead the tribe—chosen over his other eleven older brothers! This was completely contrary to the known and expected custom of the times, primogeniture, that is, the rule of the firstborn. Reuben, as the firstborn son of Jacob, was not only the logical but also the commonly recognized legal person to ascend to tribal leadership. As the logical and legal heir to Jacob, he would have received the title of tribal leader—as well as fifty percent of all Jacob's wealth. The other eleven brothers would then have shared equally in the remaining half of the estate. This is what the brothers expected. So to have the youngest—that dreamer, that braggart, Joseph—advanced above all his elders to the putative leadership of the tribe was just too much to be endured. Small wonder his brothers "...could not speak peaceably unto him...."

But then, Joseph went too far. Through his retelling of his dreams, he indicated not only that his father Jacob, but also that even God Himself wanted him to succeed Jacob. In two separate dreams, he calls first upon the Earth, and then the Heavens to witness to his ascendancy. First the products of the Earth, sheaves of wheat, bow down to his sheaf. Then the heavenly bodies—the Sun, Moon, and eleven "stars" bow down to him. Certainly this upset his brothers. Notice that Jacob does not react to the first dream; for it is only after Joseph has called on the two standard witnesses to God's will, the Heavens and the Earth, that Jacob "...kept the saying in mind." Moreover, note the astrological symbols in Jacob's immediate reply to Joseph when the latter reveals his second dream.

> "Behold, I have dreamed yet a dream: and behold, the *Sun and Moon* and eleven stars bowed down unto me." And he told it to his father and to his brethren; and his father rebuked him and said unto him: "What is this dream that thou hast dreamed? Shall *I and thy mother* and thy brethren come to bow down before thee to the earth?"
>
> Genesis 37:9-10

Jacob's immediate reaction to " . . . the Sun and Moon. . . ." is: " . . . I and thy mother. . . ." An immediate question comes to mind: if a person has eleven brothers, and eleven stars appear in a dream, then isn't the dream about the eleven brothers? In the same manner, eleven sheaves of the first dream represented the eleven brothers, and the brothers themselves recognized this to be accurate. In all events, the uniqueness of the impending change in the method of choosing tribal leadership would certainly play some part in seeking Divine sanction for such change, and in those days, dreams were considered the Divine messages.

As long as Joseph sticks to a search for divine sanction for his leadership over his brothers, all is part of a normal divinatory process, and Jacob is not disturbed. But Joseph adds a new dimension to the process. With this new addition, Joseph becomes an immediate threat to his father's leadership. For when Joseph adds the Sun and Moon to his dream, Jacob instantly recognizes the implications, and his reaction is immediate. You shall not displace me as leader! Neither I nor your mother will bow down to you! And Jacob remembers the threat, since he cannot conceive that the threat was innocent, that it was not deliberate on the part of his beloved son, Joseph.

For our purposes, we must note that Joseph uses an astrological figure of speech which is instantly recognized by Jacob who interprets or translates the *Sun and Moon* as *father and mother*. Obviously only an astrological explanation fits the facts. For the change in tribal leadership normally takes place after the death of the father-sheikh. There would be no reason to infer the subservience of the legal tribal leader to his youngest son. There is no logical reason to include the Sun and Moon in a Divine message of unique succession unless something other than succession after the death of Jacob is meant. Joseph obviously threatens an immediate succession—the Sun and Moon bowed down—and Jacob immediately sees it for what it means—neither I nor your mother will bow down—and the whole tale is played out in the best of astrological allegories. Also, do not hesitate to notice that, just after the play of events initiated by this second dream, in the very next two verses, Jacob removes Joseph from his immediate presence.

It is obvious to me that, even as early as the patriarchal period, Astrology was so much a part of the life of the people and of their leaders that the equating of the Sun and Moon to father and mother was common and readily understood. Note also that throughout the rest of the biblical narrative, the lessons Joseph learns are in humility. With the exception of his mother who died before his ascendancy in Egypt, his astrological dream is fulfilled. And Joseph's own interpretation of the lessons he had to learn, of his hardships in slavery, and of his sale into that condition:

And now, be not grieved nor angry with yourselves, that
ye sold me hither; for God did send me before you to
preserve life.

Genesis 45:5

Joseph grows to see the process of Divine will in all that
accompanied his life, from his earliest dreams of succession to the
astrologically allegorized challenge to his father's leadership, to his
humiliation as a slave, to his elevation to second in the realm to
Pharaoh. And the whole process begins with the challenge cast before
his father in explicit, astrological terms.

11

SAMSON AND DELILAH:
THE FIRST STAR-CROSSED LOVERS

The story of Samson and Delilah is in the Book of Judges 13-16. This intriguing story is about Samson and *two* women: one known only as the woman of Timnah, the name of a Philistine town. Although she becomes the wife of Samson and betrays him, she is not Delilah. Delilah enters the picture much later. Reviewing the story more closely reveals that the wife of Manoah of the tribe of Dan, being barren, is visited by a Divine messenger who informs her that she will bear a son. This son will be a Nazirite, dedicated to God from the womb; he is not to drink wine or spirits, and is never to shave or cut his hair (Judg. 13:7). When Manoah is told, he insists on being witness to this promise (Judg. 13:8) and the messenger appears a second time and repeats the conditions (Judg. 13:13-14). Although Manoah attempts to discover the messenger's name, he is unsuccessful; and eventually the messenger ascends to Heaven in the fire of a burnt offering (Judg. 13:20).

The promise is fulfilled and Samson is born and is moved to become a Divine military leader—for these are the Judges. The Judges of this period were not judges of a court of law; they were divinely inspired military leaders of each tribal unit; under Divine authority and vision, they led their tribal troops into battle usually against the Philistines, but often against other Israelite tribes. In this stage of Samson's life, we are told that God deliberately causes Samson to fall in love with a Philistine woman from Timnah in order to find an excuse to attack the Philistines 14:4. While Samson and his parents are on the journey to Timnah, they are attacked by a young lion which Samson kills bare-handed (Judg. 14:5-6). Samson is pleased with the Timnite woman, and she with him. He later returns to his home, turning aside to see what became of the lion he killed, and finds that the lion's carcass has become the home of a beehive (Judg. 14:8). He eats of the honey and gives some to his parents, not telling them of its source (Judg. 14:9). His parents make a wedding party for him in Timnah, and at the party he proposes a riddle to the guests, wagering 30 linen garments and 30 changes of clothing (Judg. 14:12-13). The riddle is:

> Out of the eater came forth food,
> And out of the strong came forth sweetness.
> [Judges 14:14]

Not being able to fathom the riddle, the guests threaten Samson's new wife with the destruction of her family unless she wangles the solution from Samson and gives it to them (Judg. 14:15). She then does so, and betrays him (Judg. 14:17). He recognizes the betrayal (Judg. 14:18) and pays the debt by killing 30 Philistines of the town of Askelon and using the spoil to pay the debt (Judg. 14:19). The father of Samson's Timnite wife then gives the wife to someone else.

Samson discovers that his wife has been given to another, and in his anger ties 150 torches to the tails of 300 foxes, setting them loose in the fields of the Philistines (Judg. 15:4-5). The Philistines discover the reason for this destruction and destroy the Timnite woman, her father, and the entire household. They in turn are attacked by Samson and destroyed (Judg. 15:6-8). The Philistines then attack the tribe of Dan, seeking the surrender of Samson. The Danites receive Samson's permission to allow himself to be bound and delivered to the Philistines (Judg. 15:11-13). After he is delivered, he breaks his bonds, and kills a thousand Philistines with the jawbone of an ass (Judg. 15:14-17). Samson then is Judge for 20 years.

It is only after these events and another minor escapade in Gaza (Judg. 16:1-3) that Samson becomes involved with Delilah. He falls in love with her and she is then paid by the Philistines to discover the source of his strength (Judg. 16:4-6). Three times Delilah implores Samson to reveal the source of his strength, and three times he tells her false stories (Judg. 16:7-15). Finally unable to endure her nagging (Judg. 16:16), he tells her the truth: his hair has never been cut. She is then able to deliver Samson to the Philistines who put out his eyes, and fetter him to a millstone in the prison in Gaza (Judg. 16:18-20). However, Samson's hair grows back, and when he is put on display during a pagan temple ritual to Dagon, Samson prays for strength.

His prayer is granted, and he brings the Temple of Dagon down upon the idol, the occupants, and himself (Judg. 16:23-30).

How can this story possibly be involved in a search for evidences of Astrology in the Bible? Neither Sun nor Moon, Heaven nor Earth, planets nor stars are mentioned in this tale. And yet I maintain that this is an astrologically oriented story. Indeed, it must be understood astrologically if its meaning is to be truly fathomed. The key to the tale lies in the names of the protagonists: Samson and Delilah.

The Hebrew word for Samson is $\overline{S}M\overline{S}WNf$, and in it we can recognize the root $\overline{S}M\overline{S}$ meaning "Sun." Literally, the name means "belonging to the Sun." The Hebrew word for Delilah is almost identical to its English transliteration $DLYLH$. It is a compound word, composed of a noun and a possessive pronoun: DLY, a "water pitcher," LH, is "hers." But DLY is also the Hebrew word for the Constellation Aquarius. Now perhaps we can understand the story a little more deeply.

The story of Samson is actually divided into two stories, or rather, into a prologue and the main tale. The prologue is the longest part of the story and is used to establish the character of Samson. According to the Bible, 20 years pass between the events of the prologue and the tale of Delilah, which strengthens all the more my contention that we are involved with an astrological tale. For the character that the prologue establishes for Samson is that of a typical Leo, and the Sun rules Leo. Moreover, the character established is that of a Leo in his youth and in the prime years of his strength; the Delilah story shows us a Leo after his prime years have passed. In the prologue the persistent mention of long hair—pride of the Leo; the prominence of the Lion, sign of the Leo, and of golden honey, food of the Leo and color of the Leo, all expose Samson as the typical Leo male. The outrageously expansive and expensive wager on the riddle and the dramatic and flamboyant manner in which the wager is paid are both hallmarks of the Leo personality. I also have no doubt that the typical Leo, Samson, saw himself as the epitome of that riddle: strong and powerful without, but sweet and gentle within. Samson's assumption that his spurned wife should docilely wait for him is also a typical Leo attitude. And so is the vengeance he wreaks for her failure to do so: destruction of the fields of the whole community which led his wife to betray him—by fire. For Leo, ruled by the Sun, is a Fire Sign. And witness the royal retribution heaped upon those who would bind him—a thousand men smitten by the jaw bone of an ass in the hands of this man of the Sun, Samson. Indeed, the entire prologue sets up our hero as the typical Leo personality, even to his insistence of having the woman he desires, even though she betrays him. And, after Samson cools off following the betrayal, we see the typical Leo forgiveness and magnanimity toward the defeated "enemy."... "But it came to pass after a while, in the time of the wheat harvest, that Samson visited his wife with a kid..." (Judg. 15:1). There should be no doubt in the mind of anyone who understands the Leo personality that we have here established such a typical Leo configuration for Samson.

After this completed effort to describe the prototype Leo man is impressed on us, enter the Aquarian woman—Delilah! Her very name in Hebrew means "she of Aquarius!" Delilah of the Cardinal Air Sign, seeking her security through the use of her communicative abilities, cajoling and entreating and using all her feminine wiles to drive Samson to distraction, seeking the secret of his strength (Judg. 16:6-17).

For do not forget that both Leo and Aquarius were Cardinal constellations at this time. I have found that all people need security, but that the Fixed Sign people (today Taurans, Leos, Scorpios and Aquarians) have little trouble finding it! Neither do the Earth Sign people have much difficulty establishing secure bases for themselves (Taurans, Virgos and Capricornians). But remember that Aquarius, Delilah was a Cardinal Air Sign at that time, and always in search of stability. Cardinals always have the fear that they are overstepping their abilities, whereas Mutables are always questioning any abilities they may have. We know that the Bible speaks of people being as "unstable as water" and we know that the wind blows from all directions. Air-and-Water-Sign people have the most difficulty in finding security. Thus, Delilah could talk herself into and out of trouble very quickly as a Cardinal Air Sign personality; and she was always subject to her own self-questioning about her abilities. Thus, she could nag Samsom out of his secret—not because she did not love him, but more for the sense of accomplishment and security that it gave her.

Samson, the typical Leo, never afraid of being burned (It cannot happen to me!); willing to play with fire—especially feminine fire—never really believing that women can be his downfall: Samson finally succumbs to Delilah's fixation for security. He gives her his secret; but first, he uses three evasions before he succumbs: first, "...bind me with seven fresh bow-strings..." (Judg. 16:7); second, "...bind me with new ropes..." (Judg. 16:11); third, "...weave the seven locks of my head with the web (of the loom)..." (Judg. 16:13).

Note the use of the number seven, one for each planet. Also note that each of the astrological Fire Signs is represented in Samson's evasions: Sagittarius (bow-strings), Leo (hair), and Aries. Although the symbolism of Leo and Sagittarius is obvious from the text, the symbolism of Aries is only evident to those who know the Bible in Hebrew. The word which is translated "new ropes" is '*BTYMf* in Hebrew: the word which is translated as "bind me" is *YASRWNY*. These two words are used in an identical manner—but with far different meaning in Psalms 118:27.

> The Lord is God, He has given us light:
> In festival procession, "link yourselves" (*ASRW*)
>   with "boughs" (*B"BTYMf*) to the "horns of the altar."

Each corner of the altar of sacrifice seems to have been decorated to represent a ram's horn (*QRNf*), and the festival procession seemed to imply that fresh boughs were woven into a rope and run along the horns of the altar, binding people to the altar, possibly as a symbol of that unbreakable bond of covenant that welded the people to God. (Excellent examples of such horned altars have been excavated recently in Israel.) It seems to me that this "binding to the altar" is an ancient ritual, at least as old as circumcision, and having the same basic origins and meanings as circumcision, and I believe that this type of "binding" was meant by Samson: a sort of semidivine, semimagical "binding" which was probably known to and accepted as efficacious by all the cultic religions of the area. Certainly, Delilah would have recognized that this was a magical type of "binding," valid to overcome the seemingly magical strength of Samson. This "binding" links the evasions of Samson to the horns of the altar and to the third Fire Sign, Aries.

(There are three Fire Signs, three Earth Signs, three Air signs, and three Water Signs. In determining their order, one begins with the sign under immediate scrutiny. When talking about Leo, Leo is the first Fire Sign, Sagittarius is the second Fire Sign, and Aries is the third Fire Sign as we proceed from Leo around (counter clockwise) the Zodiac. Had we begun with Sagittarius, then it would have been the first Fire Sign, Aries would have been the second Fire Sign, and Leo would have been the third Fire Sign.)

Note also that the use of seven bow-strings and of seven locks of hair also involve the ancient magical number seven, which refers to the seven known planets of that day, calling on them either to strengthen or to weaken an existing magical situation, that is, the strength of Samson. In addition to the use of the number seven, the weaving of the hair into the web of a loom is also a fascinating indication of the effectiveness of hair as an element in religion and in magic. We know that Samson's strength comes from the fact that his hair was never cut, nor his beard shaved. This is not only a condition of his vow alone but also it is a demand made on all Jews, and kept in these modern times only by the very orthodox and the Chassidim, a mystical Jewish group. The admonition is in the Book of Leviticus:

> You shall not round the corners of your head,
> Neither shall you shave the corners of your beard.
> [Leviticus 19:27]

Note that Jewish tradition and law indicate that the "corners of the head" and the "corners of the beard" refer to *seven points* on the face of man. Once again, the number seven is part of a ritual act.

All of these evasions were effective because Delilah recognized them as acceptable magical, astrological conditions for countering an existing magical situation; she believed them to be effective. If they did not seem reasonable to her, she would not have been taken in by them: it is not too easy to fool an Aquarian when it comes to her security, especially with words, which are her forte.

The rest of the tale is well known, and typical of the final vengeance of a Leo. But most important is this: the entire tale may well be a morality play, intended to keep Hebrew men from playing around with, and falling in love with, and marrying Philistine women. The play seems to say:

> The sceptre shall never depart from Judah....
> [Genesis 49:10]

> Judah is a lion's whelp....
> [Genesis 49:9]

Therefore (Samson) be a Leo, remember that for which you are destined, and stay away from those Aquarian females (Delilahs) who can only bring you to ruin, no matter how attractive they might seem. (Of course, they would be attractive! "Opposites attract" is an astrological aphorism, and Leo (Samson) and Aquarius (Delilah) are opposite signs of the Zodiac: 6 months and 180° apart!) Incidentally, this would not be the only time that a fairytale is included in the Bible to teach a lesson. The Book of Ruth is a fictional polemic written to support exogamous marriage, an intention diametrically opposed to the intention of the Samson and Delilah story.

12

"KNOW HOW TO ANSWER"

Let us examine two more quotations. The first is from the Book of Judges, Chapter 4 and 5. The story, which is straightforward and gives direct evidence of the word "astrologer" being used in the Bible, is about the prophet Deborah. Sisera rules and oppresses the Israelite tribes, and Deborah receives a message from God to raise an army against Sisera. Deborah then taunts Barak ben Avinoam to raise this army, which he does. He engages Sisera in battle, and vanquishes Sisera and his army on the banks of the brook Kishon. Sisera escapes to the tent of Jael, who kills him in his sleep (Judg. 5). Judges, Chapter 6 is the song of victory which was sung by Deborah:

> The kings came, they fought;
> Then fought the kings of Canaan,
> In Taanakh by the waters of Megiddo;
> They took no gain of money.
> They fought from Heaven,
> The stars in their courses fought against Sisera.
>
> Judges 6:19-20

The Hebrew language has no separate words for "Star" and "planet." Either the planet is named by name or the generic word *KWKB*, "star," is used. It is obvious that here this means that the planets in their orbits fought against Sisera. The astrological

113

indications for Hebrew victory and Sisera's defeat were present that day.

There is an even more direct reference in the Book of Isaiah 47:13:

> Thou art wearied in the multitude of thy counsels; Let now the "astrologers" (*HBRY SMYMf*), the "star gazers" (*XZYMf BKKBYMf*), the "monthly prognosticators" (*MDYYMf LXDSYMf*), stand up, and save thee from the things that shall come upon thee.

This is a direct, unequivocal and straightforward reference to astrologers as practitioners. Admittedly, the reference is in a context indicating that, although the astrologer may see the coming trends, he is powerless to affect them. We would have to agree. An astrologer is *not* a magician; he works *with* the turn of the universe, not *against* it. The negative implied here is the overdependence on Astrology by the populace. But, let us recognize what this negative implies. The implication is strong that Astrology was an integral part of the daily lives of the leadership of the community, if not of the common people.

More important than the implication of the statement is the clear fact of the existence of the statement. We know from the dating of these chapters of Isaiah that the statement had to be made during the 70 years beginning 587 B.C.E. and ending 517 B.C.E. This means that from 2,492 to 2,562 years ago at this writing, Isaiah tells us that there were at least two types of astrologers, and that the process of monthly prognostication was already developed.

In his poetic polemic, Isaiah identifies two different types of astrologers. There are the "regular astrologers" (*HBRY SMYMf*) and the "star gazers" (*XZYMf BKKBYMf*). Once again, the English translations do not begin to transmit the true meanings of the Hebrew terms. The term used for "astrologer" in Hebrew translates literally as "dividers of the Heavens." The astrologer divides the Heavens into constellations, and then interprets the horoscope so derived according to known principles. This term would apply to modern astrologers, as well.

On the other hand, the Hebrew term translated as "star gazer" really means "those who have prophetic visions from the stars." This would imply the type of person who, after casting a horoscope, uses it as a type of mandala; by concentrating on this picture of the Heavens relating to one specific person in a meditative disciplined way, the astrologer is aided in some psychic manner to understand the native, his personality and needs, and future. In the light of later Jewish tradition—which states that not only every person, but even every animal and plant has its ruling planet—this second definition of astrologer-type makes sense. I can only think of today's varied astrological disciplines, among which are those striving to define and refine the horoscope, its houses, and planetary angles (the "scientific" astrologies); and those seeking to define and refine the psychic and karmic vectors of horoscope interpretation (the "esoteric" astrologies). It may very well be that we have reflected in the Book of Isaiah, more than 2500 years ago, an already well-defined dichotomy between the two astrological disciplines, which we would call today the "scientific" and the "esoteric" schools of Astrology!

Perhaps more fascinating is the implication that monthly progressions of some type were already in use. Not only were they in use but they were sufficiently widespread to draw the fire of the prophet. Please believe me when I tell you that the Bible and its prophets were never concerned with the aberrant behavior of the person which did not affect the community as a whole.

The prophet spoke to the entire community of Israel, never to the person, unless that person was the king or the high priest, a person whose actions and decisions would affect the entire community. So, the prophets inveighed against Baal-worship, which was closely involved with the agricultural cycle, as was Astarte-worship which the prophets also decried. The prophets never spoke against an action that was not already affecting the entire community of Israel. If Isaiah speaks out against the monthly prognosticator, the "scientific" and "esoteric" astrologers, it means that these astrologers were having a profound affect on the nation. I have no doubt, if we understand the context in Isaiah correctly, that the leaders of the nation as well as the general population were making wrong use of the astrological knowledge of the day. I also have no doubt that in Isaiah's day as well as in our own, there was a minority of astrologers who were willing to be "bought" by the establishment of the day, and willing to prostitute their knowledge for personal gain. It is always much easier to tell the mob and its leadership what they want to hear, even if it means stretching the truth out of shape.

Two interesting questions now arise: What were the methods used for monthly prognostication? What kind of predictive devices were available to the astrologer of the day? The first, and simplest of the predictive devices available to the astrologer of old was the simple transit of the Moon, and the speed of the Moon's motion. Since the Moon completes its circuit of the Zodiac in approximately 28 days, it obviously will pass between any given point on Earth and every degree of every constellation in the Zodiac at least once each month. This motion of the Moon, called a *transit*, will cause the Moon to make every possible aspect to every planet and personal point (Ascendant, Midheaven, Nodes of the Moon) every single month. Knowing this, and observing the speed of the transit of the Moon, the astrologer could predict the effect of the Moon on the natal chart of the native, and give the client reasonable astrological advice.

The second and more complicated of the predictive devices available to the astrologer of Isaiah's time was the lunation. A *lunation* is any obvious change in the appearance of the Moon occurring either on a regular basis or on a predictably irregular basis. For instance, the thin sliver of the New Moon Crescent is considered a lunation, as is the full face of the Full Moon. These lunations occur with monthly regularity. Irregular but predictable lunations are partial and total eclipses of the Sun and the Moon. An astrologer may cast a horoscope for the date and time of the New Moon and the Full Moon, and compare these with the natal chart of the client. A comparison with the New Moon Chart will indicate the areas of concern in the life of the native during which new procedures and adventures might be advantageous, whereas a comparison of the Full Moon Chart might indicate those areas of life which should be delayed, because of difficulties which might attend them, were they pressed to conclusion.

The third, and most involved, of the predictive devices available to our astrologer of Isaiah's time was the Lunar Return Chart. We read in Ezekiel 21:35 the following words:

In the place of thy nativity, in the land of thine origin, will I judge thee.

Those who practice Astrology will recognize that this may refer astrologically to a Solar Return Chart; that is, to a chart, calculated yearly, which is based on the exact position of the Sun, in the current year, when it sits exactly on the Sun at the time of the original birth. Thus, each person would be judged, yearly, "...in the place of thy nativity...." at the moment of each year comparable to the moment of birth. The *same reasoning* can apply to *every planet* in the horoscope, but can be most effectively used with the Moon.

For example, in my own natal chart (Table 12.1), my Sun stands at 2° Scorpio 26'27" and my Moon stands at 11° Cancer 41'24". It is relatively easy to determine the exact date and time *each year* when the Sun will stand at that very position in the Heavens. Then I could plot

Table 12.1 Natal Chart (Rectified) of Author

Birth Data	Natal Chart Information		
Date	October 26, 1926		
Time	11:07:25 A.M. E.D.S.T.		
Place	Middletown, N.Y.		
Longitude	74 W 45		
Latitude	41 N 27		
True Local Time	10:09:45 A.M.		
Greenwich Mean Time	3:05:05 P.M.		
Sidereal Time	12:26:40		
House Cusps[b]			
10	7	Libra	16
11	9	Scorpio	04
12	8	Sagittarius	24
1	6	Capricorn	07
2	4	Aquarius	20
3	4	Pisces	49
Indicators			
Midheaven	7	Libra	16
Ascendant	16	Sagittarius	07
Sun	2	Scorpio	26:27
Moon	11	Cancer	41:24
Mercury	23	Scorpio	57:01
Venus	25	Libra	56:46
Mars	14	Taurus	16:19 Rx
Jupiter	17	Aquarius	34:23
Saturn	25	Scorpio	36:54
Uranus	26	Pisces	09:45 Rx
Neptune	26	Leo	40:07
Pluto	16	Cancer	04:24 Rx
North Node	10	Cancer	35:07

[a]*Die Deutsche Ephemeride* were used, in conjunction with the
[b]*Tables of Diurnal Planetary Motion*, A.F.A. House system is
Merinus-Kepler Meridian House System

all the other planets and personal points for that exact date and time, and use the resultant *Solar Return Chart* to derive some insight into the directions my life will take during the coming year.

However, my Moon position of 11° Cancer 41'24" will repeat itself exactly *every month*, and in May of 1976 it repeated itself twice: at 2:25:48 P.M. Eastern Daylight Savings Time on May 4th; and at 7:42:38 P.M. Eastern Daylight Savings Time on May 31st. Note that my personal *Lunar Month* is 27 days, 5 hours, 16 minutes, 50 seconds long during May 1976. The length of the Lunar Month may vary as the year progresses since its apparent month depends on its relative speed as viewed against the constellations of different times of the year. In any event, my Lunar Return Chart would, when compared to my natal chart, give me some insight into the state of my emotional health during the coming Lunar Month.

The same techniques, of course, could be applied with telling effect on the return to natal position of any of the reasonably fast-moving planets. A Mercury Return Chart could indicate communicative capacity; a Venus Return Chart could indicate attractiveness and awareness of beauty and love; a Mars Return Chart could indicate coming states of energy and its ebb, flow, and influence on the life of the native. I even feel that a Jupiter Return Chart might indicate long-term expansive potentialities. And as for Saturn, it is the planet which times our changing life-cycle in approximately 7-year periods.

However, our ancient astrologers knew of and used Moon transits, Moon changes (lunations) and Moon Return Charts; and I am quite sure that they calculated them on the basis of a Lunar Year of 354 1/3 days. For the Bible states quite specifically that time was to be calculated by the Moon (Ps. 104:19), an idea which is most strongly supported by the parallelism of Genesis 1:14 and the association of time with the New Moon in Hosea 2:13 and many other locations. But perhaps the greatest body of proof in existence is the Hebrew Calendar, which is in use to this very day.

The Hebrew calendar is a solilunar calendar. This means that the calendar is based on the physical observance of the New Moon at Jerusalem, and contains months of 30 or 29 days. It is adjusted to the yearly motion of the Earth around the Sun by adding a whole month to the year according to a particular cycle. This added month is put into the calendar three times every 7 years, and four times every 11 years, according to a cycle calculated for a specific purpose. That specific purpose is to ensure that, over the period of centuries, the correction will allow for the New Moon of the month of Nisan—the month in which the Passover falls—to remain reasonably close to the Vernal Equinox. Although originally the New Moon of every month was determined by physical observation, by the time of the destruction of the Second Temple (70 C.E.), the calculation of the calendar had replaced the observance of the New Moon, except for the New Moon of the month of Nisan. It was from the basis of the still-physical observance of the New Moon of Nisan at Jerusalem that the balance of the year was calculated—and the calendar of yearly religious festivals was decided. From an astrological point of view, I think it would be advantageous to examine the Hebrew calendar, for this will prove to be a lunation calendar based on astrological months. This calendar still rules the religious life and the festival cycles of the Jewish religious year.

The Jewish New Year occurs in the autumn or fall of the year. (Notice that the term *fall* is in itself astrological: the *Fall* (Autumn) Equinox coincides with the Descendant in the mundane chart.) However, this is not the first month of the Jewish year biblically; it is the seventh month. The Bible tells us specifically and unequivocally that the first month of the year must be that month in which Passover falls—the month of the Vernal Equinox (which begins with 0° Aries, the beginning of spring and the first sign of the Zodiac, represented by the Ascendant in the mundane horoscope. So we now also understand that the *fall* of the year, represented by the Descendant in the mundane chart, is also the beginning of the Constellation Libra.)

While the Israelites are still in Egypt, preparing for the Exodus, they are told the following:

> And the Lord spoke unto Moses and Aaron in the land of Egypt, saying: This month shall be unto you the beginning of the months; it shall be the first month of the year to you.
>
> Exodus 12:1-2

To this very day, the knowledgeable Jew recites the Hebrew calendar, beginning the recitation with the month of Nisan, the month of the Vernal Equinox in which Passover falls.

The Hebrew calendar months and their common calendar and astrological correspondencies are charted in Table 12.2. I have taken the dates corresponding to an "astrological year" which we know is a "biblical year," beginning with the Vernal Equinox of 1974. Astrological data are derived from *Die Deutsche Ephemeride Band VI* and times interpolated using the *Tables of Diurnal Planetary Motion A.F.A.*

Note that the year will usually run 11 to 12 days shorter than the solar year. This is compensated for by the addition of a second month of Adar between the regular Adar and the month of Nisan. On such

Table 12.2 Hebrew Calendar Months, Their Common Calendar and Astrological Correspondencies

Hebrew Month	No. of Days	Common Calendar	Vernal/Fall Equinoxes Aries-0°-Libra	Summer/Winter Solstices Cancer-0°-Capricorn
5734		1974		
Nisan	29	3/24-4/21	00:08:40 of 3/21	
Iyar	30	4/22-5/21		
Sivan	30	5/22-6/20		
Tammuz	29	6/21-7/19		18:38:00 of 6/21
Ab	30	7/20-8/18		
Ellul	29	8/19-9/16		
5735				
Tishre	30	9/17-10/16	09:59:23 of 9/23	
Heshvan	29	10/17-11/14		
Kislev	30	11/15-12/14		
Teves	29	12/15-1/12/75		05/57/00 of 12/22
Shevat	30	1/13-2/11		
Adar	29	2/12-3/12		
Total	354			

leap years this carries the first of Nisan beyond the date of the Vernal Equinox (0° Aries) to which it will fall back in subsequent years, until it preceeds the Vernal Equinox by too many days. At that point another leap year will occur, by adding another month in the same place, according to the pattern of the Saros cycles.

The festivals of the Jewish year are fitted into this astrological solilunar monthly pattern. There are only five holidays mentioned in the Mosaic tradition: three are called *festivals* (*XG*: pronounced Khag; compare the Arabic *Haj*, from which the term *Hajira* comes, the religious pilgrimage on foot from Mecca to Medina). These three festivals are known in Hebrew as *'LH RGL* or "Pilgrimage Festivals": they are to be celebrated at the central sanctuary each year by all eligible men who must climb the Temple Mount on foot to celebrate them. The Hebrew words *'LH RGL* mean "to ascend on foot." These three Pilgrimage Festivals are Passover (*PSX*), Pentecost (*SB'WṬ*) and Sukkot (*SKWṬ*, "Tabernacles").

The other two holidays are not given any names in the Bible.

They are known only as " . . . a day of blowing the horn unto you . . ." (Numb. 29:1) and a day on which " . . . ye shall afflict your souls . . ." (Numb. 29:7). These have evolved into the modern day *Rosh Hashanah* ("New Year") and *Yom Kippur* ("Day of Atonement"), the High Holy Days. Both of these days and one of the festivals (*Shavuot*, "Pentecost") are celebrated biblically for only one day. Passover in the Bible is celebrated for seven days with Holy Convocation on the first and seventh day; Tabernacles is celebrated for eight days, with Holy Convocation on the first and eighth days. In modern times, all of these holidays and festivals have had one day of celebration added to them, with the exception of the Day of Atonement, Yom Kippur, which is still observed as the biblical one day. Interestingly, the additional days were mandated because of the slowness of communications, lest the festival be missed or celebrated on the wrong date in lands outside of Israel.

The timing of the festivals and holidays is most revealing, astrologically. The Passover is to begin on the fifteenth day of the first month, Shavuot is to begin seven weeks later, Sukkot (Tabernacles) is to begin on the 15th day of the 7th month, Rosh Hashanah (New Year) is to begin on the 1st day of the 7th month, Yom Kippur (Day of Atonement) is to begin 10 days later. Let us look at these holidays and festivals from an astrological point of view:

Passover	Full Moon of Aries
Shavuot	7 weeks later (Note numerological significance.)
Rosh Hashanah	New Moon of Libra
Yom Kippur	10 days later (Note numerological significance.)
Sukkot	Full Moon of Libra

When Judaism added two other holidays, minor festivities surrounding the events enumerated in the Book of Macabbees (not in the Hebrew biblical Canon) and in the Book of Esther (not originally included in the Canon, either), these new minor holidays were also given astrologically oriented dates:

Chanukkah (Macabbees)	New Moon Capricorn
Purim (Book of Esther)	Full Moon Pisces

There were two other major festivals ordained in the Mosaic tradition: one occurs each week, the other each month. The former is known as the Sabbath, the latter as the New Moon. The Sabbath is the seventh day of each week, represented, incidentally, by the planet Saturn. It is the 7th, 14th, 21st, and 28th day following each New Moon. It represents, astrologically, quarter-monthly progressions, of which two—the New Moon and the Full Moon—are lunations.

The New Moon was the first day of each lunar month, and was celebrated with much pomp and revelry. As a matter of fact, the Talmud states that he who has not taken part in the New Moon festival celebration in the Temple at Jerusalem has never known happiness and joy. The New Moon observance is still honored in the Temple and Synagogue ritual today as the first day of the Hebrew calendar month arrives. The Sabbath before the New Moon, the date it will occur is announced to the Congregation with prayers that it bring peace, contentment, and prosperity. On the day of the New Moon special Psalms of Praise (*Hallel*) are read, and the New Moon is blessed in a prayer ceremonial known as *QDWS̄ HLBNH*, "Sanctification of the White One." (Those interested in the origins of the White Goddess, please note.)

Now the question about the "monthly prognosticators" in Isaiah is answerable. (Readers who have sufficient knowledge about the more sophisticated astrological techniques that are available as predictive devices may be surprised to learn that they were used so early in the history of Astrology.)

The astrologers of the time had already divided the heavens into its zodiacal constellations, and not only knew the times of solar entry into each one but also were dealing with a population to whom these solar insertions and the lunations associated with each were part of and vital to the timing of the celebrations of divinely ordained religious festivals. At the very least, these astrologers had available to them solar progressions and New Moon and Full Moon lunations, for predictive purposes. I have no doubt that they also knew of the nodal cycle (The Talmud already knows of the Nodes of the Moon as the Head and Tail of the Dragon), and could place the Moon in its place in the constellations month by month, throughout the year. Although there is some obscure biblical evidence that day-for-a-year progressions (Ezek. 4:5-6) and solar return charts (Ezek. 21:30) may have been available, these would not be necessary or even helpful for "monthly prognostications," although they are certainly still useful today for yearly predictive trends. I believe we have enough evidence here in the solar insertions and the lunations to satisfy our question with its direct answer.

I believe we have given the direct answer: that is, the direct mention of Astrology and astrologers in the Scripture. In the next chapter we will examine some other fascinating sections of the Bible, sections which have not been amenable to proper translation and understanding in their "normal" condition: but which yield easily to proper understanding when analyzed from the astrological viewpoint, and which make incredibly sophisticated sense, as well.

13

SOME FASCINATING CONJECTURES

There are many passages in Scripture which all biblical scholars admit are extremely difficult to translate. These passages usually have some idiomatic use of the Hebrew language which was well recognized in the age and to the people to whom they were spoken, but their special meaning has been lost with the passage of time, and there is really no way of understanding their impact today. Therefore, when they are translated literally, they seem to make no sense, and the literal translation is twisted so that the passages make some sort of sense in English. However, most scholars admit that the true meaning and impact of the verses involved is never captured; that, had we lived in the times these verses were preached, they would have had a much greater meaning to us, and we would have readily understood the idiom.

To give you modern examples: first, how would our children today (I have a son 21 years old, and three younger daughters) react to the idiom of our parents: "23 skidoo"? I doubt if they would even understand what their grandparents meant by the expression, and it is not 50 years from the time it was a common idiom. Second, in my youth, we spoke of good music as being "hot"; our children refer to their musical idiom as "cool". Yet, we both mean the music we enjoy. I wonder what some archeologist would make of this complete reversal of idiom, which took less than 25 years. This is the type of idiomatic usage of the biblical material that makes translation so difficult. But if one knows Astrology and also knows biblical Hebrew, some of these passages begin to make excellent and idiomatic sense. This chapter is called "Some Fascinating Conjectures" because the interpretations herein presented are being published for the first time: no professional biblical linguistic scholars have seen them.

Let us begin with a standard, although I believe erroneous, translation from the Book of Habakkuk 3:2-4:

O Lord, I have heard the report of Thee, and am afraid;
O Lord, revive Thy work in the midst of the years,   (1)

In the midst of the years make it known;   (2)

In wrath remember compassion.
God cometh from Teman, and the Holy One from Mount Paran.
    Selah.   (3)

His glory covereth the heavens, and the earth is full of His praise.

And a brightness appeareth as the light;   (4)

Rays hath He at his side; and there is the hiding of His
    power.   (5)

I find it difficult to translate the Hebrew of verses (1) and (2) as it is done above. The Hebrew reads:

(1)   *YHWH P'LKʃ BQRB ŠNYMʃ XYYHW*
(2)   *BQRB ŠNYMʃ ṪWDY'*

If one considers the astrological implications of the total passage, then there is no need to stretch the translation as it has been stretched. In verse (1), the verb *XYYHW* refers to the noun *P'LKʃ*, "Thy work" not to *YHWH*, "the Lord." It should therefore be translated as follows:

O Lord, Thy work has its life in the midst of the years,

Likewise in verse (2), the verb *ṪWDY'* refers to the same noun since the two phrases are poetically parallel, and should be translated:

...It shall be known in the midst of (or by means of) the years;

In the next phrase, "God cometh from Teman...," there is neither theological nor literary sense. However, if we take the meaning of the Hebrew $M\hat{T}YMNf$ in its astrological sense, we may have something of great meaning here. As mentioned in Chapter 8 this term refers to an astrological direction, namely, the Chambers of the South, which refer to the three winter Constellations Capricorn, Aquarius, and Pisces, in general, but to the first two, in particular; the two constellations ruled by Saturn in the ancient system. If we remember that the Hebrew name for Saturn is $\bar{S}B\hat{T}AY$, that the same root $\bar{S}B\hat{T}$ is found in the name of the day God rested, the Sabbath, that, in general, all uses of this root are linked in some way to Deity, then the idea that here an astrological direction is inferred is too strong to deny.

In the second phrase of this verse, "... and the Holy One from Mount Paran...," our sense that we are speaking of a sacred direction is confirmed. For Mount Paran is in the Sinai Peninsula, and throughout the Mosaic tradition it is used synonymously with the Wilderness of Sinai, which is south of Israel. Moreover, in the Book of Deuteronomy, chapter 33:2, Paran is identified as Mount Sinai.

> ... The Lord came from Sinai, and rose from Seir unto them;
> He shined forth from Mount Paran, and He came from the
>   myriads holy,
> At His right hand was a fiery law unto them.

From all this biblical evidence, we seem to be directed to those constellations seen as southerly from Israel, a direction confirmed by its parallel phrase directing our gaze towards the Sinai peninsula, both being affirmed as the directions from which God and His revelation appeared.

Verse (4), "... And a brightness appeareth as a light...." (Hebrew: $WNGH\ KAWR\ \hat{T}HYH$) The Hebrew AWR is another synonym for the "Sun," and in some translations this phrase is rendered: "... and a brightness shall appear as the Sun...." However, NGH is also the Hebrew synonym for both the "Moon" and the "planet Venus"—so that this phrase can be rendered: "... And the Moon (or Venus) shall be like the Sun...."

Finally, in verse (5): "... Rays hath He at His side, and there is the hiding of His power." In Hebrew:

$$... QRNYMf\ MYDW\ LW,\ VSMf\ XBYWNf\ 'ZH$$

There are no verbs at all in this phrase; the verb "to be" has no Hebrew form in many of its uses and is to be understood from the context. Since the context of this entire passage is in the imperfect tense, this phrase should also be understood in that tense. We ought to read this phrase in the following manner:

> ... will be rays at His side, and therein will lie the secret of His power."

Now, let us put it all together and see if it makes sense:

> O Lord, I have heard the report of Thee, and am afraid:
> O Lord, Thy work has its life in the midst of the years,
> It shall be known by means of the years.
> God cometh from (the direction of) Capricorn-Aquarius,
> And the Holy One (from the direction of) Mount Paran. Selah.
> And the Moon (or Venus), like the Sun, will be rays at His side,
> And therein will lie the secret of His power."

However, this is not the only possible translation of these enigmatic verses: this is one, *if* we accept the traditional phrasing of the Hebrew. However, if we use an alternate phrasing of the Hebrew which is just as legitimate as the traditional phrasing, the passage makes even more sense. The traditional phrasing of the Hebrew is:

> ... *YHWH ŠM'ṪY ŠM'Kʃ YRAṪY / YHWH P'LKʃ BQRB ŠNYMʃ XYYHW....*

This traditional phrasing is totally out of keeping with the normal phrasing of biblical poetry. Normal poetic phrasing in biblical Hebrew is usually in three-word segments, less often in two-word segments, and very rarely in four-word segments. Four-word phrasing is usually used to indicate a defeat or disaster; two-word phrasing is usually used to indicate the excitement of battle. The overwhelming phrase-division used in biblical poetry is that of three-word phrasing. We have in the text above neither the excitement of battle nor the agony of defeat; what we do have is very strange indeed—one four-word phrase and one five-word phrase. If we revert to the normal three-word phrasing of biblical poetry, and divide the nine words into three, three-word phrases, we shall discover a translation which makes even more sense than that which we have already proposed as one alternate solution to the translation problem:

> ... *YHWH ŠM'ṪY ŠM'Kʃ / YRAṪY YHWH P'LKʃ / BQRB ŠNYMʃ XYYHW....*

> ...O Lord, I have heard the report of Thee:
> I am in awe of Thy work, O Lord,
> It lives in the course of the years...

Now to complete the quotation:

> ...It shall become known by means of the years.
> God shall come from (the direction of) Capricorn-Aquarius,
> And the Holy One from (the direction of) Mount Paran (Sinai)
>   Selah.
> And the Moon, like the Sun, will be rays at His side,
> And therein will lie the secret of His power.

If the secret of God's power is in the Sun and Moon being at His side, how will that secret be made manifest? We are told by the prophet in a later verse, using the same Hebrew words AWR and NGH for "Sun" and "Moon," that God will shoot His arrows and cast His spears at them. However, once again the translators, knowing nothing of Astrology nor of the widespread use of Astrology in biblical times, mistranslated the verse (Hab. 3:11):

> The Sun and Moon stand still in their habitation;
> At the light of Thine arrows as they go,
> At the shining of Thy glittering spear.

What an awkward translation: "...at the light of Thine arrows as they go...." The Hebrew of this section of the verse is:

$$...LAWR\ X\acute{S}YKf\ YHLKW\ /\ LNGH\ BRQ\ XNY\dot{T}Kf.$$

The given translation is totally wrong. First of all, the verb in each of these phrases is plural, whereas the Sun and Moon in the previous phrase use the singular form of the verb, $"MD$. The verbs here cannot refer to the words AWR and NGH, translated here as "light" and "shining." Besides, neither AWR nor NGH can be nominative, for each is preceded by the prefix L, meaning "towards," which indicates that AWR and NGH are the objective case—the receivers, not the initiators—of the action. Indeed, both AWR and NGH are synonyms for "Sun" and "Moon," respectively; and because of the parallelism to the first phrase of this verse, they must be translated as Sun and Moon in this phrase, as well. For all these reasons, the traditional translation is utterly wrong. If we use our astrological knowledge, and proper Hebrew grammar, we can and must translate this verse as follows:

> The Sun and Moon stand still in their habitation;
> Thine arrows go towards the Sun,
> Thy glittering spear towards the Moon.

Why should God cast his arrows and spears toward the Sun and Moon? Oddly enough, as I shall elucidate in Chapter 18, this is an omen of God's love.

Now our newly revised translation makes excellent sense in the context of the prayer—for this chapter of the Habakkuk is entitled "A Prayer of Habakkuk the prophet." For the context of the prayer speaks of God's power and of the prophet's joy in God, even though the Lord will make "...The Sun and Moon stand still in their habitation..." (Hab. 3:11). An interesting sidelight of this verse is the Hebrew word used for "habitation," *ZBL*. This word is used only five times in the entire Bible. Three times it is used as the habitation of God (1 Kings 8:13, 2 Chron. 6:2, and Isa. 63:15). Once it is used as the habitation of the dead in the nether-world, $\overline{S}AWL$ (Ps. 49:15). And it is used here as the habitation of the Sun and Moon. We are indeed dealing here with a dwelling place which is not of this earth: a Divine dwelling place, an eternal dwelling place, an astrological habitation.

To sum up the meaning of the prophet's prayer in its new sense: the prophet acknowledges knowing of God's power; God's power makes itself manifest through the progression of the years, God reveals His will in the Heavens as God causes the Sun and Moon to travel through the zodical signs. God made Himself manifest in the past at Mount Sinai, from the direction wherein are found the Chambers of the South, namely, Capricorn and Aquarius. At God's will the Sun and Moon can stand still in their orbits, thus symbolizing their willing obedience to God's command. God's delight in the obedience of the Sun and Moon to His will is symbolized by His shooting His arrows and spears at them (see Chapter 18).

I believe that this interpretation not only is in accordance with the proper phrasing and interpretation of the Hebrew text but also is couched in the idiom which Habakkuk's listeners understood, and to which they were most likely to respond: an idiom which has been lost to modern biblical scholars who are not astrologically oriented or aware. Incidentally, there is an idea in this prophecy of Habakkuk that is a theme to which almost every prophet aludes, at one time or another. It is the theme of the Sun and the Moon standing still, and is usually connected to prophecies involving the "day of the Lord," on which the above-mentioned phenomenon is accompanied by the darkening of the constellations, and the fall of the Heavens. We shall discuss this fascinating set of prophecies later in this chapter. For now, let us consider another prophet.

In chapter 14:12 of the Book of Isaiah, we read the following English version of the Hebrew original:

How art thou fallen from heaven, O day star, son of the morning!
How art thou cut down to the ground, that did cast lots over the nations!

We are interested in the Hebrew of the mistranslation "... day star, son of the morning..." for a mistranslation it certainly is. The translator knew nothing of Hittite mythology, nor of Astrology. The Hebrew is:

AYKſ NPLT MSMYMſ HYLL BNſ SXR....

First, the last Hebrew word in the quote above is the one most commonly used to mean day star, or morning star, which we all know to be Venus. How then do we translate *HYLL* as "day star"? Can we legitimately translate the phrase as "... day star, son of morning..."? I think not. There is no biblical evidence that *HYLL* means day star at all: this is the *only* time the word occurs in the entire Bible! Philologists have attempted to find its root in a verb *HLL*, which means "to shine," or "to praise." There is *no other biblical evidence* that would help a philologist deduce a meaning for this word. However, there *is* biblical evidence for where one should look to solve the mystery of the meaning of this word.

The book of Isaiah 14:3-23 deals exclusively with the coming punishment of the King of Babylon and his nation for having oppressed Israel, and prophesies the doom of the King of Babylon, the loss of his power and his kingdom, the dashing to the ground of his haughtiness. It states that all other kings will sleep safely in their tombs after death, but that the King of Babylon will never sleep in his tomb, but will lie unrecognized and unburied on an unknown battlefield "... because thou hast destroyed thy land, thou hast slain thy people..." (Isa. 14:19).

As we recognize that this is indeed a prophecy against Babylon, would it not seem natural and logical for us to seek the answer to this question in the mythology of the area, and in an understanding that this may involve a feminine deity who was symbolized in the minds of the day by the planet Venus? Should we not seek out some myth in which the son of this female deity aggrandizes himself, and pays for his folly? If such a myth truly exists, would it not fit into the context of this section of Isaiah better than the present translation? Does such a myth exist? Yes, it does.

In the mythological pantheon of the Hittites, which became part of the Babylonian hierarchy of gods and goddesses, we are told of a god who ascended to some power in the pantheon by defeating Anu, the sky god. He then assumed too much authority, and was castrated, cast from the pantheon to the earth, and destroyed by the god Attu, father of all gods, with the connivance of his own mother goddess, the goddess of love and fertility, later known as Ashtar, Ishtar, Astarte—the Venus of the Roman pantheon. The name of that god, son of Ashtar-Ishtar-Astarte-Venus, who aspired too high and was dashed to the pit (Isa. 14:19) was Alalu.*

Now *HYLL BNfSXR* makes excellent sense. What better way to prophecy against the King of Babylon than to use the symbolism of his own pantheon to teach him a lesson? I have no doubt that this was the type of reference which was understood by all who heard it. It may very well be that Alalu became the epitome of the person who reached too high and was destroyed. The Greeks called it "hubris," and it had to be punished. Perhaps *HYLL BNf S̄XR* became the name identified with hubris defeated, just as in our language General Hooker lent his name to the professional ladies of the night, and Mrs. Malaprop lent hers to the wrong use of language.

We may be certain that Isaiah's listeners understood both the impact and the artistry of the message, just as we today listen to, and read, the words of the great orators of our day. For the orator's skill lies not only in the message he offers but also in the manner in which the message is delivered. The great preachers of our day are sought after for being purveyors of the highest ideals as well as for being the best linguistic entertainers. In much the same vein, the prophets were both the purveyors of the highest ethical thinking and nationalistic expression, and also entertainers of the masses. I believe it very possible that the oratory of a Socrates, a Cotton Mather, a Billy Graham, or an Abba Eban found its origins in the examples of the oratory of the prophets.

And so I believe that the audiences of Isaiah, listening to him hoist the King of Babylon by his own petard, at one and the same time

---

* See O.R. Gurney "The Hittites," New York: Penguin Press, 1969. See also John Gray, *Near Eastern Mythology* Hamlyn Publishing Group, 1969, and James Hastings (ed.), *Encyclopedia of Religion and Ethics*, Vol. 6. New York: Scribner, 1955.

convicting him with his own mythical theology and at the same instant promising the nation of Israel surcease from Babylonian domination: I am quite sure that such an audience enjoyed both the message and the consummate artistry of its presentation. And yet all of this, in the richness of its imagery and of its nuance, is lost to biblical scholars who do not recognize the mythic origin of the message because they are ignorant of the astrological components of the Bible. It is even more curious that so few people recognize how strongly this image of defeated hubris has come down to our own time: it is represented in our literature and in our decks of playing cards as the Jack, the "knave of hearts"! Even the name "knave" has an opprobrious meaning.

There is one astronomical indication in the Bible that has been picked up by the most modern translators of the Bible, notably by Dr. Harry Orlinsky and his committee, whose translation of the Pentateuch is the best available. The translation of Numbers 24:17 in the King James version of the Bible is as follows:

> I see him, but not now; I behold him, but not nigh:
> There shall step forth a star out of Jacob,
> And a scepter shall rise out of Israel,
> And shall smite the corners of Moab,
> And break down all the sons of Seth.

In the new translation, called the *Torah* and published by the Jewish Publication Society, the verse is translated as follows:

> What I see for them is not yet,
> What I behold will not be soon;
> A star rises from Jacob, a *meteor* comes forth from Israel,
> It smashes the brow of Moab,
> The foundation of all children of Seth.

This makes much better sense than the old translation because it also makes much better astrological sense. Indeed, linguistically, we ought to look for some heavenly body in the phrase to parallel "star," and "sceptre" is neither an astronomical nor an astrological parallel. The Hebrew word $\overline{S}BT$ does have the meaning of "sceptre" or "staff," but it also means "tribe" as well as "meteor." But in this context, "meteor" is the only linguistic solution available. However, it is also an astrological solution, giving added meaning and greater impact to the message of Balaam. For the meteor has always been the astrological symbol of changes in national status, of forced changes in governments; all kings were fearful of them. To say that a meteor will arise from Israel which will destroy the foundations of nations and defeat Moab and Seth presents a picture that is easily understood, and that with high drama terrorizes its readers, who all astrologically, understand the impact of the meteor and fear its appearance. Indeed, it may very well be that the other meanings of the Hebrew word $\bar{S}BT$, the meaning "sceptre, staff, tribe," may be derivative of the word's original meaning "a meteor that appears in the heavens as a fiery sceptre, announcing the legitimacy or the fall of leadership and of governments."

I know of very few people raised in the Judeo-Christian tradition who have not heard the 23rd Psalm. In Christianity, it is used at funeral services as a harbinger of the promised salvation. In traditional Judaism it has the same meaning, but it is sung as a table-song on the eve of the Sabbath, in thanksgiving to God who provides us with Sabbath rest in this world, with the means of salvation in this world, and the promise of life after death assured to all living beings. Many sermons have been preached on this psalm, and in most of them "the Valley of the Shadow of Death" figures prominently as a place of steep rocks and dangerous trails, across which the shepherds of Jerusalem had to lead their flocks when traveling from winter to summer pasture. All this is true, and yet no one has ever bothered to ask: Why was it named the Valley of the Shadow of Death? The Hebrew word for "Shadow of Death" is $\bar{S}LMW\dot{T}$. The word appears in the Bible 17 times in all of its forms. And in only four of those instances which include Psalms 23 does it mean a type of location. In 12 of the quotations, the meaning is symbolic of danger. Why? The answer may be hidden in the one quotation that may shed some light on the mystery. In the Book of Amos 5:8, we read:

> Him that maketh the Pleiades and Orion, and bringeth
>   on the Shadow of Death $(\bar{S}LMW\dot{T})$ in the morning.
> And darkeneth the day into night,
> That calleth for the waters of the sea,
> And poureth them out on the face of the Earth;
> The Lord of Hosts is His name. . . .

It looks as though this may be another astrological mystery. It seems that, since $\bar{S}LMW\dot{T}$ is linked in the same phrase with the Pleiades and Orion, it might also be a constellation. Perhaps, the "Valley of the Shadow of Death" $(GYA\ \bar{S}LMW\dot{T})$ is so named, not only because it is so dangerous to cross, filled as it is with large rocks and steep cliffs and wild animals, but also because a certain constellation hovers over it at the time of the year when it is most dangerous to cross. When would that be?

Israel has four seasons: two rainy seasons and two dry seasons. Winter in Israel is considered to be from the close of the Feast of Tabernacles (*Sukkot,* eight days after Full Moon Libra) to Passover (Pesakh, Full Moon Aries). Therefore, the flocks would be taken out to summer pasture sometime during early March (the end of Pisces) and would be returned to their winter quarters some time in the middle of November (the end of Scorpio) as is done today. At either time the flocks would be in danger, either from weakness (the forage tends to turn poor at both times) or from the attacks of wild beasts (who have been hungry all winter). In all 17 quotations, $\dot{S}LMW\dot{T}$ is linked with the loss of, or the fading of, light, and with the growing darkness. This would certainly point to the middle of November as the time, and Scorpio as the constellation involved.

Such a conjecture certainly makes sense both astronomically and astrologically. The days are growing shorter, and the longer the shepherd would wait to lead his flocks from summer to winter pasture, the more dangerous it would become. Night falls suddenly in the hills of Judea. Astrologically, it would make more sense if Scorpio were involved, rather than Pisces. For in the ancient Astrology of this period, Scorpio was ruled by Mars, whereas Pisces was ruled by Jupiter. Mars is the planet of sword and claw, violence and bloodshed, whereas Jupiter is the planet of expansion and fortune. And the violence that threatened their flocks led good shepherds to avoid the Valley of Scorpio at that season. (Remember: Uranus, Neptune, and Pluto, only recently discovered, never entered into the astrological calculations of the ancients. Many astrologers today hold that their assigned rulerships over 11th-house Aquarius, 12th-house Pisces, and 8th-house Scorpio, respectively, are questionable. Such rulership assignments certainly destroy the Kabbalistic balance of the ancient planetary rulerships.)

We know that, at this time in mankind's history, astrological considerations were used in planting crops, mating animals, and even in planning human marriage. Would it not be considered logical to think that shepherds, who use the stars for finding directions, would also use the constellations to time their journeying with their flocks? I can almost hear two shepherds talking in the Judean mountains: "We must really begin to return the flocks to winter pasture. Behold, the days grow shorter: soon $\dot{S}LMW\dot{T}$ will be seen rising above the depths of $GYA\ \dot{S}LMW\dot{T}$, and it will then be too late to cross the Valley safely." Indeed, I believe we have made a strong case for the possibility that the word $\dot{S}LMW\dot{T}$ refers to the

Constellation Scorpio, which from the biblical data available, makes more sense than that this word refers only to a specific valley near Jerusalem since it is used only *once* in the entire Scripture: that is, in Psalms 23. Logically, it would be better to suppose that the word means "Scorpio," and that the valley takes its name from this meaning, rather than to assume any other possibility. From what I have been able to determine, no better possibility exists.

Since in Astrology Mars is the planetary ruler of the constellation Scorpio, we must ask the question: Why is this planet not mentioned in the Bible? For nowhere is Mars mentioned in the Bible—at least, not by the name Mars.

The Hebrew name for the planet Mars is *MADYMf*. It is derived from the word *ADWMf*, meaning "red" or *mad*, meaning "very," or both. The precise derivation is not clear: Does *MAD* mean "very" because *MADYMf* ("Mars") is the planet of intense energy, and the word takes its meaning from the astrological understanding of the nature of the planet Mars? Or does the name of the planet Mars (*MADYMf*) take its name from the intensity of the redness of the planet and from the intensity of action implied by the adverb "very" (*MAD*)? In any event, both intensity and redness are implied in the Hebrew name of the planet, which may be translated from the Hebrew as "that which reddens" meaning astronomically, the planet with the reddish hue; and meaning astrologically, the planet that spills blood. In ancient times, Mars was known to be the planet which causes strife and war, and some of those born under its influence could become murderers, warriors, butchers, or surgeons.

Although the planet is not mentioned by name in the Bible, a perfect description of God, in the guise of vengeful warrior, does appear and is linked with the word *ADWMf*. The description which is the typical ancient astrological description of the most violent of Scorpionic, Martian personalities is in the Book of Isaiah 63:1-6. I shall quote only the first phrase in Hebrew to indicate the use of the root *ADWMf*, "red:"

MY ZH BA MADWMf . . .

> Who is this that cometh from Edom (Mars?), with crimsoned garments of Bozrah? This that is glorious in his apparel, stately in the greatness of his strength?
> "I speak in victory, mighty to save."
> Wherefore is thine apparel red (*ADWMf*) and thy garments like he that treadeth in the wine-vat?
> "I have trodden the wine press alone, and of the people—there was no man with me!

Yea, I trod them in mine anger and trampled them in my fury;
And their lifeblood is dashed against my garments,
And I have stained all my raiment.
For the day of vengeance that was in my heart,
And my year of redemption, are come.
And I looked, and there was none to help: and I
    beheld in astonishment, and there was none to uphold:
Therefore mine own arm brought salvation unto me,
And my fury, it upheld me.
And I trod down the peoples in mine anger,
And made them drunk with my fury,
And I poured out their lifeblood on the earth!"

Anyone versed in the ancient astrological concepts of those personality traits engendered by the planets will recognize this description as that of the typical Martian personality in its most violent form—even to the ascribing of righteous purpose to its violence.

Finally, let us examine the problem of the "Day of the Lord." This expression is used *only* by the prophets, and is not contained in the books of the Historic, Didactic, or Mosaic traditions. Of these 15 named prophets whose works are included by name in the Bible, 8 prophets, including both Isaiah and Ezekiel, speak of the coming of the "Day of the Lord." And of these 8 prophets, 6 link the coming of this "Day" with astrological events of the direst portent. The heavens will turn black, the lights of the constellations will not be seen, the Sun and Moon will stand still, the stars will be dashed to the ground—all of the most horrible astronomical events and astrological portents imaginable will accompany this day. But this is to be the day of God's victory over the other nations, of the restitution of the scattered remnants of Israel to their land; the day of God's return to Jerusalem. In no uncertain terms, then, the prophets seem to be indicating that all these portents that signal the destruction of their oppressors have no evil connotation for Israel. This will be an important point to remember.

The idea that the loss of light portends sadness and disaster should not be strange to those who are familiar with the biblical material. After all, the first act of God's creation was the statement "Let there be light. . . ." (Gen. 1:3) and further that the light was good (Gen. 1:4). We expect the absence of light to be a portent of coming evil, and so it is. Although the Hebrew word for darkness is normally some form of the word $X\bar{S}Kf$, in 18 verses in the Bible a form of the verb QDR is used, and in all but two of these verses, the darkening refers to the catastrophe of the Heavens losing their light. Of the other two verses, one refers to the black ice of a stream, the other to the face of a person turning black with astonishment. Of the other 16 verses, 1 refers to the natural darkening of the Heavens before a storm: 7 refer to the Heavens becoming dark as a sign of mourning; and 8 refer to the darkening of the heavens as the result of some supernatural act. Technically, we may consider only these last 8 verses as referring to the "Day of the Lord" syndrome, but I would also include the mourning verses, which in themselves depict a paranatural act. Including these verses adds two more prophetic voices, one of a major prophet, Jeremiah, and Malachi, a minor prophet, giving the three major prophets and 7 of the 12 minor prophets. All predict a phenomenon called the "Day of the Lord" on which all destroyers of Israel themselves will be destroyed; Israel will be restored, and the Temple reestablished: all orchestrated to the terrible symphony of astronomical events and astrological portents without parallel in the memory of mankind. For example:

And it shall come to pass in that day that there shall be light,
> But heavy clouds and thick:
> And there shall be one day which shall be known as the
> Lord's
> Not day and not night; but it shall come to pass,
> That at evening time there shall be light."
> > [Zechariah 14:6-7]

> Moreover, the light of the Moon shall be the light of the
> Sun,
> And the light of the Sun shall be sevenfold, as the light of
> the seven days.
> In the day that the Lord bindeth up the bruise of his people,
> And healeth the stroke of their wound.
> > [Isiah 30:26]

> Multitudes, multitudes in the valley of decision.
> For the Day of the Lord is near in the valley of decision.
> The Sun and the Moon are become black,
> And the stars withdraw their shining.
> > [Joel 4:14-15]

There should be no doubt that the prophets thought of the "Day of the Lord" as being a day of Divine Judgment. The judgment would occur against the nations that had oppressed Israel and against the sinners of Israel: For the prophets always spoke of national salvation, of national redemption, of the return and of the success vouchsafed to the righteous remnant of Israel. And the prophets believed that the day was imminent.

But why all the imagery of the fall of the Heavens? Had there been such a natural catastrophe within the immediate memory of the historical people Israel? Was there a natural catastrophe of which the Israelites took advantage during the Exodus from Egypt, later used by Moses to defeat the Amalekites (Ex. 17:8-13), still later used by Joshua to pass over the Jordan on dry land (Josh. 3:7-17), destroy Jericho (Josh. 6:1-27) and defeat the Amorites (Josh. 10:8-15)? Or were the peoples of the area so steeped in the astrological lore of their time, that calling on the cessation of all astrological certainty was an oratorical device understood by and responded to, by all listeners? Dr. Immanuel Velikovsky and Erich Von Däniken would undoubtedly lean toward the first supposition; I would lean toward the second. However, that such a supposition is available to us from the evidence of the Bible is in itself a cause for wonder and a phenomenon in its own right, unless of course, one is used to reading the Bible with an astrologically aware and open mind.

PART IV:
ASTROLOGY
IN THE
MIDRASH

14

INTRODUCTION

The Lord said ... to Abram ...: "Look to the heaven and count the stars...."

Genesis 15:5

Abram said: "My planetary fate oppresses me ...!"

Midrash Rabbah to Genesis 15:5

The Lord said to him: "It is as thy words; Abram and Sarai cannot beget, but Abraham and Sarah can beget!"

Midrash Rabbah to Genesis 15:5

There is no finer example of astrological prediction in all of Jewish literature. Why should it be given in the Midrash? Perhaps because the Midrash is a literature of hope and salvation, we find this and other astrological statements in positions of great importance in it; positions connected with our greatest leaders: Abraham, Moses, King David, King Solomon. Here are some more examples:

When Moses seeks to select men to cooperate in the governing of the freed Israelite slaves (see Exod. 18:14-23), his father-in-law Jethro advises him to use "that mirror in which kings seek their choices," that is, Astrology (Mekilta Yitro Amalek 2).

King Solomon's astrological knowledge was greater than that of both the men of the East and of Egypt (see Eccles. Rab. 7:23).

... and the Lord blessed Abraham in all things.
[Genesis 24:1]

These blessings were astrological gifts.
[Tosefta Kiddushin 5:23]

Abraham wore a large astrological tablet on his breast. Each morning the kings of the East and West would gather before him to seek his advice (see Tosefta Kiddushin 5:17, also Talmud Bavli Baba Batra 16b).

Finally, I would like to quote one particular Midrash verbatim, for it indicates not only that a particular type of Astrology was practiced, but also that the astrologer should be paid for his advice. The type of Astrology indicated is known as *Horary Astrology*, and is based on the positions of the planets at the time a particular question was asked:

> *I have seen all the works that are done under the sun....* (Eccles. 1:14).... The Rabbis say: "It is like an astrologer who was sitting at the entrance to the harbor and advised all passers-by, telling them that such-and-such wares could be sold in such-and-such a place; ought not people to be thankful to him?"
> Midrash

Indications are that the astrologer cast the horoscope for each cargo as it tied up safely at the dock, and that he expected to be paid for his merchandising advice. The last phrase quoted above, referring to being thankful, is in reality a Near Eastern euphemism for payment for services rendered. In such cases, we know from other sources that the payment involved was usually ten percent of the profit.

Astrology was also used to illustrate God's concern for Israel in the act of creating the universe:

> *In the beginning God created...*(Gen. 1:1). Six things preceded the creation of the world; some of them were already created, whereas the creation of others was already contemplated...the creation of Israel was contemplated, as it is written: *Remember thy congregation, which thou hast gotten aforetime.*" (Ps. 74:2).... R. Huna...said: "The intention to create Israel preceded everything else. This may be illustrated thus: A king was married to a certain lady and had no son by her. On one occasion the king was found going through the marketplace and giving orders: 'Take this ink, inkwell, and pen for my son,' at which people remarked, 'He has no son: what does he want with ink and pen?' Strange indeed! Subsequently, they concluded: 'The king is an astrologer, and has actually foreseen that he is destined to beget a son.'"

Thus, had not the Holy One, Blessed Be He, foreseen that after 26 generations Israel would receive the Torah, He would not have written therein *Command the Children of Israel* ... (Numb. 28:2).

Midrash

Astrology was also used by the Midrash to illustrate areas of Scripture which were questioned by the Rabbis:

Why did God proclaim His law amidst fire and darkness (see Deut. 5:20) rather than in broad daylight? This can be explained by a parable. A king, who was a great astrologer, gave his son in marriage and hung black curtains before the bridal chamber saying: "I know that my son will not abide by his nuptial promises longer than 40 days. Let not the people in days to come say that an astrologer such as I, did not know what was to happen to his son." The astrologer is God, his son is Israel, the bride is the Torah—by which Israel abode no longer than 40 days (from the Revelation to the making of the Golden Calf!).

Pirke dR. Eliezer 41

A king sentenced a man to death by fire. However, when he perceived by Astrology that the man was to beget a daughter who would become the king's bride, he said: "This man must be saved for the sake of his daughter." Thus did God (the astrologer) save Abraham (the condemned man) from the fiery furnace because of Jacob (the "daughter," destined to become Israel—the "bride" and "chosen" of God).

Midrash

A man sired a son, and an astrologer, on seeing the son, states that the son is to be a bandit chief and must be abandoned in the desert. The father of the child refused until the astrologer's father told him to do just as his son had ordered. The astrologer is Sarah, the son is Ishmael, the father of the son is Abraham—and the father of the astrologer is God.

(Deuteronomy Rabbah 4:5, referring to Genesis 21:10)

Astrologers are human; they are as prone to error as any other group of human beings. The following three illustrations of Midrashic material are about astrologers who saw the Heavens correctly, but interpreted their meaning incorrectly.

In ancient times, when a pagan desired to buy a slave, he would consult an astrologer. Thus the wife of Potifar learned that she was to have a son by Joseph, and tempted him (see Gen. 39:7-20). The stars were right, but the interpretation was in error. Joseph was indeed destined to have a son from the line of Potifar's wife—but through her daughter, whom he married (see Gen. 41:45).

Genesis Rabbah 85:2 and 87:4

Mesha, King of Moab, asked his astrologers: "Why can I not vanquish Israel?" They answered him: "Because of the merit of Abraham, who was ready to sacrifice his son." Mesha then sacrificed his son. (The astrologers did not distinguish between being willing to act and completing the act.)

Pesikta 2:13a

Haman chose the time for the extermination of the Jews (see Esth. 3:7) by means of astrological calculations. (Since he failed, his calculations were in error!)

Pirke dR. Eliezer 1

Although all of these uses of Astrology in biblical interpretation make very interesting and sometimes surprising reading, it is most important to understand the place of Midrash in Jewish religious literature to clearly understand the importance of Astrology. For if the Midrash is peripheral, unimportant literature in Jewish life, then the importance of its astrological vector can be minimized.

There is much scholarly debate concerning the dates which conclude the books of the Bible, but it is generally accepted that they were completed soon after the return from Babylonian exile in 517 B.C.E. If we allow a leeway of one century, we could say that the Bible was effectively completed about the end of the fifth century B.C.E. although the Canon of the Bible was not closed until the year 70 C.E., following the destruction of the Temple by the Roman Empire.

Contrary to popular belief, the literary and religious development of Judaism did not end with the completion of the Bible. It still continues to this very day. What was the continuation of the religious and literary tradition from the fifth century B.C.E. through the turn of the era? Basically, it developed in the same manner as the Bible itself did. First, there was a verbal, vocal tradition which was later written down by compilers. This development was of interest in itself as well as for our own consideration of the astrological contents and importance contained within it.

All Jewish literary, legal, and religious output in ancient

times—and this includes the Bible itself—was the product of an interiorized dialectic. That is to say, all biblical material began as stories passed on from father to son, as legal traditions passed on verbally from sage to novice, as cult worship instructions passed on verbally from experienced priest to neophyte, and so on. Even the right to inherit property was guaranteed through the verbal traditions of family tree recitation. When the Bible was finally written down—piecemeal—only those traditions which were important enough to remember were included. We know for instance, that King Saul was required to follow all of God's laws which Samuel "... wrote in a book, and laid it up before the Lord ..." (1 Sam. 10:25). The tradition at this time included probably most of Genesis and Exodus, and parts of Numbers. We know that later, on the return from Babylonian Exile (517 B.C.E.), the rest of the Mosaic and most of the Historic traditions had been compiled; by the time of the Sanhedrin (fourth century B.C.E.) most of the prophetic and a good part of the Didactic traditions had been copied down. We know that the final books were admitted to the Canon of Scripture in the year 70 C.E.

Now consider: If Astrology were unimportant in the lives of the population, and in the lives of its leadership and its teachers, then during the period of the winnowing of this oral tradition, surely the "unimportant" astrological elements would have been blown away with the rest of the unremembered chaff. After all, if we remember that the oral tradition of the Bible begins with the proto-Hebraic memories of Abram of Ur in the Chaldees, we are talking about a stretch of time from approximately 2,500 B.C.E. to the first writing, about 700 B.C.E.—1,800 years. Another 770 years brings us to the final close of the Canon. Surely, in a period of almost 2,600 years, that which was peripheral and unimportant, and transmitted verbally, would have been eliminated. And it was eliminated. Which means that the growing astrological information in the Bible was considered not peripheral but *central* to the needs and understandings of the people.

By the time that the Bible was completed, a new religiolegal-literary-ethical tradition was developing, and it too was a verbal dialectic. From this point on, Jews would speak of two authoritative traditions: the "written law" (*Torah shebichtav*) and the *"oral law"* (*Torah sheb'al peh*). This latter tradition is the legal-ethical-literary-religious dialectic which was never to be written down, but which eventually was compiled as Scripture was, and became the various compilations generically called by the term *Midrash*, and which also became the Mishnah-Gemarrah complex known as the *Talmud*.

It is most difficult to separate the Midrash and the Talmud. The difficulty lies in that both were dialectic in nature; that is, they were the remembered and subsequently the collected conversations of the sages in the areas of law and ethics. And very often, one area of conversation was used to illuminate the other, so that one will find many midrashic elements in the Talmud, and also many legalistic Midrashim. Another reason for the difficulty is that the same sages, who discussed the materials later collated as Midrash, were also the men who taught the legalities which were later collated as the Talmud. Therefore, for the sake of simplicity, I shall use the term *Midrash* to refer to those compiled volumes of aggadic material which are known as Midrash texts; and I shall use *Talmud* to refer to all those halachic materials that are printed in the standard format of the Talmud. (Remember, *aggadah* refers to that which was "expounded" as ethics primarily; *Halachah* refers to that which was "taught" as the "way to go" in life, primarily its legalities.)

If we were to consider the midrashic elements of the Talmud, we would see that the Midrash began as early as the halachic discussions of the Mishnah-Gemarrah complex, notably, with the return from the Babylonian Exile at the end of the sixth century B.C.E. The Midrash as Midrash continues through the thirteenth century C.E., at the least, giving us a body of information encompassing almost 2000 years. From this vast body of ethical-religious writings, samples of which opened this chapter, I would like to draw three examples and analyze them in detail. I will deal with two historic personalities vital to the development of Israel; then I shall embark with you on a fascinating trip through the lifetime of the human being as developed in the Midrash along astrological lines, exclusively.

It would be valuable at this time to review the methodology of the Midrash. The Midrash is a continuous commentary on the Bible. Its method is to quote a verse of Scripture and then to proceed along one of three different paths:

1. The commentator may comment directly on the verse quoted, indicating God's intention when He revealed the information.

2. The commentator may immediately quote another biblical verse seemingly unconnected in meaning to the first. Then by comparing the two verses in some unique way, the commentator will introduce a new meaning to the original verse. This technique is known in Hebrew as a *p'tichah*, and is usually translated as: Rabbi Jose "opened his discourse. . . ."

3. The commentator may use an example taken from life to illustrate the meaning of the verse. This is known in Hebrew as *mashal*, and means "parable."

Thus when we quote the Midrash, it will be necessary to quote the biblical verse, or verses, on which the Midrash is based, and then continue with the midrashic interpretation.

15

PATRIARCH AND LAWGIVER

Perhaps the two most important persons in the history of Israel are Abraham and Moses. Abraham was the Father of the Hebrews, the first monotheist, the man willing to leave his father's household and his native land to follow the dictates of an unseen God. Moses was the charismatic leader of the enslaved Hebrews in Egypt. He led them out of slavery to the great theophany at Mount Sinai; he welded the disparate tribes into one people and led them to the borders of the Promised Land, borders he was not allowed to cross. Astrologically, how does the Midrash deal with these men?

Abraham was born in the city of Ur of the Kasdim—and his name was originally not Abraham, but Abram. What do we know about his early life? Not very much. There are legends that his father Terach was a maker of idols, and that Abram rebelled against this. However, we do know one fact. In Hebrew, the word $K\bar{S}DYMf$ means "astrologers," and one ought to translate the name of Abram's birthplace, AWR $K\bar{S}DYMf$, "light of the astrologers." We also have some evidence that the rulers of that area of Mesopotamia during that period of history (third millenium B.C.E.) were astrologer-kings. There are clues to this in Kurt Seligman's *History of Magic*, in which he alludes to the temporal power of the Chaldean astrologers: Astrologer-kings are also mentioned in the New Testament stories of the birth of Jesus as well as in talmudic and midrashic sources of the type in the midrashic examples in the next paragraph. There is also a

151

Midrash (Yalkut Shimoni on Lech L'cha 21b v.60) which states that Abram's father Terach was an astrologer. But how does the Midrash treat Abram-Abraham?

We read in the Bible (Gen. 12:1-3) God's command to Abram, and His promise:

> Now the Lord said unto Abram: "Get thee out of thy country and from thy kindred and from thy father's house, unto a land that I will show thee. And I will make of thee a great nation, and I will bless thee and make thy name great; and be thou a blessing. And I will bless them who bless thee, and him who curseth thee will I curse, and in thee shall all the families of the earth be blessed."

And yet, by Chapter 15 of Genesis, Abram is still childless. We then have this conversation recorded between God and Abram:

> After these things, the word of the Lord came to Abram in a vision saying: "Fear not Abram, I am thy shield, thy reward shall be exceeding great." And Abram said: "O Lord God what wilt Thou give me, seeing I go forth hence childless, and he that shall be possessor of my house is Eliezer of Damascus?" And Abram said: "Behold, to me Thou hast given no seed and lo, one born in my house is to be mine heir." And behold, the word of the Lord came to him saying: "This man shall not be thine heir, but he who shall come forth out of thine own bowels shall be thine heir." And He brought him forth abroad and said: "Look now toward heaven and count the stars (Hebrew: *HBT-NA HŠMYMH WSPR HKWKBYMf*) if thou be able to count them." And He said unto him: "So shall thy seed be."
>
> Genesis 15:1-5

We must understand what was in question here, both biblically and from the point of view of the later Rabbis whose duty it was to interpret the Bible. In the Bible, the question is clear-cut. Abram is questioning the validity of God's promise in Genesis 12:1-3. He has as yet no child. How then, can the promise " . . . make of thee a great nation . . ." be fulfilled? The problem is one of Abram's questioning of the whole process of Divine Election.

How do later Rabbis handle this problem? They handle it astrologically. Let me quote from the Midrash Rabbah to Genesis:

> And Abram said: *Behold, to me thou hast given no seed* . . . (Gen. 15:3). Rabbi Samuel ben Isaac commented that Abram said: "My

planetary fate oppresses me and declares 'Abram cannot beget a child.' Said the Holy One, Blessed Be He to him: 'Let it be even as thy words; Abram and Sarai cannot beget, but Abraham and Sarah can beget.' "

What a fascinating astrological attitude is here ascribed to God. God says to Abram that indeed, you have read your horoscope well. As Abram and Sarai, before I have changed your names, your horoscope is true; you will remain childless. But because of your faith in Me, you have earned a change in name, that is, from Abram to Abraham and from Sarai to Sarah. Now if you will cast a new horoscope using the moment of your name-change as a new moment of birth, you will see that your planetary influences indicate that you will beget a child. The Rabbis put God squarely on the side of Astrology. Even more important, the Rabbis provide an insight into the importance of names both astrologically and psychologically.

From this Midrash an interesting custom derives in orthodox Jewish life. When an orthodox person is gravely ill, his or her nearest male relative will go to the synagogue on a morning on which the Torah is publicly read. The relative will ask to be called on to say the blessings for the reading of the Torah, and then during the ceremony of the reading of Scripture, he will ask that the reader say those special prayers which will "add a name" to the Hebrew name of the sick one. This ceremony of "adding a name" stems directly from this Midrash wherein God agrees that Astrology is valid, but that the giving or taking of a new name indicates the necessity of a new natal chart for the symbolic new birth.

An interesting case in point would be that of my own father. He often told me that soon after he was brought to the United States as an infant—before his first birthday—he became gravely ill, and this adding-a-name ceremony was done in his behalf. Because my father did not know his own birth time, I will use an arbitrary birth time of 6:00 A.M. (which is sunrise), and set his Sun at birth conjunct (directly equal to) his Ascendant, and use an Equal House System (each house = 30°) on which to plot the planets and personal points of his birth. My father was born in Klintsy, Russia on March 7, 1902 (Georgian date corrected from Julian calendar), 32 E 16 longitude, 52 N 45 latitude. In Figure 15.1 his natal chart is labeled Chart A.

My father's natal chart is not too happy a chart. All his planets are on one side of the chart, bounded by an opposition of two conjunctions: Uranus conjunct Midheaven opposed Pluto retrograde conjunct a stationary Neptune, and the Sun-Ascendant-Mars conjunction sits on the midpoint of this opposition, crosses the T, as

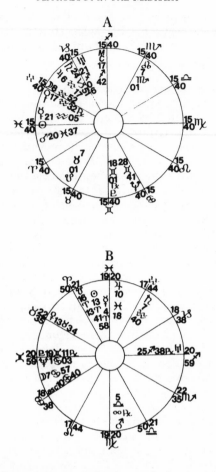

Figure 15.1 Chart A is my father's natal chart; chart B is his new natal chart at the adding-a-name ceremony.

it were. We also have a Moon-Jupiter conjunct in Aquarius in the 11th house, a Mercury-Venus conjunct in Aquarius in the 12th house, and a Moon-Venus conjunct in Aquarius across the 12th house cusp, which ties the two conjunctions together. The *only* planet not involved in a conjunction is Saturn and Saturn is in its ruling constellation, Capricorn, and therefore is a very powerful influence in the natal chart. Saturn is the only planet in a Cardinal Sign, and also the only planet in an Earth Sign, as well. And lonely Saturns can cause a lot of trouble. Now, note how close that natal Saturn is to the Jupiter-Moon conjunction in Aquarius. We know from the chapter dealing with the constellations that, in ancient times, people thought the liver was controlled by Aquarius, and that one of the diseases common to Aquarius is black jaundice. In his modern theories of cosmobiology, Reinhold Ebertin states that one of the biological indications of an afflicted Moon-Jupiter midpoint (that point in the horoscope midway between the positions of the Moon and Jupiter, in this case 7° Aquarius 34′42″) is jaundice.

When the strong, lonely Saturn in the natal chart transited Jupiter conjunct on March 17, 1903, I believe that there was the onset of a serious illness. My father was only 10 days past 1 year old, and lived in Staten Island. The disease probably hit its crisis on April 3, 1903 when Saturn transited conjunct the Moon-Jupiter midpoint, that date was a Friday. The next day was The Great Sabbath, the Sabbath before Passover. As a matter of fact, that very Sabbath night, the first Seder (ritual family dinner retelling the story of the Exodus) was held throughout the Jewish world. What better time to seek God's aid to cure an ailing, beloved son. Grandfather, of blessed memory, went to the synagogue on that Sabbath (he never missed a day from going to synagogue, unless he was ill), and most probably changed my father's name from David, son of Jacob Tsvi, to Ephraim David, son of Jacob Tsvi. (Why Ephraim? The Bible says: " . . . By thee shall Israel bless, saying, 'God make thee as Ephraim and as Manasseh'." Thus, these two names are used in giving new names, as are the names of the three Patriarchs Abraham, Isaac, and Jacob, and the name *Chayyim*, meaning "life," or *Alter*, meaning "old." For women, the names of the four Matriarchs Sarah, Rebecca, Rachel, and Leah are used, as well as the name *Chava*, or *Chaya*, meaning "life.") Since the Torah is usually read on the Sabbath at around 10:30 A.M., and since the ceremony of giving a new name is done at the time of the Torah reading, we may consider that, with the change of the name, my father had a new birth at 10:30 A.M. on Saturday, April 4, 1903 in Staten Island, New York, U.S.A., in the small synagogue near the ferry slips; 74 W 05 longitude, 40 N 38 latitude. His new natal chart is labeled Chart B in Figure 15.1 and from it we may see a new lease on life!

As you can see, the new chart has planets all over the chart and only two major groups of planets. The Sun, Mercury, and South Node are conjunct in Aries in the tenth house, and the Moon,

Neptune and Ascendant are conjunct in the 1st house, in Cancer. There are no major stellia (groups of planets) in Aquarius, and Saturn sitting there is not as powerful as it would be in Capricorn, and besides has positive aspects to it from Mars (120°, a Trine) and from the Mercury-Sun-Node conjunct (60°, a sext). Thus, we see that the new birth chart literally "opens up" new vistas for my father, and, with so many of his planets now in the Cardinal signs, ensures new beginnings.

Similar to this name-change is the Western concept of place-change: "Change your place, change your luck!" This same place-change idea is also an ancient Hebrew concept, but in Hebrew the term is *MŠNH MQWMf MŠNH MZL*, "Change your place, change your *constellation!*" As you will discover later in the discussion of Astrology in the Talmud, this really refers to the constellation on the Ascendant. Every astrologer knows that if a person changes his location, the astrologer must calculate a new Ascendant for the latitude and longitude of the new place.

There is a second commentary on this same section of Scripture, which further places God on the side of Astrology:

> *And He brought him forth abroad* (Hebrew: *HXWŚH*) *and said...*" (Gen. 15:5). Rabbi Judah ben Rabbi Simon said in Rabbi Johanan's name: "He lifted him above the vault of Heaven; hence, He says to him *"Look now towards Heaven..."* (Gen. 15:5); (Hebrew: *HBT-NA HŚMYMH*), *HBT* signifying "to look down from above."

Once again God agrees that Abram has read his horoscope correctly, that as long as Abram is under the influence of his planetary angles and his constellations, he will not be blessed with children. However, whereas Rabbi Samuel ben Isaac solved the problem by a name-change, which today we can, and still do, use in times of dire emergencies, Rabbi Judah indicates that in some miraculous fashion, God removes Abram from his natal astrological influences by physically transporting him *above* the vault of Heaven: Therefore, Abram influences the Stars, not vice versa.

The Rabbis of old realized that they were dealing with the problem of Abram's challenge to the promise of Divine Election. They answered the challenge in terms that they were used to, and in terms that their followers would understand, and those terms were astrological terms. The two Rabbis saw Divine Election in two different dimensions: Rabbi Samuel sees Divine Election as being a function of man's efforts to live the life of Godliness on earth, and he provides an earthly solution to Abram's dilemma. "Live according to God's law and will, and this will change your persona, symbolized by a change of name, and this change will mean the type of new life for you which would be akin to rebirth; so your natal chart for your new birth would symbolize and delineate the blessings of your new awareness." Rabbi Judah ben Rabbi Simon, on the other hand, sees Divine Election as being independent of man's efforts: "a miraculous gift from God tendered to a humanity unworthy of it. One becomes worthy only by direct Divine intervention"; and this Rabbi Judah symbolizes as being carried "...above the vault of Heaven..."; thus the influences of one's natal planetary positions are no longer brought into play. His attitude seems to be that one can rise above one's planetary influences only by coming into direct contact with the Divine.

Once again, we see that what seemed to us to be new religious and astrological dichotomies are revealed now to us as really being ancient ones: Rabbi Samuel is the "scientific" astrologer and the believer in the "social gospel"; Rabbi Judah is the "esoteric" astrologer and believer in "salvation through faith." Indeed, as the book of Ecclesiastes states (Eccles. 1:9):

That which hath been is that which shall be,
And that which hath been done is that which shall be done;
And there is nothing new under the sun.

Let us turn to the problem of Moses and his survival. Once again we must review the biblical narrative of events and the occurrences surrounding the birth of Moses. We are told in the book of Exodus that "...a new Pharoah..." arose who "...knew not Joseph..." (Exod. 1:8). Fearful of the growing strength and affluence of the Hebrew tribes, he orders them enslaved and oppressed. Since even this treatment did not stay their growth, he next orders the Hebrew midwives to destroy all Hebrew male newborns (Exod. 1:18). When this too proves ineffective because the midwives refuse to obey the order, the Pharaoh next decrees that his own people cast every newborn Hebrew male child into the Nile (Exod. 1:22).

Moses is born into this holocaust. His mother hid him for three months then made him an ark of rushes, floated him on the Nile and set his sister Miriam to watch over him. As you may recall from the second chapter of Exodus in which this tale is told, the daughter of Pharaoh finds the ark of rushes and adopts Moses as her own, sending Miriam to find a wetnurse for him: of course, Miriam brings Moses' own mother.

This biblical story is well known to all, and yet the Rabbis of the Midrash see in it the clue to the world's misunderstanding of the Jewish concept of mission and election, and they explain it in astrological terms. The Pharaoh who had no experience with the works of Joseph sees only a growing foreign community in his native Egypt. How shall he deal with it? First, he arouses the hatred of the indigenous Egyptians, on the basis of national security. Next, he enslaves the Israelites, then refuses them permission to leave Egypt, while at the same time attempting the earliest recorded practice of controlled genocide. And yet the very water, the Nile, that is to bury the future of Israel will become the vehicle on which Israel's future leader will ride to salvation. How do the Rabbis handle the story? Once again, let me quote directly from the Midrash:

> *Every son who is born ye shall cast into the river.*
>
> Exodus 1:22

Why did they decree that they should cast them into the river? Because the astrologers foresaw that Israel's savior would be smitten by water, and they thought that he would be drowned in the water: but as we know, it was only on account of the well of water that the decree of death was pronounced upon him...(see Numb 20:1-13 for this story).

[Exodus Rabbah 1:18]

She took for him an ark of bulrushes and she daubed it with slime and with pitch and she put the child therein, and laid it in the flags (reeds) by the river's brink.

[Exodus 2:3]

Why did they cast him (Moses) into the river? So that the astrologers might think that he had already been cast into the water, and would not search for him. (*He* and *him* refer, in general, to the expected savior of Israel; thus if they saw that *he* had been cast into the River Nile, they would rescind the order to destroy all Hebrew male newborns.)

[Midrash]

Note once again that there is no intimation at all that the astrologers of Pharaoh saw incorrectly; nor was there any indication that the astrologers were not to be believed, that they were charlatans, that they were in any way antireligious or antimonotheistic. To the contrary, the Midrash insists that the astrologers saw correctly. Moses *was* defeated because of water. They were wrong only in the identification of which body of water was to be his downfall. In addition to this: the Rabbis of the Midrash were so convinced of the essential *truth* of astrological indications, that they have Moses' mother place him in the Nile not only to hide him (after all, she hid him quite well for three months on the ground) but more important, to fool the astrologers of Pharaoh into seeing in their progressions and transits that the savior of Israel had been cast into the Nile already, and to call off the bloody hunt.

For the astrologers of Pharaoh, according to Jewish tradition, believed that everything was preordained, and that all events, past, present, and future could be seen in the transiting planets. I shall show later in this chapter that Moses was born at the first-quarter Moon in Pisces, and that he was hidden on the Nile three months later, which would be at the first-quarter Moon of Gemini. The transiting Moon about this time of year is usually very close to the cusp (0°) of Pisces, a Water Sign. And since the Moon has always been strongly associated with the ancient Hebrews, and is still the basis of our modern Jewish religious calendar, the writers of the Midrash naturally applied their knowledge of Astrology to the astrological determinism of the Egyptians, and indicated since the transiting Moon had entered the Water Sign, Pisces, the leader of the Hebrews must have been cast into the Nile. Thus did they interpret the actions of Moses' mother as a deliberate ruse; they assigned to her a knowledge of both Astrology and of the determinism of the Egyptians.

In the Bible, the word used for the Pharaoh's Egyptian astrologers is *XRTMY MṠRYMf*, and is to be translated as "astrologers of Egypt." Khartoum, which is the present capital of the Sudan, is located above the sixth cataract of the Nile River. In biblical times, it was the capital of the southern kingdom of the *MṠR*, whose northern capital was located in the Nile delta region. The two kingdoms were joined together in the dynastic society known in Hebrew as *MṠRYMf*, the "twin kingdoms of Egypt." This was always indicated by the Pharaoh's wearing of a twin-peaked mitre similar to a bishop's mitre in the Roman Catholic church, and by his carrying of a whiplike object in one hand and an orblike sceptre in the other. The whiplike object referred to the northern delta kingdom, and the orblike sceptre referred to the kingdom of the south, centered at Khartoum. It represented the bowl of the Heavens, for this city takes its name from the *XRTMY MṠRYMf*, the "astrologers of Egypt." The city was most probably given the name because the royal school of astrologers had their observatories and classrooms there. Its elevation is over 3,000 feet, at the confluence of the White Nile and the Blue Nile; this would make it much more suitable for astrological studies than the delta region, with its seamists and its fog.

Why should these astrologers think of water as being the downfall of Moses? And why should the Rabbis agree with them? After all, nowhere in the Bible is there any direct indication that Moses was destined to meet his defeat through water. The Bible just states that this is what happened (Numb. 20:1-13). Why should the Rabbis give credit to the astrologers of Egypt for spotting this in Moses' horoscope, or in the horoscope of the Pharaoh, or of the Egyptian nation? Where do the Rabbis get the astrological knowledge to give such a conjecture? For it is a conjecture most certainly based on astrological knowledge. The answer is in a quotation from the Talmud (B.T. Megillah 13b, repeated in B.T. Kiddushin 38a) that Moses was born on the seventh day of the month of Adar.

The first day of the Hebrew month of Adar is 0° Pisces, and in the lunar calendar of Judaism represents the New Moon in Pisces. Therefore, if Moses was born on the seventh day of Adar, this would be a quarter of the month of Adar, and a quarter of the lunar cycle for the month or approximately 7° Pisces and the first-quarter-Moon in Pisces. Astrologers would expect dire results from a Saturn transitting conjunct Moses' Sun in Pisces. As you recall from the chapter on the Testimony of the Planets, Saturn hinders and inhibits and blocks the forces of other planets when at a tense aspect to them, and a conjunction is a tense aspect. So, transiting conjunct in Pisces, it would indicate troubles in the life and involving the lifeforce (Sun) of Moses because of restrictions placed within its path (conjunct Saturn) and in some way involving water (Pisces).

Note that three months passed before Moses' mother places him in the ark. He would now have a transitting Sun at first-quarter Moon in Gemini, square to both a Natal Sun in Pisces and a Saturn conjunction in Pisces. Time to do something drastic, such as saving him from water by floating him above it.

The quotation from the Midrash concerning Moses does not share the same ease of transition enjoyed by the first quotation concerning Abram-Abraham. In that instance, Abram was instructed to look towards the Heavens, to count the Stars; the transition from this to an astrological interpretation is quite straightforward. Not so the Moses quotation. Here, no Heavens nor Stars are mentioned in the Bible. Why then, do the Rabbis of the Midrash bother to introduce Astrology and astrologers into their interpretations? There would be no need to introduce these elements, unless first, the Rabbis themselves were knowledgeable in, and *believers in*, the efficacy of Astrology; and second, unless their *audience* was knowledgeable enough to immediately grasp the meaning and the intent of the teacher.

16

MAN'S LIFE
THROUGH THE ZODIAC

We are all familiar with the type of literary and artistic effort which was prevalent in the seventeenth and eighteenth centuries; the type of didactic art and literature through which the sages attempted to teach the proper mode of life through morality plays. For example, art like "The Rake's Progress" which, in a series of prints displayed in pyramid form, shows the "progress" of the ne'er-do-well from a youth of dissipation to a pinnacle of middle-aged acceptance among his cronies, to a disastrous old-aged man, lying drunken in the gutter. In like manner, "literature" of the true-confession and Horatio Alger type would warn us of the evils of dissipation and the virtues of hard work.

Similarly, Midrash Tanhuma Parshat-Ha-azinu presents the life cycle of the human being totally in astrological terms. I shall quote Chapter 1 of this Midrash which uses the method 1 type commentary described in Chapter 14; that is, the commentator quotes a verse of scripture and then comments on it to clarify God's intention or meaning when He first revealed the information. To assist the reader in recognizing the astrological significance of this Midrash, I shall insert my comments at appropriate intervals.

Listen, O Heavens, and I shall speak. . . ." [Deut. 32:1] Fortunate is he born of woman who affirms the workings of the heavens. As a king says to his servants, "Listen, and heed my words," thus He says to the Heavens and to the Earth: "Be silent, until I have finished My statement! . . .

161

These words begin Deuteronomy 32:1, which is the beginning of the final section of Moses' perorations to Israel. Thus, the Midrash likens this to God telling His witnesses, the Heavens and the Earth, to be silent until He has finished giving them His instructions.

> *Listen O Heavens,* thus states the Scripture, *if Heaven above can be measured, and the foundations of the Earth be searched out beneath, then will I also cast off all the seed of Israel.* (Jer. 31:37) Since they are established forever, and Israel is also established forever, they are therefore valid witnesses that Israel shall fulfill the Torah and the commandments....

See Chapter 9 for a discussion of the biblical concept of witness, and for a discussion of the validity of the Heavens and the Earth as witnesses.

> And if—God forbid—Israel should transgress them, the hands of the witnesses shall be raised against them to destroy them first as it is written:...

This is a direct quotation from Deuteronomy 17:7. The law in ancient Israel was that the judgement of the court was executed by the witnesses who appeared against the accused. If the ruling of the court was death by stoning, then the witnesses against the accused were the first to cast the accused into the pit and stone him; their initiating act was then followed by the community, so that all shared in the carrying out of the just decision of the court. In fulfillment of this law, the Heavens and the Earth being valid witnesses, they would actively carry out God's judgement against a sinful Israel, being the first to "raise their hands" against the convicted accused, according to Jewish law.

> *He shall shut up the Heavens so that there shall be no rain, and the Earth shall not yield her fruit.* (Deut. 11:17) Thus they are proper witnesses that Israel shall establish the Torah and commandments. And if—God forbid—they refuse, then the hands of the witnesses shall be against them at the first, as it is said: *I call Heaven and Earth to witness against them.* (Deut. 31:28) Therefore, I have established them as witnesses, as is stated in the *Pesikta:*...

The Pesikta Rabbah, another and older homiletic Midrash, is the original source of this Midrash.

...Man can be compared to the 12 constellations. Beginning at birth, he is as pure as the male lamb (Hebrew: *TLH:* "Aries") and he becomes as strong as the ox (Hebrew: *ŠWR:* "Taurus"). He grows up and becomes twins (Hebrew: *TAWMYMf:* "Gemini"), that is to say, complete, ...

This will give you a clue to the Astrology involved in this statement. We are involved, not in a Sun cycle (the motion of the Sun through all signs of the Zodiac in 1 year), but in a Saturn cycle (the motion of Saturn through all the signs of the Zodiac in approximately 28 years). Each advance of a constellation (e.g., Aries to Taurus, Taurus to Gemini) is considered to be an advance of Saturn to square its previous position (Saturn in Aries to Saturn in Cancer, 90° in approximately 7 years). Thus, Taurus would indicate the strength of young childhood, Gemini the onset of puberty, Cancer the beginning of real sexual maturity, and so on. Note that until puberty, man is not considered "complete" or "whole." There are fascinating correspondencies to this idea in the *Alphabet of Rabbi Akiba* and the Prologue to the *Zohar,* in which the letter *Tsadi* in Hebrew is representative of both the concepts of justice and the male/female principle. For an expanded discussion of this, see *The Alphabet of Rabbi Akiba* in Appendix 3.

...and the evil inclination grows within him....

The evil inclination in Hebrew *(YSR HR')* is not entirely an evil thing; we are not dealing with a devil or Satan. What is implied when this term is used? Is it the human tendency to indulge in one's lusts? However, since every human being has this tendency, the trick is to guide it into constructive channels. Thus, man's lust for the satisfaction of his sexual appetite is the *first* drive that turns his attention to the opposite sex. The control of this lust, however, and the proper channeling of its energies, guarantees marriage, the establishment of a home, and a continuation of the race and the nation. Without this *first* drive, a product of the *YŠR HR',* of man's primal lust, none of the good results could follow! In the East, women were especially thought to be under this particular evil inclination

...Its beginnings are as weak as the crab   (Hebrew: *SRTNf:* "Cancer")...

Like the crab, the pinch is powerful, but the crab itself is easily destroyed.

... but as it later matures, it becomes strong as the lion (Hebrew: *ARYH:* "Leo"). If he sins, he acts like the virgin (Hebrew: *BṪWLH:* "Virgo"); ...

Virgo, the virgin, must be understood in her Near Eastern attire and not in her Western garb. In the Near East, the virgin was considered to be continually anxious to experience new phenomena. She was ripe for the plucking, and couldn't wait to be plucked! She was full of new ideas, in search of new experiences, pregnant to all the possibilities rampant in her universe. She was definitely not the prim, prissy, meticulous, demure person she is considered to be in the West. Western Astrology has been colored by the Christian Church's concept of the Virgin Birth—This concept has robbed the Western Virgo of all her seductiveness.

When the quotation speaks of the sexual sinner acting like the Virgo, it simply meant to illustrate that which the Eastern Astrologer knew of the Virgo of his time, and all too often that which is still true, but unrecognized, in the Virgo of our time, as well. In her eagerness for new experience, the Eastern Virgo also included the sexual experience, and her surrender to her animal nature; which in the finest sense of that term, led her into sexual sin: intercourse with those legally and ethically forbidden to her. For this reason the Eastern Virgin was secluded and guarded in the seraglio and harem; for the same reason the Western Virgin was locked into the chastity belt.

... If he adds sin to sin, he is weighed in the scales   (Hebrew: *MAZNYMf:* "Libra"). ...

All things are weighed in the scales; merit poured into one pan, sin poured into the other. If sin outweighs merit, then Scorpio takes on the aspect of the viper. If merit outweighs sin, then Scorpio takes on the aspect of the eagle. Scorpios are usually either very, very good, or horrid, like the little girl with the curl in the middle of her forehead, of nursery rhyme fame.

... If he continues in his rebellion, they cast him into darkness and Gehinnom like the scorpion (Hebrew: *'QRB:* "Scorpio") who is cast into the dust and the pits. ...

Hebrew has no word for, or concept of, Hell. The closest that the Hebrew language can come is a place-name in ancient Israel, *GYA BNY XYNWMf,* the "Valley of the Sons of Hinnom," or "Gehinnom," for short. This valley is located in the hills of Judea, near Jerusalem, and in this valley the worshipper of Molokh used to burn their children alive in sacrifice to their idol Moloch, which had an oven incorporated into its bodily construction, for this purpose. To the Israelite, this is the closest to a concept of Hell he could get. Remember that Jews believe that one makes one's Heaven and Hell while yet on Earth, and so this place-name came to be used by Jews as a synonym for the Christian Hell.

> ...But if he repents, he is thrown into the open as one shoots an arrow from a bow (Hebrew: $Q\bar{S}\dot{T}$: "Sagittarius")....

It is interesting that Sagittarius is associated with salvation. Note that it is ruled by Jupiter, traditionally the planet which controls concepts of justice and of religious ideas. See also Chapter 18, dealing with the arrows of God. The next part of this midrashic quotation is enclosed in brackets because it is not part of the original but rather a later parenthetical addition to it.

> ...[Thus it is proper to remember the deceased on the Sabbath, that they return not to Gehinnom....

The ancients believed that on the Sabbath, condemned souls were given rest, as all of God's creatures were told to rest on the Sabbath. (This may seem to be a contradiction of the Jewish idea of Heaven and Hell as applying to this lifetime, and not to reward or punishment after death. However, this section is *not* a part of the original Midrash but a later parenthetical addition to it, this side remark about condemned souls originated at a time when Christian ideas were absorbed by some branches of Judaism under the same conditions of duress that engendered them in Christianity.) Therefore although the Sabbath was in progress and condemned souls took respite in the divinely ordained day of rest, many believed that extra efforts on behalf of the deceased, which were made in honor of the Sabbath, would shorten the torment of the condemned.

> ...For thus it is written in the Law of the Priests:...

The section of Deuteronomy which includes Chapters 12 to 27 deals with a restatement of both ritual and community law, and is known in Hebrew as the $\dot{T}WR\dot{T}$ *KHNYMf*, "the Law of the Priests," since it was the duty of the priests to administer the ritual and to maintain community order.

...*Forgive your people Israel*... (Deut. 21:8a)—these are the living—*whom you have redeemed* (Deut. 21:8b)—these are the dead. Thus we learn that the living redeem the dead. Therefore, it is our custom to remember the dead on the Day of Atonement...

See Chapter 3. This is the Day of Atonement, when one observes a 24-hour fast of total abstinence from both food and water, and prays for forgiveness for all sins committed by all humanity the world over. It is the holiest day in the Jewish calendar.

> ...and to give charity in their behalf. Thus we are taught by the Law of Priests. Can one say that those who have died are not raised up (from Gehinnom) by means of charity? Therefore the Teaching says: ...*whom you have redeemed* (Deut. 21:8b). Therefore if we allocate charity in their behalf, we remove them, and raise them "like a shot from a bow" (Hebrew: $Q\overline{S}\hat{T}$: "Sagittarius").]

> Immediately they become direct and pure, like the kid (Hebrew: *GDY:* "Capricorn") and they are as pure as the hour they were born....

Note that Capricorn is considered to be a most positive sign. It is under the rule of Saturn, which planet in Jewish Astrology is the planet of the searcher for hidden secrets, and is considered to be the planet under whose direct influence the Children of Israel dwell. Capricorn is the solar side of Saturn, Aquarius the lunar side. The Hebrew word for the planet Saturn is $\overline{S}B\hat{T}AY$, in which you may discern the word $\overline{S}B\hat{T}$, meaning the "Sabbath."

> ...Pure water is poured upon them from the pitcher (Hebrew: *DLY:* "Aquarius")...

Note that the libation comes from Aquarius, an Air Sign. In Astrology, the 12 Signs of the Zodiac are grouped into two divisions: triplicities and quadruplicities. The triplicities are commonly known as Fire, Earth, Air, and Water Signs. The quadruplicities are known as: Cardinal, Fixed, and Mutable Signs. Thus each constellation of the Zodiac has two basic affinities which delineate its basic influence. These can be cataloged broadly as shown in Table 16.1.

Table 16.1   Basic Influences of Triplicities and Quadruplicities

Sign	Quality	Cardinal (pioneering)	Fixed (stolid)	Mutable (adaptive)
Fire:	(enthusiastic)	Aries	Leo	Sagittarius
Earth:	(rooted)	Capricorn	Taurus	Virgo
Air:	(communicative)	Libra	Aquarius	Gemini
Water:	(emotive)	Cancer	Scorpio	Pisces

However, in biblical times, the four constellations indicated in the chart as being *fixed* constellations, were *Cardinal* constellations. (The modern quadruplicities are used in the chart, to avoid comment.) Thus the sign of Aquarius was then a Cardinal, Air sign. The idea that air signs are indicators of communication is biblical. The Hebrew word for "air" or "wind" in the Bible is *RWX*. This same word is used in Genesis 1:2: "... the wind of God hovered over the face of the waters...." This is usually mistranslated as "... the Spirit of God...," which is a good indication of the manner in which Christian theology interprets Scripture as it translates. In any event, this ... *RWX ALHYMf...,"* or wind of God, is the only extension of the Divine Presence in the universe, according to Scripture, when God commands the light to appear. Thus, these two English words, "air" or "wind" of God," are identical in biblical Hebrew as *RWX* and translate as the carrier of the Divine will. Thus, "Air" Signs are communicative.

The libation of "pure water," then, is really a libation of Divine communication. It is interesting that Saturn rules two signs which indicate the difficulty of change: Capricorn (Cardinal but *Earth*) and Aquarius (Air but *Fixed*). Astrologically, Israel is warned that both in leadership and in communication it must seek to establish the Divine pattern, to stick to the "straight and narrow path," not to seek innovation for its own sake. Perhaps, the Age of Aquarius will find that such steady purpose will be communicated.

...and they abound in great pleasure, as the fish (Hebrew: *DBYMf:* "Pisces") takes pleasure in water....

Once again, the ancient interpretation of Pisces is quite different from that of today. Pisces was considered to be ruled by Joseph (each constellation had a planetary ruler and a spiritual ruler, one of the sons of Jacob). Joseph became quite an important person, and Pisceans are often most successful, not at all the dour and troubled personalities interpreted so often today. There are two reasons for this change in interpretation: one is astrological, the other reveals itself in its spiritual ruler, Joseph. Astrologically, in biblical times and well into the common era, Pisces was not considered to be a Mutable constellation, but rather a Fixed constellation.

In biblical times, the Hebrews lived through two astrological eras, the Age of Taurus and the Age of Aries. During the Age of Taurus, Egypt was the major nation, the Twin Egypts (Hebrew: MŠRYMf, a plural); and the Cardinal Signs are Gemini, Virgo, Sagittarius, and Pisces. Note that the Pharaoh wore a twin crown, that he married his sister, that the gods of Egypt often had dualistic animal-human natures and representations.

During the Age of Aries, the Paschal lamb becomes a symbol of salvation, the leading nations are always involved in bull worship (the Bull of Bashan, the Minotaur, and Bull dances of Crete, the Bulls of Assyria and Babylonia, and the Golden Calf); and the Cardinal Signs are Taurus, Leo, Scorpio, and Aquarius. (And note also the importance of the lion at this time: the Lion of Judah, the Winged Lion of Persia, and so on.)

The Age of Pisces began with the Christian Era: Note the predominance of the fish as a Christian symbol. The Cardinal Signs are now Aries, Cancer, Libra, and Capricorn. Christianity now adopts the salvation through the blood of the lamb of the Hebrew Exodus story as part of its own theology, but Jesus is now *Agnus Dei*, the "Lamb of God." Now, with the Age of Aquarius, we should expect the beginnings of Cardinal reactions from Pisces, Gemini, Virgo, and Sagittarius. We have come full circle—note how important Egypt and its political control of a liquid, oil, has become. Note also the proliferation in the world of esoteric writing of the so-called Egyptian secrets.

The other reason for the confusion in interpretation of the lives of Pisceans lies in the confusion involved in its spiritual leadership. Joseph, the spiritual ruler of Pisces, is the one son of Jacob after whom no tribe is named; instead, the tribes within Israel who represent Joseph bear the names of his two sons, Ephraim and Menasseh. The Bible relates that Jacob adopted Joseph's two sons as his own, gave them portions of his inheritance, and gave them the blessings which are due to sons. However, in Jacob's aged infirmity and blindness, he crossed his hands when blessing Ephraim and Menasseh, giving the prime blessing to the younger Ephraim, and the secondary blessing to the older Menasseh. When Joseph sought to correct his father Jacob, Jacob remained adamant, stating that the younger Ephraim would always be better than the older Menasseh. (see Gen.: 48).

Since the rulership of Joseph was not manifested directly as a tribe in Israel but only indirectly through the leadership of his two sons Ephraim and Menasseh, since these two sons received blessings from their grandfather in reversal of the natural order of blessing, since Joseph's rulership was directly evident only as it manifested itself in a foreign land, Egypt, since that leadership manifested itself only after Joseph displayed esoteric abilities in his interpretation of three dreams, would it not seem inevitable with all this confusion involved in the rulership of Joseph, that there should be confusion about the interpretation of Piscean lives and abilities, and to expect from Pisceans some esoteric interests and powers?

...And thus he bathes hourly...

This is a reference to the Ascendants of the chart, which were known in Hebrew as the hours. The righteous thrive under the planetary influence of all Ascendant constellations.

...in rivers of balm and in milk and in oil and in honey....

These represent the four "humors" or triplicities of the constellations of the Zodiac: balm: Air; milk: Water; oil: Earth; and honey: Fire. This is just a further amplification of the comment above; that is, the righteous thrive under *all* influences.

...and he eats forever of the Tree of Life...

Biblically, the Tree of Life and the Tree of Knowledge were both forbidden to man's use (Gen. 2:16-17). Eve ate of the Tree of Knowledge and fed Adam from it, and thus came about the forced exodus from the Garden of Eden. The Tree of Life becomes, in Jewish life, the key to the mystery of Creation, and is symbolized by the Tree on which are outlined the Ten Sephirot of the Kabbalah; this is metamorphosed into the symbolic body of Adam Kadmon, or primal man, and is symbolized in its perfect balance by the Magen David, the (mistranslated) Star of David. This *MGNf DWD* is in reality an astrological symbol of the Divine plan and balance and consists of two Grand Trines, one pointing to Heaven, the other to Earth. Since the Hebrew word *MGNf* also means "horoscope," this symbol is an outline of the planetary positions in the horoscope of King David; although a sinner (remember Bathsheba?), King David is to sire the Messiah. He was the most perfectly balanced of all men, thus the *MGNf DWD* indicates that his balance was ordained in God's plan. The Jewish mystic turns his efforts toward understanding this dynamic balance, symbolized by the *MGNf DWD*.

> ... which is planted in the midst of the righteous, its boughs spreading over the tables of all righteous persons, who live forever.
>
> [Tankhumah, Parshat Ha-azinu, Chapter 1]

As you can see from this chapter, Astrology played its vital and central part in delineating the lives, hopes, and ethical demands of the Jewish people, as shown by only a few Midrashic examples. In the next chapter, I shall show that, to an even greater extent, Astrology plays an essential part in the discussion of, and the development of, Jewish law.

PART V:
ASTROLOGY
IN THE
TALMUD

17

INTRODUCTION

An astrologer could determine by his calculations under which planet, in which month, and on which particular day any given nation was to undergo an attack. [Sanhedrin 95:a]

Astrology can indicate the potential of the individual. When the Pharaoh of Egypt was asked why he would place all Egypt in the hands of the foreigner Joseph, the Pharaoh answered: "I see the colors of rulership in him." (In the Talmud, Astrology and color are inextricably intertwined, see Sotah 36b.)

Joab refused to join the conspiracy of Absalom against his father David, because he (Joab) had seen David's favorable horoscope. (See Sanhedrin 49a.)

People can misinterpret the warnings of Astrology. A barber who was also an astrologer saw in his own horoscope that Jews would shed his blood. Therefore, he murdered 80 (some say 300) Jews who sought him out for his barbering services. He later converted to Judaism, and then understood that the blood to be shed by the Jews referred to his circumcision. (See Jerusalem Talmud, Avodah Zarah II 41a.)

How do we fit these and many other astrological references into the pattern of the Talmud? For unlike the Midrash, the Talmud is not in the main a book of ethical and moral interpretations of Scripture, providing great leeway to the imagination of the interpreter. On the contrary, the Talmud is the legal development of the interpretation of Scripture, a dialectic whose goal is the determination of law.

173

Throughout this book I have used the word *dialectic* to describe the postbiblical religious literature of the Jewish people. The Talmud is the prime example of what this term means. To understand the importance of any astrological material in the Talmud, it is necessary to understand the Talmudic process, the filters through which all material had to pass to find its way into this great compilation of the legal spirit of the Jew—and to remain there.

The foundation of all Jewish religious literature is the Bible. From it derives all our law, all our ethics, and all our understanding of our ancient history up to the time of the return from Babylonian Exile in 517 B. C. E. As I have already indicated, the Bible was to have retained its oral form, but even after the Bible was committed to writing, the concept of an oral law was not abandoned: an oral law which would be within the tradition of the Bible and faithful to its ethic, but more flexible and responsive to the needs of the generation propounding it. This oral law first took root in the group of post-Exilic scribes who followed Ezra. This group of men, known in Hebrew as the *ANSY KNST HGDWLH*, "the Men of the Great Assembly," developed into what was later known as the Sanhedrin, the court of 71 Rabbis. The concept of the continuity of Divine Revelation is most important in Jewish tradition, and every Rabbi today stands in a direct line of descent from this Sanhedrin; this is what the ceremony of "laying on of hands" means during the ceremony of ordination of Rabbis. Even the Hebrew word for ordination, *SMYKH*, means the "laying on of hands." The traditional statement of this Divine continuity is given in the Talmud, Order Nezikin, Tractate Abot, Chapter 1:

> Moses received the Torah at Sinai and passed it on to Joshua; and Joshua to the Judges; the Judges passed it on to the Prophets, and the Prophets to the Men of the Great Assembly....

Since this latter body developed into the Sanhedrin, and since the Rabbis of the Sanhedrin ordained their successors, this Divine continuity adhered to them and through the process of ordination, to the Rabbis of today.

One can say that the Men of the Great Assembly began the dialectic process. Dialectic is a process of discussion, a means by which the law was both expounded and expanded. The process entailed discussing each legal case as it was presented to the court, coming to a decision, remembering that decision, and using that decision as a basis for future discussion and decision making. This process was to have been a totally oral one; the law was not to be written down but to be memorized. The ancients felt that writing the law down would concretize the law and make it less amenable to needed change in the future; it would become another Bible-like document. However, by the time of Rabbi Judah the Prince (170 to 217 C. E.), many of the Rabbis had taken to keeping notebooks of the most important decisions. Rabbi Judah finally collected the best of these, and using them in conjunction with his own great knowledge, compiled the first authoritative collection of postbiblical Jewish law: the Mishnah. Once again, necessity had forced the abandonment of the concept of the oral transmission of law.

The concept of oral transmission of law was not yet dead, however. On the basis of the now-transcribed discussions called the *Mishnah*, two new oral traditions developed: One grew in the land of Judea, then ruled by Rome, and after an initial flowering, ended with the demise of the Sanhedrin following the Roman suppression of the various Jewish revolts of the time (135 C. E.). This is known as the *Palestinian Gemarrah* (completion) and its final compilation was not very extensive. The great expansion of the Mishnah took place in Babylonia where there was a large and influential Jewish community, with rabbinic courts at Sura and at Pumbeditha and their attendent schools. This expansion is known as the *Babylonian Gemarrah*, and it was finally codified in 600 C. E.; it extends to approximately 18 to 27 volumes, depending on page and type size. The Mishnah combined with the Palestinian Gemarrah is known as the *Talmud Yerushalmi* (The Jerusalem Talmud); The Mishnah combined with the Babylonian Gemarrah is known as the *Talmud Babli* (The Babylonian Talmud); and it is to this extensive work which I shall refer throughout these chapters.

You can now see the filtering process through which any astrological material had to pass to be included in the Talmud. In some manner, it had to arise in a discussion of the Bible on the part of a Court of Rabbis. Then their successors had to remember it, use it to determine law and ethics, copy it down in private notebooks, and finally it had to be deemed worthy of being included in the compilation of Rabbi Judah. Or it had to be deemed applicable to a discussion of the law as compiled by Rabbi Judah and included in the discussions of the later Rabbis whose dialectic filled the Gemarrah; and it then had to be considered important enough to be included in the final compilations of the Gemarrah in 600 C. E. In other words, the filtering process for any material in the Talmud was a testing process which covered a span of 1,100 years through the minds of thousands of sages—a process which ensured the winnowing out of any materials the Rabbis considered either spurious or unimportant.

How did Astrology come through this process? Magnificently!

The uses of Astrology for the purposes of healing are involved in discussions of the laws of the Sabbath. The ancients discussed the efficacy of astrological indications, and applied Astrology to the lives of human beings and to the growth of plants. In short, they enjoyed the full range of all astrological practices and considerations that we have today. How are these manifested in the Talmud? First of all, there are the dialectical links to the Bible and the Midrash, verses which I referred to in previous chapters. Remember that the same Rabbis were active in both the midrashic and the talmudic interpretations of the Bible; we should expect to find these links reflected in astrological references, and we do. Secondly, we ought to expect references to the efficacy and validity of Astrology, in general. Third, we should expect to find specific references to Astrology in terms of Jewish law. Fourth, if Astrology is considered an acceptable subject for discussion, we should find specific references to astrological knowledge itself. Indeed, we find all these in the Talmud.

18

TWO GREAT LIGHTS
AND THE
ARROWS OF GOD

I pointed out that the Sun and Moon were mentioned in the Bible in paranatural astrological situations. This type of biblical situation is amplified in the Talmud in *Tractate Hullin*.

R. Simeon ben Pazzi pointed out a contradiction (between biblical verses): One verse says, *And God made two great lights...* (Gen. 1:16), and immediately the verse continues... *the greater light... and the lesser light* (Gen. 1:16). The Moon said to the Holy One, Blessed Be He: "Sovereign of the Universe, is it possible for two kings to wear one crown?" (Can both the Sun and I jointly rule the universe?) He (God) answered: "Go then and make thyself smaller." "Sovereign of the Universe!" cried the Moon, "because I have suggested that which was proper, must I then make myself smaller?" He replied: "Go, and thou wilt rule by day and by night." "But what is the value of this?" cried the Moon. "Of what use is a lamp in broad daylight?" He replied: "Go. Israel shall reckon by thee the days and the years." "But it is impossible," said the Moon, "to do without the Sun for the reckoning of the seasons, as it is said: ... *and let* them *be for signs and for seasons and for days and for years* (Gen. 1:14)." (God said) "Go. The righteous shall be named after thee." (Since you were made smaller, the righteous shall be called *the Small*). And we find Jacob the Small (Amos 7:2), Samuel the Small (a

177

renowned Rabbi and Teacher of the Mishnah of the first century
C. E.), David the Small (Sam. I 17:14). Upon seeing that it (the
Moon) would not be consoled, the Holy One, Blessed Be He said:
"Bring an atonement for Me, for making the Moon smaller."

[Hullin 60b]

On the basis of this fanciful confrontation between the Moon
and God, we have a fascinating midrashic story in the Jerusalem
Talmud as well as in the Tractate Hullin, which uses a *piyyut*
("religious poem") of a Palestinian Rabbi of the time to link together
the God-Moon argument with such disparate biblical verses as those
from the prophets Isaiah and Zechariah, the Psalms and the second
book of Samuel. Also involved are two of the mystical tools for the
interpretation of the Bible. One method, known as *Notarikon*, uses
the letters of one Hebrew word as the initials of a group of Hebrew
words in the same order, and this new phrase illuminates the
meaning of the first word. The other method known as *Temurah*,
will change the order of such letters either to form a new word or two
be used in a Notarikon process. The best way to describe these two
tools is to illustrate them in connection with the quotation from the
Hullin 60b.

The Rabbis were trying to understand a problem in Scripture to
which I have already alluded in Chapter 4, the problem of "the Day of
the Lord." What did this reference mean in the Prophets? First, the
Rabbis quoted the three puzzling prophetic statements:

And there shall be one day which shall be known as the Lord's,
Not day and not night; but it shall come to pass that at eventime
There shall be light. And... the Lord shall be King over
All the Earth; In that day shall the Lord be One, and
His Name One.

[Zechariah 14:7-9]

Moreover the light of the Moon shall be as the light of
The Sun, and the light of the Sun shall be seven-fold,
As the light of seven days, In the day that the Lord
Bindeth up the bruise of His people,
And healeth the stroke of their wounds.

[Isaiah 30:26]

I have set watchmen upon thy walls, O Jerusalem,
All that day and that night....

[Isaiah 62:6]

The Rabbis of the first century C. E. used the first four words of Psalms 114:8 as a mystical key to these allusions. The Psalm reads in English as follows:

... Who turned the rock into a pool of water. ...

This seems to have absolutely nothing to do with the problem. Indeed, on the surface it does not. But remember that these men were mystics, that they believed that all secrets would be revealed by a proper mystical understanding of the Scripture; also remember that these men were absolutely at home in the Hebrew language, just as any English Ph.D. scholar of the English language would be. So let us examine the four Hebrew words involved, apply the mystically oriented interpretive directions of Temurah and Notarikon, and see how the Rabbis understood this verse:

HHPXY HṠWR AGMʃ MYMʃ. ...

Although the normal translation of this part of the verse is "... Who turned the rock into a pool of water. ..." it can also be translated in a more fanciful way, as "... Who reverses the (order of letters in the word) HṠWR ...!" Thus, the Rabbis stated that if one will reverse the order of the letters in the word indicated (the process of Temurah), then use each letter as the initial letter of a new word to form a new verse (the process of Notarikon), then that person will come to a new understanding of the Prophet's words.

Let us begin. First we shall reverse the order of letters in the indicated word HṠWR, deriving the letters in the order R W Ṡ H. Now, we are instructed to use these letters as initial letters for some well-known verse, which happens to be the verse in the piyyut (religious poem) found in the Jerusalem version:

R̲AH W̲HṪQYNʃ Ṡ̲WR̲Ṭ H̲LBNH   "He beheld, and ordained the form (size) of the Moon." (Note that the initial letters underlined above conform to the demands of both Temurah and Notarikon.)

The Rabbis immediately related this new verse of piyyut to the three prophetic verses previously quoted which involved the "Day of the Lord," stating that on that "day" the injury done to the Moon would be rectified and the Moon would be comforted. But what "day" will that "Day of the Lord" be? All we have to do, said the Rabbis, is to use the Notarikon procedure on the next two words of the piyyut quotation: AGMʃ MYMʃ.

_A_ _G_ _M_: _A_BDW _G_WYM_f_ _M_ARŚW: "...the nations are perished out of His land." (Full verse: "The Lord is King forever and ever; the nations are perished out of His land.")

[Psalms 10:16]

_M_ _Y_ _M_: _M_GDYL _YŚ_W'W_ṫ_ _M_LKW: "A tower of salvation is He to His King...." (Full verse: "A tower of salvation is He to His king; and showeth mercy to His annointed, to David and his seed, forevermore.")

[II Samuel 22:51]

And so, the Rabbis said, the day involved in the references concerning the "Day of the Lord" will be that day on which the Moon is reconciled and restored to its former glory, the day on which the foreign nations will be driven out of the land of Israel, the day that the Lord will rule from Jerusalem upon whose walls He shall set guardians "on that day"; the day when the seed of David His annointed (the Messiah, which means "annointed") will be reestablished on the throne: in other words on the Day of Judgement. However, the key to understanding this interpretation was the existence in the Talmud of the Moon/God confrontation in Tractate Hullin, and the relationship of this to the piyyut in the Jerusalem Talmud through Psalms 114:8. Another good example of the astrological link between the Talmud and the Bible is the following quotation from Nedarim 39b interspersed with my comments to assist the reader:

> Raba, or as others say R. Isaac, lectured: "What is meant by _The Sun and the Moon stood still in their course_ (Hebrew: ZBWL)? What were they doing in the ZBWL seeing that they were set in the firmament (Hebrew: RQY')? ...

Traditionally, the words ZBWL and RQY' are names given to two of the seven heavens that were created. Thus, the Sun and Moon leave their assigned places in the RQY' to ascend to a higher heaven, the ZBWL, to confront God.

> This teaches that the Sun and Moon ascended from the RQY' to the ZBWL and exclaimed before Him: "Sovereign of the Universe! If Thou wilt execute judgement for Amram's son, we will give forth our light; if not, we will not shine." ...

Moses, son of Amram, who was being confronted by Korach (Hebrew: QRX) and his rebels (Numb.:16). The Sun and Moon intercede on Moses' behalf by threatening to remain dark.

> ...In that moment He shot spears and arrows at them....

The play on words involves the Hebrew word in the text, *BRQY'*: the usual translation is to consider the *B* as the prefix meaning "in," and to translate the term as "in the firmament of." However, one may, in a flight of fancy, consider the letter *B* as an integral part of the word and read the root as *BRQ*, which means "lightening." From this to a consideration of lightening as the spears and arrows of God is not too great a leap.

> ...He chided them: "Every day men worship you and yet you give your light. For My honor you do not protest,...

God says that you have not threatened to stop shining because mankind often worships you and not Me; yet you are enough concerned with the honor of Moses that you threaten Me.

> ...yet you protest for the honor of flesh and blood! (Moses, son of Amram). Since then, spears and arrows are shot at them every day before they consent to shine....

This particular link between Talmud and Bible is of special interest to us, since I referred previously to the spears and arrows of God (Chapter 4). I am most happy that the Rabbis of the Talmud agree with my grammatical analysis.

This whole problem of the spears and arrows of God deserves more intensive study since it appears so often in both the Bible and the Talmud. What is the meaning of this imagery? It seems as though God is forcing the planets to do His will. And yet, this interpretation is totally out of phase with the Jewish concept that the planets and the entire universe do God's will voluntarily and gladly, for His glory. One can discover that this latter interpretation is in reality the truth by the following astrological quotation from the Talmud, which states the meaning of this imagery:

> R. Eleazar ben Pedath found himself in very great want. Once after being bled, he had nothing to eat. He took the skin of garlic and put it in his mouth; he became faint and fell asleep. The

Rabbis coming to see him noticed that he was crying and laughing, and that a ray of light was radiating from his forehead. When he awoke they asked him, "Why did you cry and laugh?" He replied: "Because the Holy One, Blessed Be He, was sitting by my side, and I asked Him: 'How long will I suffer in this world?' And He replied, 'Eleazar my son, would you rather I turn back the world to its very beginnings? Perhaps then you might be born at a more fortunate hour?' (Under a more fortunate planet! See Chapter 10) I replied: 'All this, and then only perhaps?' (So much trouble for only a possibility of change?) I then asked Him: 'Which is the greater life, the one that I have already lived, or the one that I am still to live?' He replied: 'The one that you have already lived!' I then said to Him: 'Even if so, I do not want it.' (Do not go to the trouble of changing the entire universe from its creation just for the possibility that I might be born under a more fortunate planet—even though You have told me that this life full of suffering is better than the life I can expect in the next.) He replied: 'As a reward for refusing it (the possibility) I will grant you in the next world 13 rivers of balsam oil as clear as the Euphrates and the Tigris, which you will be able to enjoy....' He thereupon snapped at my forehead and exclaimed: 'Eleazar my son, I have shot you with Mine arrows!'"

[Talmud Ta'anit 25a]

It is obvious from this text—and it is thus interpreted by the great commentator of the end of the eleventh century c.e., Rabbi Shlomo Yitzchaki (*RASHI*)—that the shooting of God's arrows is a sign of Divine approval. Thus must we understand the shooting of God's arrows and spears at the Sun and Moon; these are not signs of God's displeasure, rather they are marks of God's approval. These arrows are not shot at the heavenly bodies to coerce them into doing God's will, but rather they are signs of God's approval of their willingness to do His will as willing witnesses to His glory. Now we must understand that, when God chides the Sun and Moon for seemingly being more solicitous of Moses' honor than of His own, He is only joking; he secretly approves. Now we have another mystery on our minds: What does the shooting of arrows have to do with approval? One might think just the opposite.

Our search now takes us to a consideration of yet another reference in the Talmud which is often misunderstood. I refer to the Bed of Gad, the *Arsa d'Gadda*, which is often mentioned in the Talmud with reference to the laws of mourning. (Also called *Dargesh*. See Moed Katan 27a, Nedarim 56a, Sanhedrin 20a.) In a house of mourning, one is to turn over all couches and beds as a sign of mourning, except the Arsa d'Gadda or Dargesh. We are told that this particular bed, which was in every household, was not to be turned over; that indeed, if the king were in mourning, he was allowed to sit on it. This story is so ancient that by Talmudic times the reason for the existence of this bed was lost. The Talmud only relates that it was a particular type of bed of special importance—but did not give any reasons for its importance. However, there are links among the bed of Gad, the military organization of the tribes in Bible times, the arrows of the Lord, and the constellations of the Zodiac.

The following biblical verse (Gen. 49:19):

GD GDWD YGWDNW WHWA YGD 'QB

is usually translated; "Gad, a troop shall troop upon him, but he shall troop upon their heels."

What a difficult translation. No one really knows how to handle it. In modern Hebrew the word *GDWD* means "a battalion," and in ancient times it also had a military meaning, as is obvious even from the attempted translation. However, we know that in biblical times, foot soldiers were not organized into units that bore names such as squad, regiment, company, or battalion; they were organized into numbered units. The Bible speaks of tens, fifties, hundreds, and thousands, and of their leaders. The term *GDWD* in all probability meant "mounted archers" or "spearmen." If we were to translate the above statement grammatically, we should probably read it as follows: "As for Gad: although a band of mounted archers shall attack us, he will attack at their rear."

Now, which constellation is represented as the mounted archer, or in later representation as a centaur-archer? Sagittarius! And which planet rules Sagittarius? Jupiter, the planet of expansion and good fortune. Now the arrows of God, the bed of Gad, and the troop of Gad all come together and inform each other with meaning. With *astrological meaning*. We reinforce the astrological vector of this interpretation when we realize that, in the Kabbalistic scheme of spiritual rulerships by the sons of Jacob, one to each constellation, the constellation Sagittarius is ruled by Gad. We also know that Gad was the name of the Babylonian god of good fortune. All these meanings find their modern expression both in Astrology and in modern Hebrew idiomatic speech.

In modern Hebrew, a person without luck is called either *Bish Gadda* or *Bish Mazzley*. *Bish* means "without"; *Gadda* is the Aramaic form of "Gad," and *Mazzley* is the Aramaic form of the word

Mazzalot, which means "constellations." Thus, the unfortunate person is without the Divine arrows of Gad, of Jupiter, of Sagittarius, of God. Even Shakespeare picks up this nuance of meaning when he has Hamlet complain of "...the slings and *arrows* of outrageous *fortune*...." And the concept that piercing by an arrow can be pleasant is carried over in modern times through Cupid, the messenger of Venus, whose arrows smite one with love.

THE REAL ISSUE: DIVINE ELECTION VERSUS THE MANDATE FOR ASTROLOGY!

Another important astrological link, this time between Talmud and Midrash in interpretation of Scripture, deals with the Abram-Abraham problem of Divine Election (see Chapter 6). In neither of those midrashic passages was there any denial of the efficacy of Astrology in its application to Abram-Abraham's situation. However, in the Talmud we get an absolute denial of Astrology, in this particular case only!

> Rab Judah said:...(God said to Abram)..."Put aside your foolishness; Israel is not under planetary influence."
>
> [Nedarim 32a]

Let us consider this objection of Rab Judah; this is one of the great arguments that rages in the pages of the Talmud with Rabbis taking sides on the issue. It is most interesting to discover what the real issue is:

The real issue here *is not* the efficacy of Astrology. All the Rabbis of the Talmud *agree* that *all other nations of the world* are deterministically subject to the influences of the planets and constellations. (I shall illustrate this later.) Only *Israel* is not subject to the stars. There is no argument here about the validity of Astrology; that validity is accepted by all Rabbis, on both sides of the issue. The issue is *not* Astrology: The issue is the Divine Election of Israel. For if there is Divine Election, then Israel is subject *only* to God, never to his creations. Thus, argue some Rabbis, if Israel is subject to planetary influences, then he is subject to God's creatures as are all other men, and there is no Divine Election of Israel. This is the position of the most adamant deniers of astrological influences over Israel.

There is another group of Rabbis who deny the effectiveness of planetary influence over Israel, but if we examine their statements and illustrations clearly, we shall see that their position is one of equating Divine Election with the operation of Free Will in the religious sphere, that is, with the concepts of sin, salvation through works, and repentance. Finally, there are important Talmudic Rabbis who state categorically that *everything* depends on the astrological indices. The following are the relevent quotations:

Raba said: "Length of life, children and sustenance depend not on merit, but on the constellation *(MZL)*."

[Moed Katan 28a]

In the same section, Raba continues with the following illustrations of the futility of merit:

For take Rabbah and R. Hisda. Both are saintly Rabbis; one master prayed for rain and it came, and the other master prayed for rain and it came. R. Hisda lived to the age of 92, Rabbah lived only till the age of 40. In R. Hisda's house there were held 60 marriage feasts; in Rabbah's house there were 60 bereavements. At R. Hisda's house there was the purest wheaten bread for dogs, and it went to waste; at Rabbah's house there was barley bread for human beings, and that not to be had.

R. Se'orim, Raba's brother, while sitting at Raba's bedside saw him dying (lit. "going to sleep"), when he (Raba) said to his brother (R. Se'orim): "Do tell him (the Angel of Death) 'Sir do not torment me.'" R. Se'orim replied: "Are you, Sir, not his intimate friend?" [As a Rabbi, Raba was also a messenger of God (in Hebrew, *MLAKf* means "messenger," as *angelos* meant in Greek originally) therefore he ought to be able to talk to the Angel of Death on intimate terms.] Said Raba: "Since my constellation *(MZL)* has been delivered to him, he takes no heed of me."

On the other hand, the following statement is in the Talmud without any further elaboration:

Rabba Bar Bar Hanah said in the name of R. Samuel ben Martha in Rab's name, on the authority of R. Jose of Huzal: "How do we know that you must not consult astrologers? Because it is said: 'Thou shalt be whole-hearted with the Lord thy God ...' (Deut. 18:13)."

[Pesachim 113b]

The list of names of Rabbis is intended to add weight to the argument that Astrology in some way implies mistrust of God, the desire to know God's will in order to circumvent it. However, the biblical text in its context does not support their contention. Hebrew is a very specific language, and the Bible is quite forthright in saying what it means. The entire quotation, out of which the above fragment is taken, covers those methods of divination which the Bible prohibits, and are in Deuteronomy 18:9-14. This entire section enumerates quite specifically nine different types of divination, among which Astrology is conspicuous by its absence. If indeed, the Bible meant to include Astrology among the forbidden processes, there are good Hebrew words for the Bible to use. That the Bible in its specificity includes all other types of divination but does not include Astrology among those that are forbidden should be ample evidence that Astrology is accepted as a valid discipline.

The major confrontation on the issue of Astrology as it bears on Divine Election is in the Tractate Shabbat 156a-b. The lines are so explicitly drawn here and the examples given so interesting, that I shall quote the entire passage, and then discuss its implications.

It was stated, R. Hanina said: "The planetary influence gives wisdom, the planetary influence gives wealth, and Israel stands under planetary influence." R. Johanan maintained: "Israel is immune from planetary influence." (Hebrew: *AYNf MZL BYŠRAL*, "Israel has no constellation.") R. Johanan said: "How do we know that Israel is immune from planetary influence? Because it is said, *Thus saith the Lord: Learn not the ways of the nations and be not dismayed at the signs of Heaven, for the nations are dismayed at them.* (Jer. 10:2) They are dismayed, but not Israel." Rab, too, holds that Israel is immune from planetary influence. For Rab Judah said in Rab's name: "How do we know that Israel is immune from planetary influence? Because it is said, ... *and He brought him forth from abroad.* ... (Gen. 15:5; see Chapter 6) Abraham pleaded before the Holy One, Blessed Be He. 'Sovereign of the Universe,' he cried: 'I have looked to my constellation *(MZL)* and find that I am fated not to beget a child.'

(God said) 'Go forth from thy planet (i.e., cease your astrological calculating), for Israel is free from planetary influence. What is thy calculation? Because ŠDQ ("Jupiter") stands in the west on the Descendant? (because Jupiter rules children, and on the Descendant, it is a point of weakness in the native's chart.) This position is not propitious for begetting children. I will turn it back and place it in the East (on the Ascendant, a much better position)!' And thus it is written, *Who hath raised up ŠDQ* (also means "righteousness") *from the East? He hath summoned it for his* (i.e., Abraham's) *sake.* (Isai. 41:2)"

From Samuel too (we learn that) Israel is immune from planetary influence. For Samuel and Ablat (a Persian astrologer and friend) were sitting while certain people were going to a lake. Said Ablat to Samuel: "That man is going but will not return, for a snake will bite him and he will die." "If he is an Israelite," replied Samuel, "he will go and he will return." While they were sitting he went and returned. (Thereupon) Ablat rose and threw off his (the man's) knapsack, and found therein a snake, cut up and lying in two pieces. Said Samuel to him: "What did you do (to escape your fate)?" (He said) "Every day we pooled our bread and ate it; but today one of us had no bread and he was ashamed. Said I to them, 'I will go and collect (the bread).' When I came to him I pretended to take (bread) from him, so that he should not be ashamed." "You have done a good deed *(MŚWH),*" said he (Samuel) to him. Then Samuel went out and lectured (on the biblical verse): *But charity* ("righteousness," Hebrew: ŠDQH) *delivereth from death* (Prov. 10:2). And this does not mean from an unnatural death (only), but from death itself.

From Rabbi Akiba* too (we learn that) Israel is free from planetary influence. For R. Akiba had a daughter. Now astrologers told him, "On the day she enters the bridal chamber a snake will bite her and she will die." He was very worried about this. On that day (of her marriage) she took a brooch and stuck it into the wall and by chance it penetrated into the eye of a serpent. The following morning when she took it (the brooch) out, the snake came trailing after it. "What did you do (to escape your fate)?" her father asked her. "A poor man came to the door in the evening," she replied, "and everybody was busy at the banquet and there was none to attend him. So I took the portion which

* See Appendix 6.

was given to me, and gave it to him." "You have done a good deed *(MŚWH),*" said he to her. Thereupon R. Akiba went out and lectured: *But charity delivereth from death* (Prov. 10:2). And not from an unnatural death alone, but from death itself.

From R. Nachman ben Isaac, too (we learn that), Israel is free from planetary influence. For R. Nachman ben Isaac's mother was told by astrologers, "Your son will be a thief." (So) she did not let him be bare-headed, saying to him, "Cover your head that the fear of heaven may be upon you, and pray (for mercy)." Now he did not know why she spoke that to him. One day he was sitting and studying under a palm tree (that did not belong to him); temptation (Hebrew: *YŚR HR',* lit. "the evil inclination"; see Chapter 6) overcame him, he climbed up and bit off a cluster (of dates which did not belong to him) with his teeth. Thus, because of his devotion to God (symbolized by his never going bare-headed) his thievery was mitigated to only one small act.

From the discussions of Rabbi Samuel and Rabbi Akiba, it is obvious that complete freedom from astrological influences followed only on the performance of good deeds. Indeed, the modern concept that the stars impel but do not compel is classically illustrated here. In Rabbi Nachman's quotation, however, there is a different situation: Rabbi Nachman insists that the influence of astrological forces working on man must be felt in some manner. He maintains that the negative influence cannot be totally avoided, but rather will be mitigated and rendered less harmful through the exercise of one's freedom to do righteous acts. However, Rabbi Nachman insists that in every case the astrological imperatives will in some way be borne out.

This controversy in the Talmud is most revealing not only for what it states but also for what it implies. For the greatest Rabbis of the period were involved in this altercation which had profound theological overtones. But before considering any of these theological overtones, consider what this need to clarify a theological position on Astrology implies for the importance of Astrology itself. We have both Raba and Rabbi Haninah boldly stating that, in spite of the theological necessities for the validity of Divine Election and the existence of Free Will, Astrology is true, useful, valid, and that Israel is subject to planetary influences.

What does this controversy state about the status of Astrology in the Jewish world of that time? First of all, we must infer that the practice of Astrology was widespread, widely accepted and that astrologers were very respected within the Jewish community. Second, we can see from the illustrative denials of the validity of Astrology just quoted, that a very rigorous Astrology was practiced, an Astrology in which the accurate prediction of future events was not only necessary but also which was demanded by and believed by all—including those Rabbis who fought against it. The Astrology thus practiced in those days pointed to a worldview in those times which was much drawn to the fatalistic approach to life; the astrologer prepared man to face his revealed fate; and the Rabbis reacted strongly against this aspect of Astrology as it was practiced in their day.

For if we analyze the three examples of the "failures" of Astrology in the cases presented in the Talmud, we shall see that what bothered the Rabbis was not the accuracy of astrological prediction, but the necessity involved in the practice of astrologically predicted fatalism. The Rabbis did not fight Astrology; they accepted and practiced it. What they did fight was the fatalism of the day which colored astrological interpretation, as they battled for the possibility of Free Will to exist in this world as a theological necessity. For if man has no Free Will, then sin is a meaningless term and salvation is "pie in the sky." Judaism, the world's first great *salvational* religion, gave the concepts of Divine Election and Divine Salvation to the world, and the fatalism of those days denied all three: Divine Election, Divine Salvation, and Free Will. Since Astrology as practiced in those times partook of the fatalist orientation of the day, it came under the same attack as the fatalism of the times. But let us look at the wording of this attack.

In the first two examples given by the Talmud, that of the man with the knapsack and that of R. Akiba's daughter, although the dangers that had been predicted were indeed avoided, the presence of the actually predicted threat was affirmed. In each case the snake was present, and the catastrophe was avoided in an intriguing way. Neither victim knew of the prediction; neither victim, therefore, could take the common form of precaution against the danger. In each case the victim performed a good deed, a *MŚWH*, which led to seemingly random activity (i.e., cutting up bread and sticking the pin of a brooch into a porous adobe-like bedroom wall) which "saved" the victim from death.

Everything in the attitudes of both R. Samuel and R. Akiba point to a very early instance of the use of a modern statement of Astrology: "The stars impel, they do not compel." This is *exactly* the position on which both R. Samuel and R. Akiba insist: otherwise the story would not have been told in this form. Astrology is easy to ridicule; this profession lends itself easily to the ridicule of the blissfully ignorant. But the Rabbis knew too much about Astrology to indulge in ridicule. Had they done so, they themselves would have been subjects of ridicule by a population whose acceptance of fatalistic Astrology was the cause of the controversy in the first place.

The third illustration, revealed by R. Nachman ben Isaac, is even more revealing of the thrust of Rabbinic opposition at this time. For here is a Rabbi who was himself involved in an astrological prediction: The prediction was that he would become a thief. And he himself testifies that he *did* become a thief; but the stringency of the astrological prediction was mitigated because of two things. One, he never went with a bared head (a symbol of his fear of Heaven, which in Judaism means respect for God) and he continually prayed for mercy (without knowing why). Here we have the very unique combination of a statement that proves the validity of astrological prediction joined with an insistence that the stars do not impell, but only compel.

Astrology was the "hook" on which an extremely important theological confrontation took place; the confrontation between pagan fatalism and Jewish insistence on Divine Election, Divine Salvation, and Free Will; both through works (R. Samuel and R. Akiba) and through faith (R. Nachman). As we analyze these confrontations, we see that, rather than denying the validity of Astrology, the Rabbis really wanted to "modernize" Astrology, to modify it so that it would cease being the tool of pagan fatalists, and become a witness instead to the glory of God.

Rabbis in Talmudic times freely admitted to the influence Astrology had on their lives, both as clients and as practicing astrologers. For instance:

> R. Hisda said: "Astrologers...told me I would become a teacher...."
>
> [Yebamot 21b]

One of the greatest Rabbis was also an astrologer, as demonstrated in a discussion of pictures that were permitted and those not permitted:

> *Mishnah:* If one finds utensils upon which is the figure of the Sun or Moon or a Dragon, he casts them into the Dead Sea (a symbol of utter destruction)...
>
> *Gemara:* ...Abaye explained:... but in regard to the making of images for worship, they (heathens) do so only of these three objects which are especially honored by them. R. Sheshet used to collect difficult B'raithot

(extra-Mishnaic passages, that is, legal discussions found in notebooks other than the ones collected into the Mishnah by R. Judah the Prince: They were still considered valid since they were part of the Oral Tradition contemporaneous to the Mishnah, and were often quoted as legal precedents) and expound them: "Pictures of all planets are permissible except that of the Sun and the Moon . . . and all figures are permissible except that of the Dragon." Rabban Gamliel had a picture of the lunar diagrams in his upper chamber, in the form of a chart hanging on the wall, which he used to show to the unlearned (those who were acting as witnesses to the advent of the New Moon without having previous knowledge of what a New Moon phase was supposed to look like.)

[Avodah Zarah 43a]

These passages are also repeated in at least two other Tractates of the Talmud (Rosh Hashanah 14a, Hullin 40a), and indicate their importance. In other places Rabban Gamliel is referred to as an astrologer, and defends his possession of the charts he needed on the basis of a ruling which I shall quote later; he also claims to study Astrology while bathing, lest it take him away from the study of Torah, and he also demands that an astrologer who has given good advice should be paid in proportion to the money saved for, or earned by, his client. But note that in these quotations the primary objection to depicting the Sun, Moon, and Dragon (symbolic of the Moon's nodes) is *not* an objection to Astrology, but rather a defense against accusations of idolatry. Representations of all other planets are permitted.

Even more important are the implications of the following quotations from the Talmud (with my comments interspersed to assist the reader):

Our Rabbis taught: He who sees the Sun at its turning point, . . .

This can refer either to the insertion of the Sun into the equinoxes and solstices or it can refer to the Great Cycle (an explanation of the Great Cycle is given further on in this series of quotations.).

. . . the Moon in its power, . . .

When it causes the great spring tides, after the Vernal Equinox.

... the planets in their orbits and the signs of the Zodiac in their orderly progress, ...

As a result of the precession of the equinoxes, approximately 50.1″ of arc per year, it appears that the signs of the Zodiac progress, and this is what the Talmudic sages believe. One who lives long enough to witness this progression through his observations is to say this blessing on confirming the observation.

... should say: "Blessed be He, Who has wrought the work of creation." ...

This is one of the many formula-type blessings of Jewish life, which are meant to impress on a person the sanctity of each moment of life. There are such blessings over food and drink, blessings on seeing the power of God evident in a waterfall or a falling meteor; there is even such a blessing to be said on seeing a beautiful woman ("Blessed art Thou O Lord our God, Ruler of the Universe, Who has created such a thing in the universe."). As you can see, there is also one such blessing to be said on verifying astrological observations. What better proof can there be for the importance of Astrology in Jewish life.

... And when does this thing happen? Abaye said: "Every twenty-eight years when the Cycle begins again ...

This means the Great Cycle of 28 years, that is, a Saturn cycle. Taking a year as calculated by Samuel (the Julian Year; see Chapter 8), every *Tekufah* ("start of a new season") occurs 1.25 days later in the week on each consecutive year. Every 4 years each *Tekufah* would occur at the same hour of the day, but 5 days later. After 28 (4 x 7) years, the *Tekufah* recurs not only at the same hour of the day but also on the same day of the week. This is known as the Great Cycle.

Please note that the 28 years of the Saturn cycle is an extremely significant numerological indicator. It is composed of the product of the four seasons (cardinal points of the Zodiac, primary directions, and so forth) and the seven days of the week (seven days of Creation, which includes the mystery of the Sabbath, and so forth).

As we shall see the traditional time of Creation was Tuesday at 6:00 P.M., a Saturn-ruled hour (also see Chapter 20). Thus, to be able to witness the turn of the Great Cycle according to our calculations, three things had to coincide:

1. The Vernal Equinox (0° Aries) had to occur at 6:00 P.M. (This is a Saturn-ruled hour on Tuesdays.)

   2.   The Vernal Equinox had to occur on a Tuesday.
   3.   Saturn had to be rising at that every moment.

   ... and Nissan (month begun by the Vernal Equinox is 0° Aries)
   falls in the Saturn (hour) on the evening of Tuesday, going into
   Wednesday.

See Chapter 8 for a discussion of the traditional Day of Creation
(Tuesday at 6:00 P.M., considered to be the first hour of the night of
Wednesday). This hour is ruled by Saturn. According to the
computations of a great Rabbinic commentator on the Bible and
Talmud, Rabbi Sh'lomo Yitzchaki *(RASHI)* who lived in France in
the last half of the eleventh century C.E., this day and time coincides
with the rising of Saturn.

   R. Zutra ben Tobiah said in Rab's name: "... he who is able to
   calculate the Cycles [This includes both the *Tekufah* Cycles and
   the Great Cycle of Saturn of 28 years.] and planetary courses but
   does not, one may hold no conversation with him." R. Simeon
   ben Pazzi said in the name of R. Joshua ben Levi on the authority
   of Bar Kappara: "He who knows how to calculate the Cycles and
   the planetary course but does not, of him the Scripture saith,
   ... *but they regard not the work of the Lord, neither have they
   considered the operation of His hands.* (Isa. 5:12) R. Samuel
   ben Nachmani said in R. Johanan's name: "How do we know
   that it is one's duty to calculate the Cycles and planetary courses?

   Because it is written: ... *for this is your wisdom and understanding in the sight of the peoples....* (Deut. 4:6) What wisdom
   and understanding is "in the sight of the peoples"? It is the
   science of the Cycles and the planets."

All peoples can see the glories of the Heavens. The Rabbis in their
interpretation of this verse emphasize the necessity for the existence of
a kind of wisdom and understanding to which all peoples can be
witness. The Rabbis see the Heavens as being the witness to the truth
of one God, a truth to which Judaism is bound to give witness and
expression to in the world. All intelligent humanity, seeing the Unity
of the Heavens, must be helped by that Unity to understand the
existence of one Creator. Thus, those Jews who know the Divine
Science of Astrology and refuse to use their knowledge to witness to
the one God, are sinners. Astrology is the only wisdom and
understanding that qualifies as being universally available to all
peoples.

If anyone should need "proof-texts" for the importance of Astrology in the development of the Jewish religious heritage, these Talmudic texts would be the only ones necessary. For it would be possible, I suppose, to infer that the necessary knowledge was *astronomical* not *astrological*, and that this knowledge was needed to calculate the religious calendar for the year, and for no other purpose. If only the equinoctial and solstitial insertions were mentioned, this might be true. However, in reality by the time of the Talmudic period, the *only astronomical* observation that was used to determine the religious calendar was the observance of the *New Moon after the Vernal Equinox:* all other holidays were calculated mathematically from this one observation. Not even the other solar insertions of the seasons were needed to determine the *Tekufot* (plural of *Tekufah,* that is, "start of spring each year, 0° Aries"). So why were they included when they had nothing to do with the religious calendar? Why did they include the ability to calculate the orbits of the planets, their time of complete cycle, and the Great Cycle of Saturn when these had *nothing* to do with the religious year and were *only useful in the calculation and interpretation of horoscopes.*

However, the Rabbis of the Talmud not only insisted that this knowledge was legitimate but also they reiterated in three different quotations that this knowledge was *divinely* demanded of man. The Rabbis quote *scripture as proof-text* insisting that one who *does not use* his ability to cast horoscopes is not fulfilling his *religious responsibility* to give witness to God's glory nor is he fulfilling his *religious duty* to practice his *God-given wisdom.* Such a person is to be ostracized; which is what the statement of R. Zutra means: "... one who knows how to calculate the cycles and planetary courses, *but does not,* one may *hold no conversation with him.*"

Indeed, if no other statement were needed, then the unique statement that one had to approach the study of Astrology with the blessing of the Divine Name on his lips should direct our sensitivities to the high estate in which both Astrology and the astrologer were held. Both declared the "Glory of God" before all the peoples of the world, and both had the responsibility of being diligent, accurate, and oriented to the Divine, as they spoke of His love and His will among the people.

One can see that the Rabbis themselves heeded the advice of astrologers from the following intriguing tales, the result of which has been historically verified:

R. Abin the Levite said: "Whoever tries to force his constellation *(MZL)* will be dogged by ill fortune, and whoever forgoes his good constellation will postpone his ill fortune." This we can illustrate from the case of Rabbah and R. Joseph. For R. Joseph was *Sinai* (i.e., he had an encyclopedic knowledge of the Jewish legal traditions) and Rabbah was an 'uprooter of mountains' (i.e., skilled in dialectic). The time came when they were needed (to head the academy at Pumbeditha). The colleagues (at Pumbeditha) were sent there (to Judea) to ask: "As between *Sinai* (R. Joseph) and an 'uprooter of mountains' (Rabbah), which should be our preference?" They (the colleagues in Judea) sent answer: "*Sinai*, because all require the 'owner of wheat' (a euphemism for one who knows the authentic traditions)." Nevertheless, Rabbi Joseph would not accept the post, because the astrologers had told him that he would be head (of the academy at Pumbeditha) for only 2 years. Rabbah thereupon remained head for 22 years, and R. Joseph after him for 2.5 years. During all the time that Rabbah was head, R. Joseph did not so much as summon a cupper to come to his house. [Since heads of the academy are appointed for life, the astrologers predicted R. Joseph's death after 2 years of occupancy. During the 22 years of Rabbah's leadership, R. Joseph had such perfect health that he did not even get a boil. After occupying the head chair at the academy for 2.5 years, he died.]

Why did I state that this quotation and the intriguing astrological prediction in it were historically verified? Rabbah headed the academy at Pumbeditha in Babylonia for 22 years, from 309 to 330 c.e. After his death, R. Joseph took over as head and died in 333 c.e. The statement about the cupper is an indication that when R. Joseph did not "push his luck" and refused to take the position when it was offered 22 years earlier, he was rewarded by such good health that even a cupper who normally treats minor injuries was not needed.

Cupping was an ancient method of increasing the blood supply to an area of infection. It was still being used in the United States 40 years ago, and may still be in use in parts of the world. In Yiddish, cupping was known as *beinkes*. In this process small glass cups, having necks and mouths smaller than their bodies, were heated to drive the air out of them. They were then placed on the necessary area of the skin, mouth down. As the cups cooled, a partial vacuum was formed in the large body of the cup, and blood would be drawn to the afflicted area. Often round welts were left on the skin, and sometimes burns, as well.

As indicated, legal decisions bearing on biblical prohibitions (not to make representations of anything) were interpreted as applying *only* to the three major astrological indicators of the time;

for example, the Sun, the Moon, and the Dragon (an imaginary line connecting the North Node and the South Node of the Moon, known as the Head and the Tail of the Dragon, respectively: The mythical line was known as the Line of the Dragon). This was not the only major legal decision involving astrological matters. An interesting question arises concerning the Sabbath.

A very large part of the Tractate Shabbat deals with the problem of what constitutes "work" on the Sabbath. For the Bible states and restates in clear terms and in many different passages that no kind of work is to be done on the Sabbath, not by the individual Jew, not by his wife nor by his children—not by his servants nor animals, not even by the non-Jew who lives within a totally Jewish community. It thus becomes very important to define with the utmost exactness those activities which are considered to constitute work.

However, all stringencies placed on work are modified when it comes to saving a life. What happens if a possible danger to life arises on the Sabbath? Is one allowed to travel beyond the proscribed distance usually permitted on the Sabbath to fetch a doctor? Is the doctor allowed to carry his instruments and medicines on the Sabbath? To operate on a patient on the Sabbath? To write a prescription on the Sabbath? For all these activities—traveling, carrying, cutting, writing—are not permitted on the Sabbath; they are all considered work. Is the doctor allowed to perform this "work" to save a life? The answer is yes, and the general rule is: All commandments and injunctions can be disregarded to save a life, except three; one cannot deny God, commit murder, or commit adultery to save a life. But what has all this to do with Astrology?

Astrologers of that day were also involved in medical Astrology, in what today we would call astrodiagnosis. But they were also involved in prescribing drugs and in writing astrological amulets for the prevention and cure of disease. There is a long and fascinating discussion of the proofs of validity for these astrological amulets in Tractate Shabbat 61a-b. In essence, the astrological practioner is approved *by the Rabbinic Court* if he has written astrological amulets that have cured three different people by three different amulets. The *amulet* itself is approved if it has cured three times; either the same person or others who have worn it.

Thus, we now have the following problem, dealing with work on the Sabbath, with which to contend: A man is ill, and an astrologer writes an amulet or prepares an herbal or metal amulet (akin to copper bracelets) for him to wear. Is this amulet necessary to the saving of life; is it medicinal? Or is this astrologically prepared amulet to be considered only an ornament? To carry or wear an ornament on the Sabbath, on a chain around your neck, or on a bracelet around your wrist, or pinned to your garment is considered working on the Sabbath and is therefore forbidden. In the quoted section of Tractate Shabbat, the law is stated as follows: A proven amulet, or an amulet prepared by a proven astrologer, is medicine; it is *not* an ornament; it *may be worn or carried on the Sabbath.*

The decisive factor in this discussion comes in a section of this same Tractate Shabbat which deals with work done by animals. Remember that animals were also prohibited from working on the Sabbath, and that included carrying. This particular section deals with those parts of an animal's domestic gear which an animal can wear and carry with it on the Sabbath, without transgressing the law prohibiting work on the Sabbath. What about an amulet? (Astrologers wrote amulets to cure domestic animals as well as people.) Let us pick up the argument at this point:

> Mar said: "(One cannot wear on the Sabbath) an amulet, though it is proven." But we learnt: "Nor with an amulet that is *not* proven." Hence if it is proven, is it not permitted? That means proven with respect to human beings, but not with respect to animals. But can they be proven with respect to human beings yet not with respect to animals? Yes; for it may help man, who is under planetary influence, but not animals, who are not under planetary influence.
>
> [Shabbat 53b]

And so the law is: If you are wearing any amulet of a planetary or zodiacal nature designed to bring the curative forces of the planets and constellations to aid your health (such as copper bracelets), you may wear them on the Sabbath.

To summarize the main points of this chapter:

1. Throughout 1,100 years of a dialectic winnowing process, Astrology has made its unique impact on, and contribution to, the Talmudic literature.
2. The Rabbis have used Astrology in its own right; they themselves have been astrologers who have believed in Astrology and consulted with other astrologers, and have given their own personal witness to its validity.
3. When Astrology seemed to come under attack, it is quickly apparent that it was not Astrology, but pagan fatalism that denied Divine Election, Divine Salvation, and Free Will

that was under attack. All evidence in the Talmud itself indicates that an Astrology which is true to the modern astrological statement "The stars impel but do not compel" is in every way valid in Judaism.

4. Astrology itself is involved in making Jewish law and involved in legal decisions affecting two basic issues in Judaism: the Sabbath, and idolatry. In neither of these areas is Astrology found to be at fault; it is cleared, and honored with the imprimatur of the *Rabbinic Court.*

Finally, if we turn aside from the Talmud itself and turn to an old commentary on the Talmud, there is an interesting note which validates this thinking. In Otsar HaG'onim Shabbat 477, there is a long commentary on the astrological discussions in the Tractate Shabbat. The discussion deals with the issue of the validity of Astrology for Israel. The general idea of the discussion is this: There are two types of astrologers: One group insists that all aspects of a person's life, including one's very desires and appetites, are determined by his stars, and that one has no ability to add to or detract from that which is coming to one astrologically. The other group of astrologers insists that one's soul and will are of greater power than his stars, and that man can change his astrologically indicated fate; Free Will is a Divine gift which can be used to mitigate one's planetary and constellational difficulties. It is to this latter group that most modern Astrologers belong, and it is to this latter type of astrological practice that the Rabbis of the Talmud tried to direct the Divine Science. Modern Astrology has at last caught up with Talmudic Rabbinic Astrology, 1,375 years late.

We have seen examples of the type of Astrology of which the Rabbis approved and which was applied to the "fates" predicted for Israelites. What about the type of Astrology of which the Rabbis did not approve, the type accepted by too many Israelites and pagan non-Israelites? There is an example of this type also in the Tractate Shabbat, and although a Jew profits by a Gentile's loss, the story is told for a different purpose, that is, to convince Jews that the observance of the Sabbath is its own reward.

Joseph Mokir Sh'vi (Sabbath-observer) had in his neighborhood a gentile who owned much property. Astrologers told the gentile, "Joseph will consume all your property." So he sold all his property and bought a precious stone with the proceeds, which he set in his turban. As he was crossing a bridge, a wind blew it into the water and a fish swallowed it. Subsequently the fish was hauled up in a net and sold to Joseph for the Sabbath meal. He opened the fish, found the jewel and sold it for thirteen roomfuls of golden denarii. And an old man said to him: "He who lends to (prepares for) the Sabbath, the Sabbath repays him."

[Shabbat 119a]

With all of the Rabbinic involvement with Astrology in discussions of vital legal and theological matters, and with all the Rabbinic first-person witness to the efficacy of Astrology, one might be curious about the amount and type of astrological information the Rabbis possessed. One Rabbinic dictim of this period states: "All is in the hands of Heaven, except the fear of Heaven (Hebrew: *HKL BYDY ŠMYMf XWŠ MYRAṪ ŠMYMf)*." The Hebrew word for "fear" used here, *YRA*, has the same root as the word for "teacher *MWRH)* and the word for "awe" (NWRH) and the word for "Scripture" itself *(TWRH)*. Although the phrase in this quotation is usually translated as above, it can also legitimately be translated as: "All is in the control of the Heavens except the knowledge of the Heavens!" Thus, in the light of the evidence in this chapter, it was *incumbent* on the leaders of society to be most familiar with the "awesome knowledge" of the heavens; otherwise the community would be at the complete mercy of astrological influences, not knowing how to act to "avert the severe decree." So one might ask again: How much of what kind of knowledge of Astrology did the Rabbis of the Talmud possess? I shall answer this question in the next chapter.

20

HOURS, DAYS, MONTHS

Now the earth was formless and void, and darkness was upon the
face of the deep; and the spirit of God hovered over the face of the
waters. And God said: "Let there be light." And there was light.
And God saw the light, that it was good; and God divided the
light from the darkness. And God called the light Day, and the
darkness He called Night. And there was evening and there was
morning, one day.

[Genesis 1:2-5]

In this manner does Scripture indicate the original division of
day and night. Note that a full "day" begins with sunset and darkness,
and ends with the next sunset. Theologically, life begins in the
unknown, and ends in the light of Divine Salvation. And so the
Astrology of the Talmudic Rabbis conforms to this scriptural and
theological pattern. There are 7 planets, 7 days of the week, 24 hours
in the day. Thus, the pattern of hourly occurrences repeats itself in
each week. What do I mean by the pattern of hourly occurrences? It
would be helpful at this time to review the concept of planetary
rulerships in Talmudic Astrology.

As described in Chapter 4, each constellation had as its guiding
spirit one of the 12 sons of Jacob. However, each constellation was
also ruled by a planet; and each planet had its guiding spirit, an
archangel. Please pay particular attention to Table 20-1; you will
begin to understand the complexity and the depth of meaning
inherent in the Talmudic concept of the balance of forces in the
Zodiac.

201

Table 20.1 Biblical References to the Constellations

Constellation	Spirit	Genesis 49[a]	Deuter-onomy 33[a]	Planet	Archangel
Aries	Benjamin	27	12	Mars	Ma'admiel[b]
Taurus	Reuben	3-4	6	Venus	Haniel[c]
Gemini	Simon	5-7	—	Mercury	Raphael[d]
Cancer	Levi	5-7	8-11	Moon	Gabriel[e]
Leo	Judah	8-12	7	Sun	Michael[f]
Virgo	Zebulun	13	18-19	Mercury	Raphael
Libra	Issachar	14-15	18-19	Venus	Haniel
Scorpio	Dan	16-18	22	Mars	Ma'admiel
Sagittarius	Gad	19	20	Jupiter	Zidkiel[h]
Capricorn	Asher	20	24-25	Saturn	Zophikiel[i]
Aquarius	Naphtali	21	23	Saturn	Zophikiel
Pisces	Joseph	22-26	13-17	Jupiter	Zidkiel

[a]In the verses from Genesis: 49 and Deuteronomy:33, the blessings given to each of the sons by Jacob and by Moses are enumerated. These blessings are used by the Rabbis of the Talmud to help enumerate both the Sun-Sign potentials and the Ascendant-Sign potentials of the respective constellations.

[b]The Lord makes angry.

[c]The Lord makes beautiful.

[d]The Lord makes swift (also implies healing). Mercury is the planet of communication, transportation (Gemini), and of the healing arts (Virgo). As the symbol of communication, he wears winged shoes (and is thus swift), and as the symbol of healing, he carries the caduceus.

[e]The Lord makes powerful.

[f]Who is like the Lord?

Note the balance of the planetary rulerships in the Zodiac. The Sun rules Leo and the Moon rules Cancer. From this base, the planetary rulerships are assigned to the constellations in the order of their distance from the Sun in the Solar System:

1. The first constellation solar to Leo (Virgo) and lunar to Cancer (Gemini) is ruled by Mercury.
2. The second pair of constellations solar to Leo (Libra) and lunar to Cancer (Taurus) is ruled by Venus.
3. The third pair of constelations solar to Leo (Scorpio) and lunar to Cancer (Aries) is ruled by Mars.
4. The fourth pair of constellations solar to Leo (Sagittarius) and lunar to Cancer (Pisces) is ruled by Jupiter.
5. The fifth pair of constellations solar to Leo (Capricorn) and lunar to Cancer (Aquarius) is ruled by Saturn.(Let us bear in mind that in a solar constellation, the life force, physicality, is expressed, whereas in a lunar constellation, the emotions are expressed.)

[h]The Lord makes righteous.

[i]The Lord causes to become a searcher of secrets.

In addition to these planetary rulerships over the constellations, there were also planetary rulerships over the days of the week:

The Sun	rules	Sunday
The Moon	rules	Monday
Mars	rules	Tuesday
Mercury	rules	Wednesday
Jupiter	rules	Thursday
Venus	rules	Friday
Saturn	rules	Saturday (the Sabbath)

In addition to the daily planetary rulerships, there were also the planetary rulerships of the Ascendant, as well as planetary rulerships of each hour, which were independent of the Ascendant. The pattern of hourly rulerships mentioned at the beginning of this chapter are given in Table 20.2. Please note that the complete pattern is repeated each week, and that the first "hour" of the new 24-hour period of a day corresponds to 6:00 P.M. of the previous "day." This corresponds with the theological creation time implied in our Scriptural quotation in Genesis. Thus if someone in the Talmud states that an astrological event occurs in the third hour of the night or the seventh hour of the day, he is referring to 8:00 P.M. and 12:00 noon, respectively.

I have stated that the Hebrew calendar was basically a lunar calendar corrected for the seasons of the year (the solar insertions into the Equinoxes and Solstices). The Talmud gives rules for such solar insertions. I shall quote Erubin 56a, and again insert my comments for the reader's convenience.

> Samuel stated: "The Vernal Equinox begins only at one of the four quarters of the day, either at the beginning of the daylight (6:00 A.M.) or at the beginning of the night-dark (6:00 P.M.) or at midday or at midnight. . . .

According to Jewish tradition, the first Vernal Equinox following Creation (which occurred at 0° Libra) occurred on the beginning of a Wednesday night (6:00 P.M.). Since the length of a year is 365 days and approximately 6 hours, representing 52 weeks and 1.25 solar days each season can be no longer than 13 weeks (52/4) and 7.5 (1.25 solar days equals 24 hours plus 24/4 or 6 hours equals 30 hours. One-quarter of 30 hours is 7.5 hours). Therefore, the second year after Creation the Vernal Equinox occurred at midnight; the third year after Creation, at 6:00 A.M.; and the fourth year, at noon (these latter three times occurred on Thursdays). Thus, the pattern repeats itself every 4 years, and the Vernal Equinox advances by 1 day every 4 years. For this reason, the corrections are made in the lunar calendar.

"... The Summer Solstice only occurs either at the end of 1.5 or at the end of 7.5 hours of the day or the night. The Autumnal Equinox only occurs at the end of 3 or 9 hours of the day or night, and the Winter Solstice only occurs at the end of 4.5 or of 10.5 hours of the day or night. . . .

If the first Vernal Equinox was at the first hour of the night on Wednesday (6:00 P.M.), then the first Summer Solstice was 13 weeks, 7.5 hours later. Since the planetary hours repeat themselves weekly, we need to be concerned only with the 7.5 hours. The first Summer Solstice occurred on a Thursday at 1:30 A.M. (7.5 hours of the night). The second occurred at 7:30 A.M. Thursday (1.50 hours of the day), the third at 1:30 P.M. Thursday (7.5 hours of the day), and the fourth at 7:30 P.M. Thursday (which is 1.5 hours of the night of Friday).

According to our continuing calculations, the first four Autumnal Equinoxes would have occurred at 9:00 A.M. Thursday (3rd hour of the day), 3:00 P.M. Thursday (9th hour of the day), 9:00 P.M. (3rd hour of the night of Friday) and 3:00 A.M. Friday (9th hour of the night).

The Winter Solstices in those first four years would have occurred at 4:30 P.M. Thursday (10.5 hours of the day), 10:30 P.M. Thursday (4.5 hours of the night of Friday), 4:30 A.M. Friday (10.5 hours of the night) and 10:30 A.M. Friday (4.5 hours of the day). Thus, the next 4-year cycle would begin with a time 7.5 hours later than the *beginning* of this 1st solstice, and the Vernal Equinox of the fifth year would begin at midnight on a Friday.

> ... The duration of a season of the year* is no longer than 91 days and 7.5 hours; and the beginning of one season is removed from that of another by no more than half a planetary hour." ...

Since there were seven known planets and seven days in the week, the *hourly* planetary rulerships repeated themselves each week. Thus if the *beginning* of each season was 13 weeks 7.5 hours later than the beginning of the previous season, and 13 weeks 7.5 earlier than the beginning of the coming season, we can disregard the 13 weeks as far as hourly planetary rulerships is concerned, and deal only with the 7.5-hour difference. With seven planets, each ruling 1 hour, and with a 7.5-hour difference between the start of one season and the start of the next season, it should be obvious that the last half-hour, at least, of

---

* See the calculations of duration for the first three Vernal Equinoxes.

the season should be ruled by the same planet that ruled at the beginning of the season. Every season thus begins half a planetary hour later than the previous one. To illustrate this timing, see Table 20.2 Hourly Planetary Rulers and Table 20.3, Timing of Planetary Rulers.

As you can see, the next cycle which will begin with the next Vernal Equinox will begin with midnight Friday as indicated in the progression given in the Talmudic quotation.

> ...Samuel further stated: "The Vernal Equinox never begins under Jupiter but that it breaks the trees, nor does a Winter Solstice ever begin under Jupiter but that it dries up the seed. This, however, occurs only when the New Moon occurred in the Moon-hour or in the Jupiter-hour."

To begin on a Jupiter-ruled hour, the Vernal Equinox must fulfill two conditions. First, it must occur at midnight or noon, 6:00 A.M. or 6:00 P.M. Second, it must fall on a day on which those hours (the first and sixth hours of the day or night) are ruled by Jupiter. There are four days in the week when this can occur: Sunday at 6:00 P.M., Tuesday at Noon, Thursday at 6:00 A.M., and Saturday at midnight. But if the Vernal Equinox occurs at one of these times and if the Talmud is correct in its procession of the equinoxes, then the following is true: If this event occurred, for example, at midnight Saturday in 1974, then it will occur in 5-year cycles, the next two occurrences being Thursday 6:00 A.M. in 1979 and Tuesday at noon in 1984. Given the same conditions as these calculations warrant, then the four weekly days on which the Winter Solstice could fall on a Jupiter-hour are Monday at 3:00 P.M., Wednesday at 9:00 A.M., Friday at 3:00 A.M. and Saturday at 9:00 P.M. Thus if we assume the Vernal Equinox insertion on a Saturday midnight in 1974, the next possibilities for a Winter Solstice insert in a Jupiter-hour would be nonexistent; for the Jupiter-ruled hours and the Winter Solstice insertion-times never coincide with the assumption of a 1974 Vernal Equinox that "... breaks all the trees. ..." We would have to use a different assumption to provide a proper example. In any event the astrological indications would be rare, for in order to have this Winter Solstice insertion "...dry up the seeds," it would have to be accompanied by a New Moon on a Moon-hour or a Jupiter-hour. The Jupiter-hours and the Moon-hours are listed in Table 20.4.

With this information some of the passages of the Talmud which link Astrology to the practice of Medicine are understandable. In Talmudic times it was unthinkable that a physician would not

Table 20.2 Hourly Rulerships of the Week According to the Talmud

Corresponding Times Today

Evening day → Day	Talmudic Hours of the Night												Hours of the Day												Day
Talmudic hour	1	2	3	4	5	6	7	8	9	10	11	12	1	2	3	4	5	6	7	8	9	10	11	12	
Clock (P.M. → Mid A.M. → Noon P.M.)	6	7	8	9	10	11	12	1	2	3	4	5	6	7	8	9	10	11	12	1	2	3	4	5	
Saturday → Sunday	My	Mo	Sa	Ju	Ma	Su	Ve	My	Mo	Sa	Ju	Ma	Su	Ve	My	Mo	Sa	Ju	Ma	Su	Ve	My	Mo	Sa	Sa Day 1
Sunday → Monday	Ju	Ma	Su	Ve	My	Mo	Sa	Ju	Ma	Su	Ve	My	Mo	Sa	Ju	Ma	Su	Ve	My	Mo	Sa	Ju	Ma	Su	Su Day 2
Monday → Tuesday	Ve	My	Mo	Sa	Ju	Ma	Su	Ve	My	Mo	Sa	Ju	Ma	Su	Ve	My	Mo	Sa	Ju	Ma	Su	Ve	My	Mo	Mo Day 3
Tuesday → Wednesday	Sa	Ju	Ma	Su	Ve	My	Mo	Sa	Ju	Ma	Su	Ve	My	Mo	Sa	Ju	Ma	Su	Ve	My	Mo	Sa	Ju	Ma	Ma Day 4
Wednesday → Thursday	Su	Ve	My	Mo	Sa	Ju	Ma	Su	Ve	My	Mo	Sa	Ju	Ma	Su	Ve	My	Mo	Sa	Ju	Ma	Su	Ve	My	My Day 5
Thursday → Friday (Shabbat eve)	Mo	Sa	Ju	Ma	Su	Ve	My	Mo	Sa	Ju	Ma	Su	Ve	My	Mo	Sa	Ju	Ma	Su	Ve	My	Mo	Sa	Ju	Ju Day 6
Friday → Saturday (Shabbat)	Ma	Su	Ve	My	Mo	Sa	Ju	Ma	Su	Ve	My	Mo	Sa	Ju	Ma	Su	Ve	My	Mo	Sa	Ju	Ma	Su	Ve	Ve Day 7

Table 20.3 Timing of Planetary Rulers

Season	Begins	Ruler	Ends	Ruler
Vernal Equinox	Wed. Night hr. 1 Wed. 6:00 P.M.	Sun	Wed. Night hr 7.5 Thurs. 1:29 A.M.	Sun
Summer Solstice	Wed. Night 7.5 hr. Thurs. 1:30 A.M.	Sun	Thurs. Day hr 3 Thurs. 8:59 A.M.	Sun
Autumnal Equinox	Thurs. Day hr 3 Thurs. 9:00 A.M.	Venus	Thurs. Day hr 10.5 Thurs. 4:29 P.M.	Venus
Winter Solstice	Thurs. Day hr. 10.5 Thurs. 4:30 P.M.	Venus	Thurs. Night hr 6 Thurs 11:59 P.M.	Venus

Table 20.4 Jupiter Hours and Moon-Hours

Day	Moon-Hours		Jupiter-Hours	
Sunday	2, 9 AM;	4, 11 PM	4, 11 AM;	6 PM
Monday	6 AM;	1, 8 PM	1, 8 AM;	3, 10 PM
Tuesday	3, 10 AM;	5 PM	5 AM; 12 noon:	7 PM
Wednesday	Midnight; 7 AM;	2, 9 PM	2, 9 AM;	4, 11 PM
Thursday	4, 11 AM;	6 PM	6 AM;	1, 8 PM
Friday	1, 8 AM;	3, 10 PM	3, 10 AM;	5 PM
Saturday	5 AM;	Noon: 7 PM	Midnight; 7 AM;	2, 9 PM

also be well-versed in Astrology. Many of the medicinal prescriptions were astrologically determined. The Talmud even states that every plant used for medicinal purposes had its own planet that influenced it. We know that cupping was used to encourage blood circulation at the site of a bruise or sore, and we know that bleeding was a common remedy for high blood pressure. However, there is always danger of hemorrhage during any cutting procedure, especially during bleeding, when a vein would be opened for a specific length of time. Here is what the Talmud (Ps. 116:6) says about bleeding as a curative process, in terms of Astrology:

> Samuel also said: "The correct time for bloodletting is on a Sunday, Wednesday, or Friday but not on a Monday or Thursday because the Heavenly Court and the Human Court are alike then. . . .

In Talmudic times the Courts of Justice met on market days, which were Mondays and Thursdays. Today, the Torah is read in the Synagogue on Mondays and Thursdays in remembrance of those court sessions. Many also believed that the Divine Court held its sessions at that time to judge the deeds of man. Since each man was to consider himself a sinner in the eyes of God, it was considered too dangerous to tempt the Court On High into an easy decision to end one's life simply because one was being bled for medicinal reasons. Thus, these two days were eliminated.

> ". . . Why not on a Tuesday? Because the planet Mars rules at even-numbered hours of the day. . . .

The 6th hour of the night (11 P.M. Monday) the 1st hour of the day (6 A.M. Tuesday) and the 8th hour of the day (1 P.M. Tuesday): Two out of the three rulerships are even-numbered hours.

> ". . . But on Friday, too, it rules at even numbered hours? Since the multitude are accustomed to it, *The Lord preserveth the simple. . . .* (Ps. 116:6)."

The 4th hour of the night (9 P.M. Thursday) the 11th hour of the night (4 A.M. Friday) and the 6th hour of the day (11 A.M. Friday). Again, two out of three rulerships are on even-numbered hours. (Those who know something of numerological theory will recognize that the Talmud considered even numbers as being unfortunate.)

Although Friday is as astrologically unfortunate as is Tuesday, the common people were used to being bled on the eve of the Sabbath, perhaps feeling that this type of preparation of the body for the observance of the Sabbath would be the type of Mitzvah (religiously motivated good deed) which would negate the astrological contraindications. Rabbi Samuel's rather facetious answer to this common practice is the well-read religionist's equivalent of "ignorance is bliss!" The full quotation will indicate that it is aptly applied from Samuel's astromedical point of view: it does speak of danger overcome by Divine aid:

> The Lord preserveth the simple;
> I was brought low, and he saved me.
> [Psalms 116:6]

21

THE IMPORTANCE
OF THE ASCENDANT

The Talmud even deals astrologically with psychological ills, and speaks of persons who are suddenly frightened or seized with sudden ill feelings, without being able to determine the source. In a commentary on the verse in Daniel 10:7 we find the following:

> And I, Daniel, alone saw the vision; for the men that were with me saw not the vision; but a great quaking fell upon them, and they fled to hide themselves." (Dan. 10:7). Who were these "men?" R. Jeremiah, or some say R. Hiyya be Abba, said: "These were Haggai, Zechariah and Malachi. They were superior to him (Daniel) and he was superior to them. They were superior to him because they were prophets and he was not a prophet....

It was not enough to see visions to be considered a prophet, even though the visions seen were accurate. A prophet must use his vision to admonish the people and to exhort them to a higher level of ethical conduct. The measure of the prophet is not the ability to foretell the future, but rather the commitment to foretell the demands of God for ethical conduct. Thus Haggai, Zechariah, and Malachi were prophets, but Daniel, Ezra, and Nehemiah were not.

> ...He was superior to them, because he saw (on this occasion) and they did not see. But if they did not see, why were they frightened? Although they themselves did not see, their star saw."...

This means the planet ruling the constellation on the Ascendant. We shall clarify this below.

> ... Rabina said: "We learn from this that, if a man is seized with fright although he sees nothing, (the reason is that) his star sees."

This matter of the Ascendant is of utmost importance in Talmudic Astrology. As you can see above, it figures in the psychological strength of the native. The Talmud also tells us in the words of two different sages, in two different tractates, that the Ascendant also directly affects the health of others with whom we come in contact.

> R. Abba ben Hanina said: "He who visits the sick removes a sixtieth part of his pain ... if his planetary hour is the same."
> [Nedarim 39b (Also said by
> Mar, Baba Metzia 30b)]

The meaning of identical planetary hours is simple: the two must be Ascendant twins! And since each planet rules one of the series of weekly planetary hours in a known distribution which repeats itself weekly, the "hourly-rulership-planetary-twin" will also remove pain. And do not be confused by the number 1/60. It seems at first glance to be a minor fraction of one's pain. However the number 60 is an important number astrologically and Talmudically, and does not mean an actual amount of that size. It means, in fact, quite a sizeable amount. The number 60 is a euphemistic number in both the Bible and the Talmud, as are the numbers 7, 10 and 40. The number 7 means fortunate; the number 10 means more than is needed for sufficiency and even for wealth; the number 40 means the timespan of one generation. The number 60 (60 seconds, 60 minutes, 6 x 60 degrees in perfection; 60/2, 60 and 60 x 2 degrees in free-flowing aspects: all are astrological uses of the number) is an ancient Babylonian unit of measure, and is used euphemistically to mean "a significant amount." Here then is a fascinating conjecture for my readers who are interested in faith healing, the ability to read, to respond to, and to heal by means of auras, and other methods. Is it possible that one is more successful in these healing arts if one is an Ascendant-twin or an hourly, ruler-twin of the patient?

There is also an astrological vector to biblical interpretation regarding accidents involving animals and men. The following two statements are made in Scripture:

And if an ox gore (Hebrew: *YGX*) a man or a woman that they die. . . .

[Exodus 21:28]

And if one's ox collides with (Hebrew: *YGPf*) his neighbor's ox so that it die. . . .

[Exodus 21:35]

The Rabbis of the Talmud ask: Why is the word *YGX*, "to gore," used with reference to a man or woman, and the word *YGPf*, "to collide with," used with reference to another animal? Their answer is astrological:

Man who possesses ruling constellations (Aramaic: *D'iṪ LeY MaALeY*, the planetary ruler of his Ascendant forewarns him) is as a rule injured by a willful goring (a deliberately intentioned act on the part of the ox)."

[R. Eleazar and R. Papa in Baba Kama 2b]

As you realize by now, the Ascendant and the hourly ruler were most important in Talmudic Astrology. They were also very important for the type of psychological and personality trait delineation that is so popular in modern Astrology, and usually attributed to the Sun Signs, which, of course delineate only the basic life drive of the native. In any event, the types of statements which are made today about the Sun Signs were made, in Talmudic times, on the basis of day, hour and Ascendant rulerships. The following *long* excerpt from the Talmud is quoted verbatim and with my comments inserted parenthetically so that none of its "feel" is lost:

It was recorded in R. Joshua ben Levi's notebook (and therefore *important*. See Chapter 19): "He who is born on the first day of the week (Sunday, Sun-ruled) shall be a man without one thing in him." What does 'without one thing in him' mean? Shall we say without one virtue? R. Ashi said: "I was born on Sunday (and I am not without one virtue!)" Hence, it must surely mean without one vice? But R. Ashi said: "I and Dimi ben Kakuzta were born on Sunday: I am a king (head of the Academy) and he is the captain of thieves (shades of organized crime!)." Rather it means either completely virtuous or completely wicked (i.e., completely in tune with one's mode of life, with no internal conflicts of one's life-principle, whatever it might be). What is the reason? Because light and darkness were created on that day (hence, one's nature shall be one or the other).

He who is born on the second day (Monday, Moon-ruled) will be bad-tempered. Why? Because the waters were divided thereon (See Gen. 1:6-8. Water is the astrological symbol of emotionality, and to divide waters is to interrupt one's emotional life, and would lead to bad temper). He who is born on the third day (Tuesday, Mars-ruled), will be wealthy and unchaste, because herbs were created on that day (and the sale of herbs and spices— especially those used as aphrodisiacs—would lead to wealth, see Gen. 1:11-12).

He who is born on the fourth day (Wednesday, Mercury-ruled) will be wise and of a retentive memory, because the luminaries were suspended on that day (see Gen. 1:14-18. The luminaries enlighten the world, remain in orbit, and retain their position of instructing the world; see Chapter 5).

He who is born on the fifth day (Thursday, Jupiter-ruled) will practice benevolence, for fish and birds were created on that day (see Gen. 1:20-22. [Because of their abundance, both fish and birds become symbols of God's largesse and providence. Also during Talmudic times, neither fish nor fowl were considered meats which were forbidden to be used with dairy products (based on the Scripture Exod. 23:19). Therefore they became symbols of everything permitted for enjoyment—and from this source we get our modern expression that something is neither fish nor fowl].

He who is born on the sixth day (Friday, eve of the Sabbath, Venus-ruled) will be a seeker. R. Nahman ben Isaac commented: "A seeker after good deeds."

He who is born on the Sabbath will die on the Sabbath, because the great Day of the Sabbath was desecrated for him (literally, "on his account": although God rested on the Sabbath and declared that no work should be done on it, the native was permitted to be born—thus to do work and to cause work to be done—on the Sabbath). Raba son of R. Shila observed: "And he shall be called a great and holy man (only the great and the holy die on the Sabbath).

R. Hanina said to them (his disciples, who were referring to the notebooks): "Go out and tell the son of Levi (R. Joshua, whom we have been quoting above) Not the constellation of the day (either the daily ruler or the ruler of the Sun's constellation) but that of the hour (either the ruler of the Ascendant's constellation or the planetary hour ruler) is the determining influence. He who is born under the constellation of the Sun (Ascendant in Leo) will be a distinguished, bright, handsome (the Hebrew means all of these) man. He will eat and drink of his own (providing) and his secrets will lie uncovered (he will not be able to dissemble). If a thief, he will have no success.

He who is born under Venus (Ascendant in Taurus or Libra) will be wealthy and (sexually) immoral. What is the reason? Because fire was created therein (during the Age of Aries, Taurus is the 1st house ruler).

He who is born under Mercury (Ascendant in Gemini or Virgo) will be of a retentive memory and wise. Why? Because it (Mercury) is the Sun's scribe.

He who is born under the Moon (Ascendant in Cancer) will be a man to suffer evil, building and demolishing, demolishing and building, eating and drinking that which is not his, and his secrets will remain hidden. If a thief, he will be successful. (Like the Moon, his fortunes will wax and wane; the Moon shines by reflected light, having no "food" of its own, and is often hidden by clouds and rarely shows its full face (Full Moon) and never shows its back; it 'steals' its light from the Sun.)

He who is born under Saturn (Ascendant in Capricorn or Aquarius) will be a man whose plans will be frustrated. (The Chaldaic equivalent of the Hebrew name for Saturn, $SB\hat{T}Y$, is BTL, which in Hebrew means 'to frustrate.' This is a play on words in two languages!) Others say: "All nefarious designs against him will be frustrated."

He who is born under Jupiter (Hebrew: $\hat{S}DQ$; 'Ascendant in Sagittarius or Pisces') will be a person who does righteousness (Hebrew: $\hat{S}DQNf$). Rabbi Nahman ben Isaac observed: 'Righteousness in (the form of) charity.'

He who is born under Mars (Ascendant in Aries or Scorpio) will be a shedder of blood. R. Ashi observed: 'Either a surgeon, a thief, a slaughterer (butcher) or a ritual circumciser.' Rabbah said: 'I was born under Mars (and I am none of these!).' Abaye retorted: 'You too inflict punishment and kill!' (As a judge you make decisions involving both capital and corporal punishment. which would be covered under a Mars-ruled Ascendant)."

It would be superfluous to comment on the foregoing passage at any length: those who are familiar with Sun Sign delineations in modern Astrology will be quick to identify the correspondencies between Talmudic knowledge and that of modern times. Those to whom the delineation of the Ascendant has become a "lost art" may be encouraged to think more deeply about the importance of this personal point in the chart. However, the real importance of the passage for modern astrologers does not lie in the very brief delineations described herein. To the true students of the Divine Science, the importance of this quotation is the direction it must give to research into two related areas of astrological concern:

1. It is a well known procedure in Astrology that, if the birth time of the native is unknown and there is neither time nor inclination (and perhaps not the skill) on the part of the astrologer to do a rectification of the chart, the astrologer may set an arbitrary birthtime at 6:00 A.M. (Talmudic "first hour of the day"), calculate the Sun's position for that time, set it exactly conjunct the first house cusp thus using it as an Ascendant in an Equal House Natal Chart, and delineate surprisingly accurate information from such a chart! Although the Ascendant has always been considered one of the five "personal points" in a natal chart (Sun, Moon, Ascendant, Midheaven, Node), not enough work has been done regarding its relationship to the Sun and its delineations. Hopefully, other astrologers will become intrigued with the problem and do some of the serious study necessary to illuminate these relationships.

2. I must surmise from the Talmudic importance of the Ascendant, that the concept of astrological theory now included in the general term "Arabian Points," is proven to have had its origin at least four or five centuries earlier, in the Talmudic Rabbinic astrologer's concern with the Ascendant and with their corollary points, the Descendant (see Chapter 7) the Midheaven and the Nadir (the four

points together being known in the Talmud as the "corners" of the chart). Nicholas Devore, in his *Encyclopedia of Astrology** defines the location of 40 such points. But Abraham ibn Ezra (1093 to 1167) in *The Beginning of Wisdom*,† defines 97 such points, which he calls "fates of the houses!" It seems that since the beginning of the twelfth century we have lost more than half of such knowledge. In all cases, the points are calculated with reference to the Ascendant or to a house cusp dependent on the Ascendant. I believe that it would be true to indicate that perhaps all of our newest techniques of midpoint delineation may have had their origins in the Talmudic period, which set the tone for later astrological work.

We also know that the Rabbis of the Talmud continued their interest in that area of Astrology for which the Divine Science was originally birthed: Mundane Astrology. And as was the case in all of ancient mundane astrological practice, the ruler was most anxious to know specifically of his own country first. Therefore the example of Mundane Astrology below is naturally directed toward answering the questions of the Children of Israel:

R. Meir said: "When the Sun is in eclipse, it is a bad omen for idolators; when the Moon is in eclipse, it is a bad omen for Israel, since Israel reckons (time) by the Moon and idolators by the Sun.

"When the Sun is (seen) eclipsed in the East it is bad for dwellers in the East. When (the Sun is seen eclipsed) in the West, it is bad for dwellers in the West. When (the Sun is seen eclipsed) in the center, it is bad for the whole world.

"If (during the eclipse) the Sun's face is red, it means war; if it is dark and gloomy, it means famine. If (the eclipse is seen) at sunset, trouble will take time in coming; if (the eclipse) is seen at dawn, trouble is coming fast. The Sun is eclipsed for four reasons:

1. A president of the Sanhedrin who died and was not mourned properly

---

* Nicholas Devore, *Encyclopedia of Astrology*. New York: Philosophical Library, 1947, pp. 14-15.

† Abraham ibn Ezra, *The Beginning of Wisdom*, Vol. 4. Baltimore: Johns Hopkns, 1926, Chapter 9.

2. A betrothed maiden who cried "rape!" in a city, and none helped her (see Deut. 22:24)
3. Sodomy
4. Two brothers who were murdered at the same time.

"The Moon is eclipsed for four reasons:

1. Forgery
2. Giving false witness
3. Raising animals that forage in the fields of others
4. Those who destroy good trees."

[Sukkah 29a]

The proper analysis of this unique list of reasons for solar and lunar eclipses leads us into an historical astrological confrontation that will, hopefully, become the basis of an article to be published at a later date. Just one tantalizing view: Reasons given for solar eclipses all involve tragedies which occurred *only* under foreign occupation of the Holy Land, whereas reasons given for lunar eclipses involve transgressions against the property of others.

It is almost impossible to exhaust all references to Astrology which are found in the Talmud. As a matter of fact, it is almost impossible to exhaust any references to any particular subject in the Talmud. In Jewish tradition, these volumes are known as the *Yam HaTalmud*, the "Sea of the Talmud," and the longer one either swims or fishes in it, the more one finds there is to discover. In this first work my object has not been to be exhaustive but to be tantalizing, and to score a polemical point. Let me just say that this is a book of apologetics in defense of the Faith; a defense which I shall summarize in the last chapter.

22

SIMAN TOV U'MAZZAL TOV!

Siman Tov Umazzal Tov Y'hey Lanu v'al kol Am'cha Yisrael!

This last chapter begins with a wedding song. Translated, it says: "May we, and all Thy people Israel, have good luck!" It is a joyous song, and it is sung over and over by the happy participants, who never realize its true meaning.

The words *Siman Tov uMazzal Tov* mean, very simply, "Good aspects and good constellations!" The song really means:

May we, and all Thy people Israel, enjoy good planetary aspects in fortunate constellations.

When Jews greet each other with the words *Mazzal Tov*, by which they mean "Congratulations," they rarely realize that what they are really saying is "May you have fortunate constellations." Expressions such as these do not become part of a language (there is no other way of saying "Good Luck" in Hebrew) unless backing them up are centuries of use during which the basis for the expression was believed in and acted on.

The Talmud tells us that every home possessed a piece of furniture known as a *Dargesh* (Moed Katan 27a-b, Nedarim 56a, Sanhedrin 20a, and others; see also Chapter 18). This piece of furniture was not treated in the same manner as other couches or beds, to which it was similar, during periods of mourning. It did not have to be overturned, nor stood against a wall as the other pieces of furniture. Another name for the *Dargesh* was the *Arsa d'Gadda*, which is Aramaic for "Bed of (the constellation) ruled by Gad" (Sagittarius). In other words, it is the Couch of Jupiter, and one does not overturn it because one does not wish to overturn his own good fortune.

What am I trying to convey in these last words of summation? I am trying to reclaim our Jewish astrological heritage for my people. I am trying to show that Astrology, far from being an aberration in Jewish life, a one-time departure from sanity from which we thankfully recovered, has ever been a growing, developing, maturing, and greatly respected part of our Jewish heritage. If I have succeeded in providing a background for this understanding, then I have done more than just reclaim Astrology for Judaism: I have also indicated a direction, that can be taken by our daughter religion Christianity, towards reclaiming an integral portion of its lost, or deliberately abandoned, heritage.

How did we Jews come to lose our bearings in this manner? The answer is all too simple. In our rush to become accepted as citizens of the Western world, following the turn of the eighteenth century (and this has not happened yet; e.g., Germany under Hitler and the Soviet Union, today), we accepted the *Weltanschauung* of the Western world and abandoned our own. We believed that we could perceive the universe differently in our worldly affairs, and not have that perception affect our understanding of our religious universe. We were wrong, for a change of perception in one area of life also affects a change in our perception of all areas of life; the entire universe is one. The Western world perceives its universe linearly, and therefore thinks in linear terms (see, for example, Marshall MacLuhan, *The Medium Is the Message**). At one time, until our pseudoemancipation began, we Jews did not perceive linearly. Let me try to explain the difference in linguistic terms.

There are five senses with which we are familiar; sight, sound, smell, touch, and taste. Two of these senses are the ones most often used by man to perceive the universe around him, sight and sound. In man, the other three senses are rather limited. Man does not even speak of them very often. But dogs rely very heavily on their sense of smell. They become aware of the presense of other dogs and of their physical condition long before they are visible. Even lower forms of animal life have different means of perceiving their environments.

* Marshall MacLuhan, *The Medium Is the Message*. New York: Random House, 1967.

According to Dr. Frank A. Brown, Jr., Morrison Professor of Biology at Northwestern University, animals such as crustaceans exhibit such behavior in their environments that "No clear boundary exists between the organism's metabolically maintained electromagnetic fields (auras? Ed.) and those of the geophysical environment.* One could say, then, that crabs and clams and the like experience their environments electromagnetically. Yet in another species, butterflies and moths, the environment is experienced through the ability to "taste" the air with their antennae and to locate their own kind through identifying pheramones secreted by them.

Now, in man's language, he has always used a sensory equivalent as a synonym for the verb "to understand." Supposing each of the above-mentioned animal species, as well as man, had developed some kind of linguistic sensory descriptive synonym for the verb "to understand." Then we would have the following list of exclamatory phrases meaning, to each species, "I understand":

> The dog would say: "I smell it!"
> The clam would say: "I electrograv it!"
> The butterfly and moth would say: "I taste it!"
> Western man does say: "I see it!"

But the Hebrew word used to imply understanding is the Hebrew verb *SM'*, meaning "to hear." Therefore in the past, the Jew would understand a thing, and exclaim: *"ANY SWM'"*—"I hear it!" The difference between hearing and seeing is very great. As a matter of fact, seeing is the most spatially limiting yet detailingly intensive sense that man has. One can see clearly only in a cone of approximately 23°, only in the direction in which the head is turned. One must turn the head to become aware of anything else visually. However, one can hear through a complete circle of 360° and in all planes. Thus one becomes the *center* of a perceived and a perceiving *universe*. In the same manner, the taste of the butterfly, and the smell of the dog, and the electromagnetic sense of the crustacean all permit their possessors to operate at the center of a perceived universe, but *the sense of sight does not permit this!* Therefore, with Western man came a linearly perceived universe, a quid-pro-quo linear process of reasoning, and thus a linearly defined science, and man became a slave to his science.

However, the Jew still has at the beginning of his most important prayer the word *SM'*—"Hear!" "Understand!" "Perceive!" This word is linked in this prayer to the concept of unity.

---

* *American Scientist*, Vol. 60 (No. 6), November-December 1972, pp. 756-766.

SM' YSRAL YHWH ALHYNW YHWH AXD!
Hear, O Israel! The Lord our God, the Lord is One!

Each Jew is supposed to perceive himself as being at the *center* of the Universe that is perceived as *one unit*, and with which the *individual* must *interact* as an integral part of that Unit, as must be since both the *individual* and the *universe* were created by *one God*—Who stands at the *other epicenter* of the universe. Living in a Universe thus perceived, it is imperative that the *totality* of the Universe be taken into account in one's life. Within this *totality*, Astrology stands as an important *interpreter* of man's relationship with this Total Universe. This is the basic understanding of the mystic, and within the very origins of Jewish mysticism the exalted place of Astrology is emphasized as being the tool one uses to fathom the Divine will for the person.

    Esau sold his birthright to Jacob for a mess of pottage, and Jews have always held Esau up to our children as a bad example. But because of the exigencies of time and space (in our prayerbooks this is expressed as "we were exiled for our sins"), we have sold our heritage for a mess of scientific pottage! We have contributed our abilities to the development of the greatest mathematicians, doctors and scientists, which is good: the Universe is to be understood. But to make this contribution to the Western world, we had to appropriate the *Weltanschauung* of the Western world. We "saw," and conquered the world of linearity, losing in the process our perception of the Divine totality. It is this Divine totality to which I would have my people respond once again. Astrology may be one key to the gate which leads to the path of this understanding.

    SM' YSRAL! ! Hear, O Israel! Learn, O Israel! Understand, O Israel! *YHWH ALYHNW ! !* The Lord is Our God ! ! *YHWH AXD ! !* The Lord is ONE ! ! !

It is only in the understanding of the *universal totality* of this statement, and it is only in the understanding that *man* and *God* stand at the two *epicenters* of this *totality*, that the words of our opening greeting make their ultimate, *real* sense:

    Siman Tov uMazzal Tov!
    May you be blessed with favorable planetary aspects in pleasant
       constellations!

Appendices

Appendix 1. Hebrew Transliteration

Letter Name	Sound	Number Value	Transliteration	Hebrew Letter
Alef	Silent	1	A	א
Bet	B	2	B	ב
Gimel	G	3	G	ג
Daled	D	4	D	ד
Hey	H	5	H	ה
Vav	V	6	W	ו
Zayin	Z	7	Z	ז
Khet	CH (gutteral)	8	X	ח
Tet	T	9	T	ט
Yod	Y	10	Y	י
Kaf	K	20	K	כ
Kaf sofit	K (final form)	(500)*	Kf	ך
Lamed	L	30	L	ל
Mem	M	40	M	מ
Mem sofit	M (final form)	(600)*	Mf	ם
Nun	N	50	N	נ
Nun sofit	N (final form)	(700)*	Nf	ן
Samekh	S	60	S	ס
'ayin	Silent	70	'	ע
Pey	P	80	P	פ
Pey sofit	P (final form)	(800)*	Pf	ף
Ṣadi	TS in le*ts*	90	S̟	צ
Ṣadi sofit	TS (final form)	(900)*	Ṡf	ץ
Quf	K	100	Q	ק
Resh	R	200	R	ר
Shin	SH in hu*sh*	300	S̄	ש
Taf	T	400	T	ת

Hebrew Transliteration—continued

* These high values for the final forms of the five letters indicated, are rarely used in the numerological interpretation of Scripture, which is known as Gematria. Usually, the final form is given the same value as the normal form of the letter.

Please note that, in Hebrew, all forms of the letters are consonants. There are no letters which are vowels in Hebrew. The vowels are never written in the Sacred Scrolls, nor is there any punctuation in them. Likewise in modern Hebrew books and newspapers, there are no vowels printed, although there are punctuation marks. When vowels are printed as aids to the beginner, they take the form of dots and dashes above and below the consonants.

In some cases, both the Vav (W) and the Yod (Y) are used as matri lectionis, or aids to reading. In those cases, the W has the sound of a long "o," as in home; the Y has the sound of the English "y" when used as a vowel. Thus:

TWRH would be pronounced *ToRaH;* but

W'D would be pronounced Va'eD.

YQWMf would be pronounced YaKooM (Y here is a consonant, and sometimes W is used to indicate the *oo* sound)

QWMY would be pronounced KooMee (Y here is a vowel)

All transliterations in this book will indicate *only* the consonants as printed in Scripture, and not the *sound* of the word.

Appendix 2

Rulership in the Bible

ROOT: MSL

RULERSHIP IN ISRAEL

Genesis	37:8
	45:8
	45:26
Deuteronomy	15:6
Judges	8:22
	9:2
	14:4
I Kings	15:11
	5:1
Isaiah	3:4
	3:12
	5:8
Jeremiah	22:30
	30:21
Psalms	33:26
	105:21
	106:41
I Chronicles	26:6
II Chronicles	9:26

RULERSHIP: OTHER NATIONS

Joshua	12:2
	12:5
Isaiah	14:5
	16:1
	19:4
	49:7
	52:5
Jeremiah	51:46
Ezekiel	19:11
	19:14
Habakkuk	1:14
Psalms	105:20
Proverbs	6:7
	17:2
	19:10
	23:1
	28:15
	29:2
	29:12
	29:26
Ecclesiastes	9:17
	10:4
Daniel	11:3
	11:4
	11:5
	11:39

LORD RULES

Judges	8:23
Isaiah	40:10
	63:19
Psalms	22:29
	59:14
	66:7
	89:10
	103:19
Job	25:2
I Chronicles	29:12
II Chronicles	20:6

MESSIAH TO RULE

I Samuel	23:3
Micah	5:1
Zechariah	6:13
	9:10
II Chronicles	7:18

DOUBLE ENTENDRE*

Isaiah	28:14
Joel	2:17

HEAVENLY BODIES RULE

Genesis	1:16
	1:18
Psalms	136:8
	136:9

SELF-CONTROL/EXAMPLE

Genesis	3:16
	4:7
Exodus	24:2
	21:8
	8:7
Psalms	12:24
	19:14
Proverbs	16:32
	22:7
Daniel	11:43
Nehemiah	9:37

* Note: In these two verses, there is a pun—a play on the two meanings of the *M-SH-L* root, in which both the concept of rulership and the concept of example exist.

Bible Verse Analysis

The books of the Bible, the number of their verses, the frequency of appearance of the word "heavens" in each book, and their physical versus paraphysical uses in each book.

Book	Verses	Astro. Verses	% of Total	Phys. Verses	% of Total	Parap. Verses	% of Total
Genesis	1,533	49	3.20	31	2.02	18	1.17
Exodus	1,210	18	1.49	9	0.74	9	0.74
Leviticus	812	2	0.25	1	0.12	1	0.12
Numbers	1,289	3	0.23	2	0.15	1	0.08
Deuteronomy	953	47	4.93	22	2.31	25	2.62
Joshua	658	15	2.28	11	1.67	4	0.61
Judges	618	13	2.10	8	1.29	5	0.81
I Samuel	811	10	1.23	4	0.49	6	0.74
II Samuel	694	16	2.30	7	1.01	9	1.29
I Kings	816	24	2.94	6	0.74	18	2.20
II Kings	719	20	2.78	3	0.42	17	2.36
Isaiah	1,290	105	8.14	6	0.46	99	7.68
Jeremiah	1,364	114	8.36	6	0.44	108	7.92
Ezekiel	1,273	10	0.78	3	0.23	7	0.55
Hosea	197	5	2.54	1	0.51	4	2.03
Joel	73	6	8.22	—	—	6	8.22
Amos	146	15	10.27	—	—	15	10.27
Obadiah	21	1	4.76	1	4.76	—	—
Jonah	48	2	4.17	1	2.08	1	2.08
Micah	105	2	1.90	—	—	2	1.90
Nahum	47	4	8.51	2	4.25	2	4.25
Habakkuk	56	4	7.14	—	—	4	7.14
Zephaniah	53	3	5.67	—	—	3	5.67
Haggai	38	15	39.47	—	—	15	39.47
Zechariah	211	54	25.59	4	1.89	50	23.70
Malachi	55	27	49.09	1	1.82	26	47.27
Psalms	2,518	100	3.97	16	0.63	84	3.34
Proverbs	915	7	0.76	2	0.22	5	0.54
Job	1,069	33	3.09	11	1.03	22	2.06
Song of Songs (Canticles)	117	2	1.70	1	0.85	1	0.85

Ruth	85	—	—	—	—	—	—
Lamentations	154	5	3.25	3	1.95	2	1.30
Ecclesiastes	222	38	17.12	37	16.67	1	0.45
Esther	167	—	—	—	—	—	—
Daniel	357	39	10.92	15	4.20	24	6.72
Ezra	280	9	3.21	1	0.35	8	2.86
Nehemiah	406	13	3.20	3	0.74	10	2.46
I Chronicles	943	10	1.06	2	0.21	8	0.85
II Chronicles	821	26	3.17	4	0.49	22	2.68
Totals	23,144	866	3.74	224	0.97	642	2.77
Torah	5,797	119	2.05	65	1.12	54	0.93
Prophets	9,293	465	4.97	64	0.69	401	4.28
Writings	8,054	282	3.50	95	1.18	187	2.32
Mosaic	4,844	72	1.49	43	0.89	29	0.60
Historic	8,076	242	3.00	86	1.06	156	1.93
Prophetic	4,977	367	7.37	25	0.50	342	6.87
Didactic	5,247	185	3.52	70	1.33	115	2.19

Appendix 4

Uses of "Heaven" and "Earth"

The use of the word "Heaven" (Heb *SMYMf*) in the Bible, when used *alone*.

USED AS PHYSICAL PLACE ONLY

Genesis	1:8	Jeremiah	49:36
	1:9		51:9
	1:14		51:53
	2:19	Hosea	7:12
	2:20	Nahum	3:16
	7:11	Zechariah	2:10
	8:2	Psalms	57:11
	11:4		104:12
	15:5		107:26
Exodus	17:14		139:8
	32:13	Proverbs	23:5
Deuteronomy	1:10		30:19
	1:28	Job	12:7
	2:25		20:6
	7:24		28:21
	9:1		38:29
	10:22		41:3
	11:11	Lamentations	3:66
	25:19		4:19
	28:26	Ecclesiastes	1:13
	28:62		2:3
	29:19		3:1
	30:4		10:20
	30:12	Daniel	2:38
Joshua	8:20		4:9
Judges	20:40		4:22
I Samuel	5:12		5:21
	17:44		7:2
	17:46		7:27

II Samuel	18:19		8:8
	21:10		9:12
I Kings	8:27		11:4
	14:11	Ezra	9:6
	16:4	Nehemiah	1:9
	21:24		9:23
II Kings	14:27	I Chronicles	27:23
Jeremiah	4:25	II Chronicles	2:5
	8:7		6:18
	9:9		28:9

USED AS PLACE OF GOD'S ABODE

Genesis	21:17	Psalms	53:3
	22:11		57:4
	22:15		68:34
	28:17		80:15
Exodus	9.8		103:19
	9:10		115:3
	9:22		123:1
	9:23	Job	2:12
	10:21		22:12
	10:22		22:14
	20:22	Lamentations	3:41
Deuteronomy	4:36		3:50
	26:15	Daniel	4:23
	33:26		4:28
II Samuel	22:14		4:30
I Kings	8:22		4:31
	8:30	Nehemiah	9:13
	8:32		9:27
	8:34		9:28
	8:36	II Chronicles	6:13
	8:39		6:21
	8:43		6:23
	8:45		6:25
	8:49		6:27
	8:54		6:30
Isaiah	51:6		6:33
	63:15		6:35
Psalms	2:4		6:39
	11:4		7:14
	14:2		20:6
	20:7		30:27
	33:13		32:20

SUBJECT TO GOD'S WILL

II Samuel	22:10
I Kings	8:35
Jeremiah	14:22
Psalms	33:6
	78:26
	96:5
	115:16
Proverbs	30:4
Job	15:15
I Chronicles	16:26
II Chronicles	2:11

HEAVENS AS WITNESS

Genesis	26:4
Exodus	16:4
Deuteronomy	33:28
Isaiah	34:5
Jeremiah	2:12
Malachi	3:10
Psalms	50:6
	89:6
	89:30
	148:1
	148:4

USED AS OMEN FROM GOD

Genesis	19:24	Jeremiah	10:13
Exodus	24:10		51:16
Deuteronomy	4:11	Ezekiel	1:1
	28:24	Psalms	18:14
Joshua	10:11		105:40
Judges	13:20		144:5
I Kings	18:45	Job	1:16
II Kings	1:10	Daniel	4:10
	1:12		4:18
	1:14		4:20
	2:1		7:13
	2:11		12:7
	7:2	Nehemiah	9:15
	7:19	I Chronicles	7:1
Isaiah	34:4		21:26

"GOD OF HEAVEN" (LIKE "LORD OF HOSTS")

Genesis	24:7	Ezra	6.9
Psalms	136:26		6:10
Daniel	2:18		7:12
	2:19		7:21
	2:28		7:23
	2:37	Nehemiah	1:4
	2:44		1:5
	4:34		2:4
	5:23		2:20
Ezra	1:2	II Chronicles	36:23
	5:12		

USED IN IDOLATRY		ASTROLOGICAL INDICATIONS	
Jeremiah	7:18	Judges	5:20
		Psalms	36:6
			89:3
		Job	35:5

The use of the word "Heaven" (Hebrew *SMYMf*) in the Bible when it appears with the word "Earth" (Hebrew *ARS*) in the same verse, or in immediately contiguous verses having the same relationship of meaning.

USED AS A PHYSICAL PLACE ONLY

Genesis	1:1	Ezekiel	8:3
	1:15		31:6
	1:17		31:13
	1:20	Zechariah	5:9
	1:26		6:5
	1:28	Psalms	57:12
	1:30		73:25
	2:1		76:9
	2:4*		85:12
	6:7		102:20
	6:17		108:6
	7:19		113:6
	7:23		135:6
	9:2	Job	28:24
	22:17		35:11
	27:28		37:3
	28:12	Lamentations	2:1
Exodus	20:4	Ecclesiastes	5:1
	20:11	Daniel	4:8
	31:17		4:13
Deuteronomy	4:17		4:17
	5:8		4:19
I Kings	8:23		4:20
Isaiah	13:5	I Chronicles	21:16
	55:9		

*NOTE: This verse is counted twice, since the phrase is used twice, with two different meanings.

231

ASTROLOGICAL INDICATIONS		OATH: "GOD OF HEAVEN & EARTH"	
Isaiah	47:13	Genesis	24:3
Psalms	119:89		

HEAVEN/EARTH ARE INTELLIGENT		GOD TAKES OATH	
Proverbs	3:19	Deuteronomy	32:40

The heavenly bodies as they appear in Scripture. These are: Sun, Moon, Stars, Lights, Hosts of Heaven, Constellations (as a generic term), Constellations (specifically by name), Planets by name, Stars by name.

THE SUN ALONE

SUN IN ITS PHYSICAL SENSE: HEAT, LIGHT, TIME, DIRECTION

Genesis	15:12	Isaiah	45:26
	15:17		49:10
	19:23		59:19
	28:11	Jonah	4:8
	32:32	Nahum	3:17
Exodus	16:21	Zechariah	8:7
	17:12	Malachi	1:11
	22:2	Psalms	50:1
	22:25		58:9
Leviticus	22:7		104:22
Numbers	21:11		113:3
	25:4	Job	8:16
Deuteronomy	4:41	Canticles	1:6
	4:47	Ecclesiastes	1:3
	11:30		1:5
	16:16		1:9
	23:12		1:14
	24:13		2:4
	24:15		2:11
Joshua	1:4		2:17
	1:15		2:18
	8:29		2:19
	10:27		2:20
			2:22

Joshua	12:1	Ecclesiastes	3:16
	13:5	(3)	4:1
	19:12		4:3
	19:27		4:7
	19:34		4:15
	23:4		5:12
Judges	(1) 8:13		5:17
	9:33		6:1
	11:18		6:5
	(1) 14:18		6:12
	19:14		7:11
	20:43		8:9
	21:19		8:15
I Samuel	11:9		8:17
II Samuel	2:24		9:3
	3:35		9:6
	12:11		9:9
	12:12		9:11
	23:4		9:13
I Kings	22:36		10:5
II Kings	3:22		11:7
	10:33	Daniel	(2) 6:15
Isaiah	41:25	Nehemiah	7:3
		II Chronicles	18:34

OMEN FROM GOD		_WITNESS TO DEEDS_	
Judges	5:31	Psalms	72:17
Isaiah	38:8		84:12
Jeremiah	15:9		
Amos	8:9		
Malachi	3:20		
Job	30:28		

SUBJECT TO GOD'S WILL		OWNED/RULED BY GOD	
Genesis	2:4*	Amos	9:6
	14:19	Jonah	1:9
	14:22	Zechariah	12:1
Deuteronomy	4:39	Psalms	73:9
	10:14		89:12
Joshua	2:11		102:26
Isaiah	40:22		115:15
	42:5		121:2
	44:24		124:8
	45:12		134:3
	45:18	Daniel	4:32
	51:13	Ezra	5:11
	51:16	Nehemiah	9:6
	66:1	I Chronicles	29:11
Jeremiah	10:11	II Chronicles	2:11
	23:24		6:14
	32:17		6:18
	51:15		

(b) AGENT FOR BLESSING		(c) AGENT FOR CURSING	
Genesis	37:39	Leviticus	26:19
	49:25	Deuteronomy	11:17
Deuteronomy	28:12		28:23
	35:13-16	I Samuel	2:10
Isaiah	45:8	II Samuel	22:8
	49:13	Isaiah	13:9-10
	65:17		13:13
Jeremiah	33:22	Jeremiah	4:23
Hosea	2:20		4:28
	2:23		7:33
Joel	3:3		15:3
	4:16		16:4
Haggai	2:21-23		19:7
Zechariah	8:12		34:20
Psalms	78:23-24		51:48
	103:11	Ezekiel	29:5
	108:5		32:4
	115:16		32:8
	146:5-6		38:20
	147:8	Hosea	4:3
I Chronicles	16:31	Joel	2:10
		Amos	9:2
		Zephaniah	1:3
		Haggai	1:10
		Psalms	79:2
		II Chronicles	7:13

HEAVENS AS GOD'S WITNESS

(a) WITNESS TO GLORY		(b) WITNESS TO DEEDS	
Deuteronomy	3:24	Deuteronomy	4:26
Judges	5:4		4:32
I Kings	8:23		11:21
	8:27		30:19
II Kings	19:15		31:28
Isaiah	14:13		32:1
	37:16	Isaiah	1:2
	40:12		44:23
	63:19		48:13
Jeremiah	10:12		51:6
Habakkuk	3:3		55:10
Haggai	2:6-9		66:22
Psalms	8:2	Jeremiah	31:37
	18:8-10		33:25
	19:2	Psalms	50:4
	57:6		68:9
	69:35	Proverbs	8:22-32
	96:11		25:3
	97:4-6	Job	11:7-8
	104:2		20:27
	113:4-6		26:11
	136:5-6		26:13
	148:13		38:31-33
Job	9:8		
	38:37-38		
Daniel	6:28		

IDOLATROUS USE		ASTROLOGICAL INDICATION	
II Kings	23:11	Micah	3:6
Ezekiel	8:16	Psalms	19:5-6

NOTE: Of the 137 times the word "Sun" is used in the Bible, five different words are used in Hebrew. The overwhelming majority use is the word *SMS*. It is derived from the verb meaning "to serve," "to function," "to attend." This is already an astrological derivation! It is used 126 times. The other four words are used a total of 8 times, and they are indicated in the listing above and below by numbers in parentheses. These are as follows:

(1) *XRS* (twice) from Hebrew root meaning golden
(2) SMSA (once) Aramaic form of SHeMaSH
(3) XMH (thrice) from Hebrew root meaning hot
(4) AWR (twice) meaning is light

THE SUN IN COMBINATION
WITH OTHER HEAVENLY BODIES

THE SUN: GOD'S WITNESS

Deuteronomy	33:14 (6)	Joel	2:10 (11)
Joshua	10:13 (6)		3:4 (6)
	10:19 (6)		4:15 (11)
Isaiah	13:10 (7)	Habakkuk	3:4 (4,14)
	24:23 (3, 5, 6)		3:11 (6)
	30:26 (3, 5, 6)	Psalms	72:5 (6)
	60:19 (6)		74:16 (13)
	60:20 (6)		89:37-38 (6)
Jeremiah	31:35 (11)		104:19 (6)
Ezekiel	32:7-8 (11)		136:7-9 (11)
			148:3 (11)
		Ecclesiastes	12:2 (11)

237

IDOLATROUS USE		ASTROLOGICAL INDICATIONS		
Deuteronomy	4:19 (7)	Genesis	37:9	(11)
	17:3 (10)	Psalms	121:6	(6)
II Kings	23:5 (9)	Job	9:7	(1, 12)
Jeremiah	8:2 (10)	Canticles	6:10	(3, 5, 6)
Job	31:26 (4, 5, 6)			

NOTE: In this listing and the listing "All Other Astrological Bodies," the verses contain either a different root word for "Sun," as indicated above, or for "Moon," as indicated below. The other numbers indicated which specific heavenly bodies are used in the same verse, in combination.

(5) *LBNH* root meaning "white," used for Moon.
(6) Sun, Moon
(7) Sun, Moon, Stars, Hosts of Heaven
(8) Sun, Moon, Stars, Constellations
(9) Sun, Moon, Hosts of Heaven, Constellations
(10) Sun, Moon, Hosts of Heaven
(11) Sun, Moon and Stars
(12) Sun and Stars
(13) Sun and Lights
(14) Sun and Venus

ALL OTHER ASTROLOGICAL BODIES

AS WITNESS TO GOD'S DEEDS/GLORY			ASTROLOGICAL INDICATIONS		
Numbers	24:17	(19)	Genesis	1:14	(18)
Amos	4:13	(21)		1:15	(18)
	5:8	(23)		1:16	(16)
Psalms	8:4	(15)	Judges	5:20	(19)
	72:7	(17)	Isaiah	14:12	(21)
Proverbs	4:18	(21)		14:13	(19)
Job	3:9	(19)		47:13	(19)
	9:9	(22)	Amos	5:26	(19)
	25:5	(15)			
	37:9	(25)		AS PHYSICAL	
	38:31	(23)		ENTITIES ONLY	
	38:32	(24)			
Daniel	12:3	(19)	Job	22:12	(19)
				37:9	(25)
			Obadiah	1:4	(19)

(15)	Moon and Stars	(21)	Venus Only	
(16)	Stars and Lights	(22)	Ursus, Orion, Peliades, Chambers of the North	
(17	Moon Only	(23)	Pleiades, Orion	
(18)	Lights Only	(24)	Ursus, Hyades	
(19)	Stars Only	(25)	Chambers Only	

NOTE: The "Chambers of the North" (Hebrew *XDRY TYMNf*) refer to the three winter zodiacal constellations: Capricorn, Aquarius, Pisces.

Appendix 5

Use of Words and Concepts
in Part III

THE HOSTS OF HEAVEN

The Hebrew word *SBA*, commonly translated as "hosts," is one of the more fascinating words in the Scripture. It is used to mean an army ready to do battle for the king. The host was always available to enforce the will of the king.

In all biblical use, the word "hosts" is always identified as to the nationality or the control of the hosts, i.e., "The hosts of Israel," "The hosts of Edom," "the hosts of the king," etc. In a very few instances, almost all of them in the Book of Exodus, the word "hosts" means divisions; i.e. "... the tribes of Israel according to their hosts ...," "He led them out of Egypt according to their hosts ...," etc. Once, in the Book of Daniel, the word is used to mean "powerful," as an adjective, a derivation which is easily understood.

In 26 places in the Bible, the word "hosts" is used to mean the heavenly bodies in general and in toto. The word is either linked directly to the Heavens linguistically, the Heavens being the identifying group as nations were identifying groups above, or the word "hosts" is found in verses whose context leaves no doubt that the hosts of Heaven are indicated. An example of the former would be:

> ... I saw the Lord sitting on His throne, and all the hosts of Heaven *(SBA HSMYMf)* standing by Him on His right hand and on His left.
>
> [II Kings 22:19]

An example of the latter would be:

> And the Heavens and the Earth were finished, and all their hosts *(SBAMf)*. ...
>
> [Genesis 2:1]

240

HOSTS AS GOD'S WITNESS

I Kings	22:19 (1)
Isaiah	24:21
	34:4
Psalms	103:21
	148:2
Daniel	4:32
II Chronicles	18:18 (1)

HOSTS SUBJECT TO GOD'S WILL		IDOLATROUS USAGE		
Genesis	2:1	Deuteronomy	4:19	
Jeremiah	33:22		17:3	
Nehemiah	9:6	II Kings	17:16	
Daniel	8:10		21:3	(2)
	8:11		21:5	(3)
	8:12		23:4	
	8:13		23:5	
		Jeremiah	8:2	
			19:13	
		Zephaniah	1:5	
		II Chronicles	33:3	(2)
			33:5	(3)

NOTE: (1)-(1); (2)-(2); (3)-(3): These three pairs of verses tell the identical story of a series of events, first reported in Kings, then repeated in Chronicles.

APPEARANCE OF SLMWT ("SHADOW OF DEATH") IN THE BIBLE

Isaiah	9:1		Job	3:5
Jeremiah	2:8			10:21
	13:16			10:22
Amos	5:8	(1)		12:22
Psalms	23:4	(2)		16:16
	44:20			24:17
	107:10			28:3
	107:14			34:22
				38:17

(1) Here astrologically linked to other named constellation Orion and Pleiades.

(2) This is the only use of the term as a place-name.

USE OF QDR IN THE BIBLE

DARKENING OF HEAVENS PARAPHYSICAL CONDITION		DARKENING OF HEAVENS AS SYMBOL OF MOURNING	
Isaiah	50:3	Jeremiah	14:2
Jeremiah	4:28	Malachi	3:14
Ezekiel	31:15	Psalms	35:14
	32:7		38:7
	32:8		42:10
Joel	2:10		43:2
	4:15	Job	5:11
Michah	3:6		

DARKENING OF THE HEAVENS AS SYMBOL OF BEING APPALLED		DARKENING OF THE HEAVENS AS A NATURAL OCCURRENCE	
Jeremiah	8:21	I Kings	18:45
		Job	6:16

"THE DAY OF THE LORD"

It would be almost impossible to list for the purposes of this book all the passages which refer to this "day." For example, almost the entire Book of Joel deals with the "Day of the Lord." However, the prophets involved in the exposition of this concept are:

Isaiah	Obadiah
Jeremiah*	Micah*
Ezekiel	Zephaniah
Joel	Zechariah
Amos	Malachi

*These two prophets symbolize the "Day of the Lord" astrologically, but do not use the name specifically.

YHWH SBAWT "LORD OF HOSTS"

This is one of the most used phrases in the Bible, and its meaning is made very clear. It means *YHVH*, the commander of the armies of Heaven, which are composed of the various mythical beings conceived of at that time, and also the Sun, Moon, Stars, Planets, and Constellations, and Luminaries, all of which have been linked to the hosts of Heaven linguistically and contextually throughout the Bible. As any good army obeys its commander, so do the hosts of Heaven obey *YHVH*.

242

This term is used 276 times, in 274 verses in the Bible! Two facts about its use are most interesting:

1. The term *YHWH SBAWT* is *never* found in the Bible prior to I Samuel in its meaning as Lord of the Hosts of Heaven.
2. The term *YHWH SBAWT* is *never* found in the Bible after I Samuel in any other meaning!

NOTE: The term is found only *once* prior to I Samuel—in Exodus 12:41, but the words are reversed, and the meaning is made obvious that we are dealing with human beings:

...YSAW KL-SBAWT YHWH MARSf MSRYMf.
...all the hosts of *YHVH* left the land of Egypt.

Note the difference vocalization of the root *SiBAWT*, not *SBaAWT*.

BIBLICAL VERSES IN WHICH YHWH SBAWT OCCURS

I Samuel	1:3	Jeremiah	46:10
	1:11		46:18
	4:4		46:25
	15:2		48:1
	17:45		48:15
II Samuel	5:10		49:5
	6:2		49:7
	6:18		49:26
	7:8		49:35
	7:26		50:18
	7:27		50:25
I Kings	18:15		50:31
	19:10		50:33
	19:14		50:34
II Kings	3:14		51:5
	19:31		51:14
Isaiah	1:9		51:19
	1:24		51:33
	2:12		51:57
	3:1		51:58
	3:15	Hosea	12:6
	5:7	Amos	3:13

	31:4		6:12
	31:5		6:15
	37:16		7:3
	37:22		7:4
	39:5		7:9
	44:6		7:12*
	45:13		7:13
	47:4		8:1
	48:2		8:2
	51:15		8:3
	55:5		8:4
Jeremiah	2:19		8:6
	5:14		8:7
	6:6		8:9
	6:9		8:11
	7:3		8:14
	7:21		8:18
	8:3		8:19
	9:6		8:20
	9:14		8:21
	9:16		8:22
	10:16		8:23
	11:17		9:15
	11:20	Zachariah	10:3
	11:22		12:5
	15:16		13:2
	16:9		13:7
	19:3		14:6
	19:11		14:17
	19:15		14:21*
	20:12	Malachi	1:4
	23:15		1:6
	23:16		1:8
	23:36		1:9
	25:8		1:10
	25:27		1:11
	25:28		1:13
	25:29		1:14
	25:32		2:2
	26:18		2:4
	27:4		2:7

*Quote appears twice in each verse.

APPENDIX 6:

THE ALPHABET
OF RABBI AKIBA

The Alphabet of Rabbi Akiba is a text which equates each letter of the Hebrew alphabet to a moral or ethical precept. Thus, the Hebrew letter *S* (pronounced *TSADI*) is the first letter of the Hebrew word *ŠDQ*, meaning "righteousness."

The Prologue to the *Zohar* introduces the Alphabet of Rabbi Akiba in a new and exciting form to explain why the Bible begins with the second Hebrew letter, the *Bet*, and not the first Hebrew letter, the *Alef*, and why the first two letters are *Bet* and the letters beginning the third and fourth words in the Bible are the *Alef*.

In Jewish mysticism the Bible was considered to be the blueprint of Creation, therefore the first letter in the Bible was thought of as being that letter with which the process of creation was initiated. All the letters of the alphabet were considered to be the tools and the molds with which God created the Universe. Thus, the letters were extremely important; they were thought of as having individualities of their own and as being able to enter into discussion with God. Therefore, my quotation from the Prologue to the *Zohar* speaks of the letters coming before God, each one to argue its merits, in order to begin the Bible and therefore the process of Creation. The following quotation will include the first four verses of the Zohar's third commentary on the first word of the Bible, *BRASYT*, the comment of Rab Hamnuna the Venerable: it will then skip to the consideration of the letter *Sadi*, and conclude with the last three verses, explaining

247

the first two words as beginning with *Bet* and the next two as beginning with *Alef.*

> *In the beginning....* Rab Hamnuna the Venerable said: "We find here a reversal of the order of the letters of the alphabet, the first two words *(BRŜYṪ BRA—In the beginning He created....)* commencing with *Bet,* whereas the two words following *(ALHYMſ AT,* "God the...") commence with the *Alef.* The reason is as follows. When the Holy One, Blessed Be He, was about to make the world, all the letters of the alphabet were still embryonic and for 2000 years the Holy One, Blessed Be He contemplated them and toyed with them. When He came to create the world, all the letters presented themselves to Him in reverse order...."

> ...Enters the Sadi and says: Lord of the Universe, may it please Thee to create with me the world, inasmuch as I am the sign of the righteous *(SDQYMſ)* and of Thyself who art called "righteous" as it is written: *For the Lord is righteous, He loveth righteousness* (Ps. 11:7), and hence it is meet to create the world with me. The Lord made answer: "O Sadi, thou art Sadi and thou signifiest righteousness but thou must be concealed, thou mayest not come out in the open so much lest thou give the world cause for offense. For thou consisteth of the letter *Nun* surmounted by the letter *Yod* (representing together the male and female principles). And this is the mystery of the creation of the first man who was created with two faces (male and female combined)." In the same way the *Nun* and the *Yod* in the *Sadi* are turned back-to-back and not face-to-face, whether the *Sadi* is upright or turned downwards. The Holy One, Blessed Be He, said to her further: "I will in time divide thee in two, so as to appear face to face, but thou wilt go up in another place. She then departed...."

> ...Then the Holy One, Blessed Be His Name, made higher world letters of a large pattern and lower world letters of a small pattern. It is therefore that we have here two words beginning with *Bet (BRAŜYṪ BRA)* and two words beginning with *Alef (ELHYMſ AT).* They represent the higher world letters and the lower world letters which two operate, above and below, together as one.

In the first paragraph of the quotation above the reason that the *Bet* appears before the *Alef:* the letters appear before God in reverse order and the *Bet* is chosen before the *Alef* gets its chance to appear. Each letter goes through the same process as did the Sadi in the quotation above, enumerating its virtues in order to be chosen the first letter of the Bible—the "Beginning of Creation." God systematically rejects all letters as he does the Sadi, by finding an intrinsic reason that the letter is unfit.

The interesting factor in God's rejection of the Sadi is that the rejection is based on the shape of the letter. God insists that this is true whether we are dealing with the lowercase letter or the uppercase (final) form. Let us examine these shapes:

Lowercase Ṣadi: **צ** breaks down to lowercase *Nun* **נ** and *Yod.* **י**

Uppercase Ṣadi: **ץ** breaks down to upper case *Nun* **ן** and *Yod.* **י**

Note that the "heads" of the letters (the tittles on their tops) face away from each other; the text refers to the letters as being "back-to-back." The Nun refers to the female principle (*NQBH*) and the *Yod* refers to the male principle, being shaped like the male organ in repose. Thus, the text speaks of the first man being created androgynous, both male and female in one body! But this man is destined to be divided into two persons, male and female, and sexuality will be created. This is the meaning of the text "...but thou wilt go up in another place." It means that the Ṣadi will have its fulfillment in the Creation through the process of creating. The whole argument including the androgynous creation of man and of man's subsequent division into male and female sexes is based on the interpretation of the biblical creation story, specifically in Genesis 1:27 and Genesis 2:21-22. The first Creation is considered by the commentators as being an androgynous creation, and the second as being the separation of the sexes (Ṣadi becoming *Nun* and *Yod* face-to-face).

In the Kabbalah, especially in its expansion of the mystery of the Tree of Life, the left-hand column of the Tree *(BYNH, GBWRH, HWD)* is considered to be the seat of power, and feminine: the right-hand column *(XKMH, XSD, NSX)* is considered to be the seat of mercy, and masculine: the middle column *(QṬR, ṬPARṬ, YSWD, MLKWṬ)* is considered to be the resultant Divine balance of the two

APPENDIX 7:

ASTROLOGY AND KABBALAH

WHAT IS MYSTICISM?

Our present attitudes toward mysticism are an amalgam of misunderstanding, lack of knowledge, fear of the unknown; there is the sudden and recent exposure to the mysteries of the Far East and a plethora of gurus, as well as images of the Maharishi Mahesh Yogi, American youths transmuted into shaved-headed, yellow-robed, begging quasi-Buddhist monks at airports, and the followers of Sun Myung Moon being married, hundreds at a time, in Madison Square Garden. We also assign to followers of mysticism the most absurd claims of those who deal with the paranormal, and lump all these together with UFO sightings and people who claim to have been abducted by space aliens. And we deal with out ignorance and fear and confusions the same way we have always dealt with the Other: we either destroy them, enslave them—or make jokes about them.

We need a good definition of mysticism. What is it? Etymologically the word is taken from the Greek *mystes,* which means "one initiated into the mysteries." Its origin is in a linguistic description of the reality of the day: to become an intitiate into a mystery religion! I believe that an understanding of mystery religions of ancient times can put us on the right track to understanding mysticism today.

Religion has its beginnings in the curiosity and fears of our most ancient ancestors as they attempted to understand the physical universe

251

around them: Rain, storms, wind, sunlight; the moon and stars; plants and animals and food; fertility, birth, life, death. These questions still occupy our thoughts in modern times. The answers to questions involving the forces of the physical universe seem to be found in the sciences—but our control of these forces takes the form of physical protections from their ravages; we still cannot control the forces themselves! And all too often our protections prove themselves to be ephemeral. We still do not have the answers to fertility, birth, life, death. These are mostly still mysterious processes to us, whose blessings and ravages we try to multiply or mitigate through modern medicine—and ancient faith.

At the heart of every religion there lies a mystery; and each religion has its own, unique mystery. It is through the contemplation of this mystery that the mystic attains his or her goal. When we define the goal of the mystic, we shall have defined the phenomenon we call mysticism.

Moshe Idel, one of Judaism's finest modern scholars of mysticism, defines the term as "the search for an experience of direct contact with God." The Oxford Dictionary defines mysticism as "a belief in the possibility of union with the divine nature by means of ecstatic comtemplation; reliance upon spiritual intuition as a means of acquiring knowledge of mysteries inaccessible to the understanding." R. C. Zaehner, in an article in the encyclopedia *Man, Myth and Magic,* defines it as "a direct apperception of eternal being."

Medieval Christianity defined two branches of theology: mystical theology and speculative theology. Speculative theology dealt with God as Supreme Being, as Supreme Goodness, and with the relationship of God and human being. Mystical theology dealt with God as Supreme Lover, supremely lovable, with God alone. These are the words of the seventeenth-century French saint, Frances de Sales: "What is our topic of conversation in prayer? God. None else. After all, what does a lover talk about but his beloved?" In medieval times prayer and mystical theology were identical.

If you believe in God, then you are a mystic! But you believe in a being—if you posit God as a divine being—whose existence is nevertheless still the subject of scholarly speculation, still debated according to the four antinomies of philosophy. The word *antinomy* means "contrary to law," and the four antinomies are four philosophical problems that can never be truthfully resolved. For there are only two ways through which a person may acquire certainty of knowledge. One is empirically—by means of the senses. If we can experience a phenomenon by means of light or sound, touch, taste, or smell, we can be certain that the phenomenon truly exists. The second is logically. If the phenomenon can be delineated logically so that the conclusion about its existence leads to a definitive response—yes, it exists, or no, it cannot possibly exist—then we can be certain of our statement about the existence of that phenomenon.

But the four philosophical antinomies can never be experienced empirically. And the consequences of logical study lead us to the proposition that each can be logically proven to exist—and also not to exist! Three of these propositions deal with religion, one—oddly enough—deals with physics. Let me state the three religious antinomies as positive propositions.

1. There is a God.

2. The Universe was created.

3. Man has free will.

It is easy to see that none of these statements can be empirically verified. And each of these statements can be proven equally well as a logical positive or a logical negative. Any choice one makes must be made on faith alone.

Incidentally, the fourth antinomy—dealing with physics—is: Matter is infinitely divisible. Particle physics and wave theory are trying to decide this issue empirically.

Each religion takes a stand—either positively or negatively—on each of these three antinomies. Judaism and Christianity stand on all three positives: there is a God; the universe was created; man has free will. Islam stands on two positives and one negative: there is a God; the Universe was created; but man has no free will—all is ordained *(kismet)*. Buddhism stands on two negatives and one positive: There is no God; the universe eternally existed and was not created; but man has free will *(nirvana, karma,* and *thalami)*.

The problem with our former battle with communism was that it was not recognized as a religion. But it was a religion because it took a stand on the antinomies. All were negative: There is no God; there was no creation; man is determined by external, economic forces.

Each religion has its own mystery. And each religion's mystics—in their approach to reaching a state of identity with the divine—meditates upon the mystery proper to that religion.

The mystery in Christianity is the Resurrection. The Christian mystic tries to attune the self with the moment of resurrection, the moment that the universe is recreated, that life begins anew, that the Christian mystic is "born again." In Christianity, mysticism is for the individual who practices the discipline. It is personal to the mystic. There is no communal motive involved—for the mystical experience cannot be defined, verbalized, demonstrated: it must be experienced.

The mystery in Islam is *kismet*, fate, the lack of free will. As the Islamic mystic contemplates this mystery, he seeks union with the God who controls all being. At that moment of unity, he knows the reason for and purpose of his life—and becomes God-like.

The mystery in Buddhism is *nirvana*, the desire to escape the wheel of *karma* and *dharma*, to cease the endless series of death, metempsychosis and rebirth, and merge with the endless Being of the universe.

The mystery in Judaism is Creation. How did God create the universe? Here the search for identity with the Divine Essence may be individual and personal, but the search is for a solution to the eternal communal conundrum. When and how will all living beings become one with the Divine Essence? When will the Messiah come? How can my community best survive life until redeemed?

Finally, today we find a type of mysticism that is not related to any theological mysteries whatsoever. It could be called nature mysticism, a search for cosmic consciousness, a perception of the whole of reality in the loss of individual identity. As Zaehner quotes Alfred Lord Tennyson:

> All at once, as it were, out of the consciousness of individuality, individuality itself seemed to dissolve and fade away into boundless being, and this is not a confused state, but the clearest, the surest of the sure, utterly beyond words—where death was an almost laughable impossibility—the loss of personality (if so it were) seeming no extinction, but the only true life.

WHAT IS KABBALAH?

Our mystical journey now takes us to the Kabbalah. the word *kabbalah* means "that which is received." The term is taken from an understanding of the theophany at Sinai, when Moses ascended the mount to receive the Decalogue directly from God. The term used in this direct reception from God is *KIBEL*, "he received." Jewish tradition states that Moses not only received the Ten Commandments; he received all knowledge, both that which is universally revealed and the hidden esoteric knowledge as well. The Talmud begins with a "genealogy" of the transmission of this knowledge: *MOSHE KIBEL TORAH MI SINAI*, "Moses received the Torah (all knowledge) at Sinai," and passed it on to Joshua, who transmitted it to the Elders, who passed it on to the Judges, who transmitted it to the Prophets, who passed it on to the Men of the Great Assembly. The Men of the Great Assembly were the rabbis who returned from Babylonian exile in 517 B.C.E., and who were the founders of the Sanhedrin. The word used for transmitting the tradition, however, was not *KIBEL*, "to receive," but *MASAR*, "to instruct." Now, for the first time, we have implied that the esoteric knowledge needed to attain the mystery involved can be taught to others by an inititate, an adept in the mystery. In Kabbalah, the mystery is creation, and in the developmental history of the investigation of this mystery, we see the investigation take two directions, the transcendent and the immanent.

In Kabbalah, the attack upon the mystery is addressed through Scripture. Since Scripture was considered to be the true word of God, the answers to all of life's processes and problems were initially sought for in the text of the Bible. The same is true in the search for the mystery. There were two sections of Scripture that were used as the starting point for the search: one was the chapter dealing with Creation itself (Genesis 1). The other source was the vision Ezekiel had of God Himself, seated upon His throne in his chariot, surrounded by His ministering angels (Ezekiel 1).

The Ezekiel vision is one of transcendence: God is visible, but not available. Surrounded by His minions, God is too well protected to be approached by any person. One could only hope to be able to place one's self in the vicinity of God and bask in the reflected glory of the deity. There was no hope of speaking to God, or of even having God acknowledge one's presence; one could only rejoice in the proximity. This concept of God's transcendence led to the development among the mystics of what has come to be known as the *heykhalot* literature. The word *heykhal* means "divine dwelling," the Holy Temple. These mystics saw the palace of God made up of many chambers—as many chambers as there were Sefirot, or divine emanations of Creation. They saw the twenty-two paths among these Sefirot as being guarded by angels, and saw the need to devise passwords and incantations so that their souls could proceed upon the paths in safety, until they reached the Divine Presence. Then, through the return trip, also in safety, the soul would be reunited with the body, and the mystic would have achieved the ultimate experience. The whole process was one of meditation proceeding to disassociation, then to reintegration. It was basically a selfish process, having nothing to do with the community or the needs of anyone else. It was the ultimate self-fulfillment—but it was not directed toward unity with God! God would afford the adept no recognition whatsoever.

The contemplation of the mystery of Creation was to merge with an immanent God. The mystical thinkers of creation mysticism focused upon the biblical fact that man and woman were created in the image of God, and were seen to be very good. Thus the concept of the indwelling God became the key to the search for unity. For do not the Psalms (8: 5–7) say, "What is man that You consider him, or man's offspring that You should recognize him? Yet you have created him but little less than God and crowned him with glory and honor! You have given him authority over the works of Your hands, You have spread all beneath his feet." It was but a step in the thinking of the mystic to believe that God was immanent, available—that indeed God sought the unity as well. God was seen as an indwelling reality—not the *imitatio dei*, the imitation of divinity in Christianity, and not the *ayatollah*, the shadow of Allah, in Islam—but the actual presence of God within each human being. Thus, the nature of the union with God did not partake of a tremendous journey outside the self into realms protected by angels and demons, but rather a search within, where God not only was present, but a Presence willing to meet one halfway. This concept of the indwelling divinity and the authority of humanity become crucial elements in the development of three outgrowths of kabbalistic philosophy: Alchemy, Magic, and Western concepts of Astrology. We shall leave the fascination of Alchemy and Magic for another time. We shall concern ourselves with Astrology as it manifests itself in one particular work of Kabbalah—the Sefer Yetzirah, or Book of Formation.

THE CREATIVE PROCESS

Having discussed the origin of the term Kabbalah and the biblical foundations of its two branches—the transcendent *heykhalot* or palace mysticism in Ezekiel's vision of the divine chariot and the immanent creation mysticism in the first chapter of Genesis, we must now delve a little more deeply into the mystic's conception of God and of the creative process.

In Judaism the concept of God presents us with an eternal, omnipotent, omniscient, and omnipresent power. If God is eternally all-powerful, all-knowing, and everywhere-present, how can matter come into existence in a universe totally full of an all-powerful, total energy that is God? This problem was not solved until the rise of the brilliant and charismatic sixteenth-century teacher, Isaac Luria—and the Lurianic Kabbalah became the standard for all further thinking and speculation in Jewish circles. Furthermore, from that point on all Western mystical thought based itself on the fascinating mystical speculation of Isaac Luria, known in Judaism as ha-Ari, from the three initial letters of the title he was given: *HA-ELOHI RABBI YITZKHAK*, "the divine rabbi Isaac," the only person to be given the title "divine" from the beginning of our history to the present day. The problem was "solved" by the Ari's introduction of the concept of *tzimtzum*, shrinking, or withdrawal.

At the time, the concept of the ten Sefirot and the twenty-two paths among them was well known. These Sefirot were divided into three groups of three each, with each superior group shedding its influence upon the next group below, with the tenth Sefirah, Malkhut, receiving the final influence of all nine. The first three Sefirot, Keter (Crown), Chokhmah (Wisdom), and Binah (Understanding), made up the Olam ha-Beriah, the World of Creating. The second three Sefirot, Chesed (Mercy), Gevurah (Power), and Tiferet (Beauty), made up the Olam ha-Yetzirah, the World of Formation. The third three Sefirot, Netzach (Victory), Hod (Glory), and Yesod (Foundation), made up the Olam ha-Ta'asiyyah, the World of Fabrication. The last of the ten Sefirot, Malkhut (Kingdom), was the final recipient of all the transformed divine powers that were used in this final form to create the universe.

To this system the Ari added another world, Olam ha-Atzilut, the World of Emanation, which was placed philosophically above the first of the *sefirotic* worlds, and which solved the problem of God's universal power and presence. The Ari posited that Creation was a direct result of the Divine Will, and that God knew that no universe could exist in the presence of timeless infinite power. And so God deliberately removed Himself from the space-time continuum, withdrawing Himself into a mathematical point of infinite power. This first level was known as the Ain, the nothingness. But in order to have matter come into existence in a totally empty universe, God had to get back in, as it were, and create matter from His own infinite power. And so the second stage of the World of Emanation was known as the Ain Sof, the infinite, without end. If one thinks about infinity mathematically, there is no difference between negative infinity—the Ain—and positive infinity, the Ain Sof. The third stage of the World of Atzilut was to prepare divine energy to reenter the universe in a form that was not destructive, but creative. This stage of the World of Atzilut was called Ain Sof Or, the infinite, unending light. This light is what is referred to in the creation story as "Let there be light." Physical light was not created until the fourth day (Genesis 1: 14–19). This light—specially prepared for its creative duties by a God who would invest the universe with His presence—is now emanated through the Sefirot to accomplish the process of Creation. For the word *sefirah* does not mean sphere. The Hebrew word for sphere is *galgal*. The word *sefirah* is the feminine form of the word *sapir*, from which we get the English word *sapphire*. The Sefirot were not circles of influence; they were conceived of as jewelled lenses through which God could modify His own essence and use it in the process of Creation so that matter could exist, could be organized, could gain intelligence, and finally, could become ensouled—the soul being the actual essence of God within. Also, one must not conceive of the Sefirot as physical entities that existed in a universe already created; they are only contemplative constructs of human mystical minds attempting to conceive of a process proceeding in the Divine Mind! And even to speak of a "Divine Mind" implies an anthropomorphism that can only be a tool of human contemplation. As the Talmud says, human beings cannot speak of God in any other than human language—we do not know "God-speak." Therefore, it is necessary to understand that the entire concept of Sefirot and emanation is the attempt of brilliant mystical minds to speak of an indescribable process of Divine Creation.

The Sefirot and the paths among them are traditionally pictured in the form of three triads distributed across three columns, with the tenth Sefirah at the bottom of the design, directly below the central column (fig. A.1). The more familiar version is known as the Tree of Life, with its twenty-two paths among the Sefirot invested with astrological influences (fig. A.2). At the time of its development, there were twelve zodiacal constellations and seven planets, for a total of nineteen "powers." Since the process was one of creation, Fire, Air, and Water completed the twenty-two influences; Earth was the end result of the *sefirotic* creation process.

The Tree of Life is often superimposed upon the figure of a man standing with legs akimbo and arms outspread. This is the form of Adam Kadmon, primal Man, who is identified in Jewish mysticism with Enoch, who did not die a natural death: "And Enoch walked with God, and he was not; for God took him" (Genesis 5: 24). In Jewish mystical writings Adam Kadmon/Enoch becomes Metatron, the leader of the Heavenly Host.

This lays the foundation for understanding how Astrology becomes involved in the life of the universe and of humanity. For the concept of ensoulment involves the emanation of the Divine Essence into all living things. And since the Divine Essence must come through the *sefirotic* process, all living things upon conception are invested with the astrological influences inherent in the Sefirot and the paths. This transference comes to us through the ten Sefirot and the twenty-two paths, which together are known as the thirty-two Paths of Wisdom. We are thus—through astrological influence—linked to the first Sefirah, Chokhmah (Wisdom), and God's Wisdom becomes available to us because God's Essence has been emanated into us! The horoscope then becomes the means through which we understand the Divine Plan for our lives.

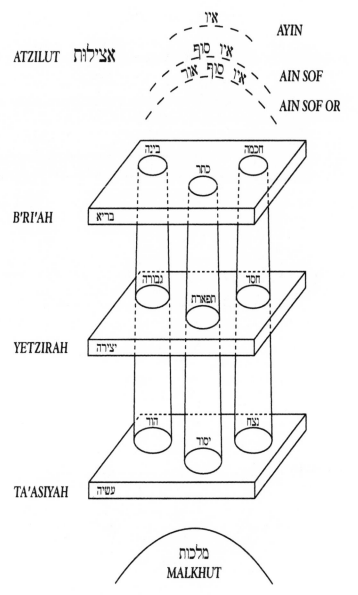

ATZILUT אצילות

איז AYIN
אין סוף AIN SOF
אין סוף אור AIN SOF OR

B'RI'AH בריא
בינה חכמה
כתר

YETZIRAH יצירה
גבורה חסד
תפארת

TA'ASIYAH עשיה
הוד נצח
יסוד

מלכות
MALKHUT

Figure A.1

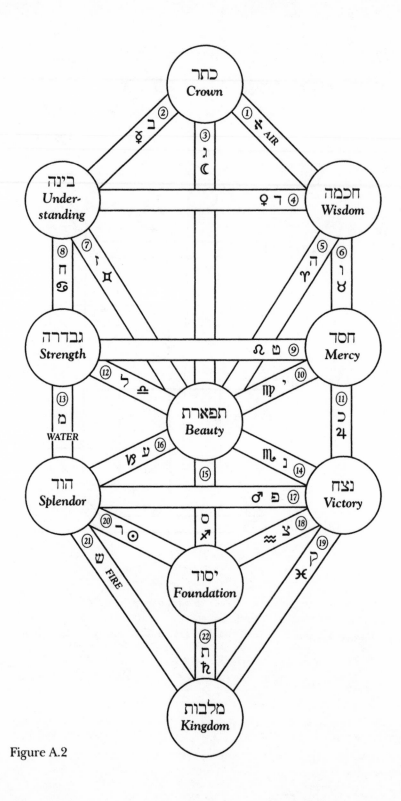

Figure A.2

But . . . how did God create the universe?

HOW DID GOD CREATE?

Having established the philosophy behind the creative process, the question remains, how did God create the universe? It is surprising that the answer to such a profound question is simple and easily available—in Scripture! If we analyze the first chapter of Genesis, we have the answer to the question standing before us.

And God *said,* "Let there be light!" (Gen. 1: 3)

And God *said,* "Let there be a firmament. . . ." (1: 6)

And God *said,* "Let the waters under the heaven be gathered to gether. . . ." (1: 9)

And God *said,* "Let the earth put forth grass. . . ." (1: 11)

And God *said,* "Let there be lights in the firmament of the heaven. . . ." (1: 14)

And God *said,* "Let the waters swarm with swarms of living creatures. . . ." (1: 20)

And God *said,* "Let the earth bring forth the living creature after its kind. . . ." (1: 24)

And God *said,* "Let us make man in our image. . . ." (1: 26)

God created the universe through saying: the act of Creation was an act of divine communication! As Jewish tradition states: *HU AMAR V'YEHEE—HU TSEEVAH V'YA'AMOD!,* "He spoke and it came into existence—he commanded and it was established!" Thus, language was the mechanism through which the creative process manifested itself. And—although God spoke in "God-language," which no human can fathom—the mystics created a link between the Hebrew language, the original language of Scripture through which God makes His will manifest, and the paths linking the Sefirot. The twenty-two paths represent twenty-two astrological influences, and there are twenty-two letters in the Hebrew alphabet. Thus, each letter of the alphabet represents one astrological influence and one path in the Tree of Life. The Sefer Yetzirah, the Book of Formation, refers to the Olam ha-Yetzirah, the

World of Formation of the Tree of Life, and builds upon this one-to-one relationship of letter to path, planet, constellation, and element (Fire, Air, and Water) to develop a system for creation.

Sefer Yetzirah begins with the following words:

> By thirty-two mystical paths of Wisdom did Yah, the Lord of Hosts, God of Israel, Living God, King of the Universe, El Shaddai, the Merciful and the Gracious, High and Exalted Who dwells in Eternity and Whose Name is Holy and who is Lofty and Holy, create His Universe: with three means of communication [Hebrew: *sefarim*, literally, "books"]: with letters, numbers and words.

> Ten Sefirot of Nothingness and twenty-two Foundation Letters: Three Mother [letters], seven Double [letters], and twelve Simple [letters].

The ten Sefirot of Nothingness might better be translated as ten infinite Sefirot—since they exist only in the mind of God. Since they represent the ten cardinal integers (0 through 9), there is a profound implication that mathematics is an infinite and divine science! The twenty-two letters are divided into their groups by sound. Since all direct communication between people involves sound, the different vibrations involved in the production of sound were considered to be creative forces. Letters, numbers, and words were considered to be the "power tools" with which God created the universe.

The three Mother Letters were considered to be the representatives of pure sound vibrations from which all other sounds derived. These were the Hebrew letters *MEM* (M, the perfect labial, OMMM), *SHIN* (the perfect sibilant, SHHH), and *ALEPH* (silence). All other sounds were thought of as being created from different combinations and permutations of these three pure sound vibrations.

The seven Double Letters are letters of the Hebrew alphabet that had two different pronunciations, depending on their grammatical positions in the sentence. They are *BET* (B) or *VET* (V), *GIMEL* (G) or *GHIMEL* (G guttural); *DALED* (D) or *THALED* (TH); *KAF* (K) or *KHAF* (KH guttural); *PEY* (P) or *FEY* (F); *RESH* (R) or *RRESH* (trilled R); *TAF* (T) or *SAF* (S).

The twelve Simple Letters never change their sounds. They are *HEY* (H); *VAV* (V); *ZAYIN* (Z); *KHET* (KH guttural); *TET* (T); *YOD* (Y); *LAMED* (L); *NUN* (N); *SAMEKH* (S); *AIN* (very light guttural, almost silent); *TSADI* (TS); *KUF* (K).

Plato's concept of the *Idea* is a useful analogue for understanding how the letters "work." Plato conceived of the *Idea* as being the perfect

Form, existing in the heavens alone, and of which all matter on earth is but a pale copy. Thus, there is the perfect tree, upon which all material trees are modeled; the perfect man and the perfect woman, of which we are but poor copies, and so on. The concept in Sefer Yetzirah is similar; however, the universe and humanity are not seen as poor copies of already existent perfect forms. Through the process of emanation, the Essence of God is poured into the physicality of the universe, through the process called time and the human being—and there is the promise of attaining perfection on Earth.

Using the image of letters as "power tools" of the Divine Will we find that to each letter is attached a perfect action or attribute in the Divine Mind. In the process of emanation, that action or attribute is passed into the universe, time, and humanity.

The three Mother Letters represent, in the Divine Mind, the perfection of merit *(MEM)* the perfection of guilt *(SHIN)* and the perfect balance *(ALEPH)* between them. Why have a perfect guilt in the Divine Mind? Could not God have created the universe without guilt, without the evil for which to feel guilt?

The origin of evil and guilt is a theological question that cannot be answered here. We can, however, investigate some of the different answers to the problem of good and evil that have been put forth. Zoroastrianism, for example, posited two gods—Ahura Mazda, god of good, and Ahriman, god of evil. These two gods were equal in eternity and in power, and either or both could be worshiped at the same or different times! Christianity posits a Devil as the source of evil, equally— it seems—as powerful as God in this world, with the struggle between their forces to be decided at a final Armageddon at the end of time. Judaism posits only one God—who must be responsible for all things in the universe of his creation—including the existence of evil. Or, as reported by the prophet Isaiah (45: 6–7), ". . . I am the Lord; and there is none else; I form the light, and create darkness. I make peace, and create evil; I am the Lord that doeth all these things." This is a difficult position to defend; but if there is one God, omnipotnet, omniscient, and omnipresent, there cannot be another God in this universe!

These perfections in the Divine Mind emanate to create the universe: *MEM* creates Earth, *SHIN* creates the Heavens, and *ALEPH* creates the atmosphere, the balance between the Heavens and Earth.

They also emanate to create time: *MEM* creates the cold season, *SHIN* creates the hot season, and *ALEPH* creates the temperate seasons, the balance between hot and cold, the regions between the Poles and the Equator, so to speak.

They also emanate to create the human being: *MEM* creates the gonads (the reproductive system), *SHIN* creates the head, and *ALEPH* creates the torso, the balance between them. These correspondences are presented in table A.1. Note that the gonads are emanated from perfect merit *(MEM)* and the head from perfect guilt *(SHIN)*. We may derive from this that human sexual problems originate, not in the reproductive organs, but rather in the brain. We get into trouble because of how we think, and communicate, sexually.

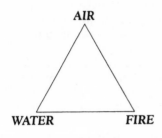

Table A.1: THREE "MOTHER" LETTERS

	M מ	A א	SH ש
DIVINE WILL	MERIT	BALANCE	GUILT
UNIVERSE	EARTH	ATMOSPHERE	HEAVENS
TIME	COLD	TEMPERATE	HOT
MAN	GONADS	TORSO	HEAD

Both the Heavens and the Earth were emanated using the Mother Letters as divine power tools. Now, the universe will be represented by both Heaven and Earth in the emanation process. Therefore, the divine actions and attributes will now be emanated into heaven, earth, time, and humanity through the seven Double Letters and the twelve Simple Letters.

The seven Double Letters represent perfection of opposites within the Divine Mind. Because they could be pronounced differently, they were seen to have "hard" and "soft" pronunciations, therefore representing "hard" and "soft" aspects of reality.

BET/VET represents the perfect dichotomy of wisdom and folly, emanating into the Heavens as the Sun, into Earth as height, into time as Sunday, and into humanity as the right eye.

GIMEL represents wealth/poverty, emanating as the Moon, depth, Monday, and the right ear.

DALED represents increase/devastation, emanating as Mars, east, Tuesday, and the right nostril.

KAF represents life/death, emanating as Mercury, west, Wednesday, and the left eye.

PEY represents ruler/slave, emanating as Jupiter, north, Thursday, and the left ear.

RESH represents peace/war, emanating as Venus, south, Friday, and the left nostril.

TAF represents beauty/ugliness, emanating as Saturn, the central holy palace, the Sabbath, and the mouth.

These may seem rather strange at first glance, but all planets known at that time were present, as were the known divisions of time. A closer study of the emanations to Earth will indicate that a perfect cube of space is described: east, west, north, south (the cardinal directions); above and below, the "ceiling" and "floor" of our contained space; and the center. The center is where we stand as human beings, standing with Saturn, whose Hebrew name is Shabtai, and which represents the seeker of mysteries. Is this not where we all stand? According to Kabbalah, each person is the center of a totally perceived universe and measures all distances, accomplishments, successes, and failures from that center, which is us. Likewise, the most important organs of human perception and communication are emanated here. We, too, perform an act of creation every time we are involved in an act of communication. And our creative, communicative acts can be either beneficial or detrimental to ourselves and to others. The mystics who developed this system showed deep insight into human life by emanating these from the Double Letters, yet linking all our efforts to the possibilities of Divine Perfection.

Table A.2: Seven Double Letters

	B ב	G ג	D ד	K כ	P פ	R ר	T ת
DIVINE WILL	WISDOM FOLLY	WEALTH POVERTY	INCREASE DEVASTATION	LIFE DEATH	RULER SLAVE	PEACE WAR	BEAUTY UGLINESS
HEAVEN UNIVERSE EARTH	☉ HEIGHT	☽ DEPTH	♂ EAST	☿ WEST	♃ NORTH	♀ SOUTH	♄ HOLY CENTER
TIME	SUNDAY	MONDAY	TUESDAY	WED.	THURS.	FRIDAY	SHABBAT
MAN	RIGHT EYE	LEFT EYE	RIGHT EAR	LEFT EAR	RIGHT NOSTRIL	LEFT NOSTRIL	MOUTH

The twelve Simple Letters represent unchanging attributes of the Divine Mind. The first five represent the processes of receiving input from the senses; the next three represent important functions in life; the next two involve the psyche; the final two involve input from non-sensory sources.

HEY represents sight and emanates as Aries, northeast, the Hebrew month of Nisan (coinciding with the zodiacal month), and the right hand.

VAV represents hearing and emanates as Taurus, southeast, the month of Iyyar, and the left hand.

ZAYIN represents smell and emanates as Gemini, above-east, the month of Sivan, and the right foot.

KHET represents speech and emanates as Cancer, below-east, the month of Tamuz, and the left foot.

TET represents eating (taste and touch) and emanates as Leo, above-north, the month of AB, and the right kidney.

YOD represents sexual intercourse and emanates as Virgo, below-north, the month of Elul, and the left kidney.

LAMED represents labor and emanates as Libra, northwest, the month of Tishre, and the liver.

NUN represents motion and emanates as Scorpio, southwest, the month of Kheshvan, and the spleen.

SAMEKH represents wrath and emanates as Sagittarius, above-west, the month of Kislev, and the gall bladder.

AIN represents mirth and emanates as Capricorn, below-west, the month of Tebet, and the stomach.

TSADI represents meditation and emanates as Aquarius, above-south, the month of Sh'vat, and the small intestine.

KUF represents sleep and emanates as Pisces, below-south, the month of Adar, and the colon.

It is interesting to note that all middle distances are emanated in the universe, so that directions may encompass the totality of universal space. Now, we have the space-time continuum within which humanity lives, loves, works, and creates, all with the possibility of contacting the God within and striving for the perfection that is thus implied.

There is much more to be found in Sefer Yetzirah that is not germane to a book on Astrology. There is Numerology, Mathematics, a guide to the creation of magical amulets, and much more. A very fine and detailed study of this text can be found in Aryeh Kaplan's *Sefer Yetzirah: The Book of Creation* (York Beach, Maine: Samuel Weiser, 1990).

Table A.3: Twelve Simple Letters

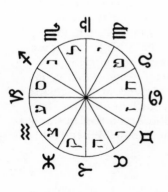

	ה H	ו V	ז Z	ח KH	ט T	י Y	ל L	נ N	ס S	ע '	צ TS	ק Q
DIVINE	SIGHT	HEARING	SMELL	SPEECH	EATING	SEXUALITY	LABOR	MOVEMENT	WRATH	MIRTH	MEDITATION	SLEEP
HEAVEN UNIVERSE EARTH	♈ NORTH EAST	♉ SOUTH EAST	♊ ABOVE EAST	♋ BELOW EAST	♌ ABOVE NORTH	♍ BELOW NORTH	♎ NORTH WEST	♏ SOUTH WEST	♐ ABOVE WEST	♑ BELOW WEST	♒ ABOVE SOUTH	♓ BELOW SOUTH
TIME	MAR 21 APR 19	APR 19 MAY 20	MAY 20 JUN 21	JUN 21 JUL 22	JUL 22 AUG 22	AUG 22 SEP 23	SEP 23 OCT 23	OCT 23 NOV 22	NOV 22 DEC 21	DEC 21 JAN 20	JAN 20 FEB 19	FEB 19 MAR 21
	NISAN	IYAR	SIVAN	TAMMUZ	AB	ELUL	TISHRE	KHESH	KISLEV VAN	TEVET	SHEVAT	ADAR
MAN	RIGHT HAND	LEFT HAND	RIGHT FOOT	LEFT FOOT	RIGHT KIDNEY	LEFT KIDNEY	LIVER	SPLEEN	GALL	STOMACH	SMALL BOWEL	COLON

INDEX

Aaron, 20, 119
Abraham, 7, 15, 32
  biography, astrology in, 151–53, 156–57, 187–88
  Father of the Hebrews, 151
  grandson of. *See* Jacob
  and practice of astrology, 143–44
  son of. *See* Isaac
Abraham ibn Ezra, Rabbi, 68, 217
Abram. *See* Abraham
Adam Kadmon, primal man, 169, 258
air signs, 29*t*, 55*t*, 110, 111, 167*t*. *See also* triplicities
Akiba, Rabbi, 188–89, 190, 191. *See also* The Alphabet of Rabbi Akiba
alphabet, Hebrew, 69
  Double Letters, 262, 265, 266*t*
  Mother Letters, 262–65, 264*t*
  Simple Letters, 262, 267, 268*t*
The Alphabet of Rabbi Akiba, 163, 247–49
Amos, Book of, 79*t*, 80*t*
aphelions, as variable forces, 59
Aquarians, attributes, 41, 66–67, 68, 110
Aquarius
  Age of Aquarius, 30–31, 32, 41, 168
  attributes, 29*t*, 46, 55*t*, 155, 167
  biblical references to, 202*t*
  Earth sign, 167*t*
  eleventh house, and Uranus, 135
  Fixed, mid-winter, 25, 110, 127
  linked to Delilah (DLY), 109
  and Naphtali, son of Jacob, 34*t*
  ruled by Saturn, 45, 127
Archangels, listed, 202*t*
the Ari, Isaac Luria, 256–57
Arians, attributes, 43, 62, 67
Aries
  Age of Aries, 30, 31–32, 34, 168
  attributes, 29*t*, 46, 55*t*
  and Benjamin, son of Jacob, 34*t*, 43
  biblical references to, 202*t*
  Cardinal, beginning of spring, 25, 167*t*
  Fire sign, 111, 167*t*
  ruled by Mars, 45
  symbolic representation, 110–11, 163
  zero⁰. *See* Vernal Equinox

See also constellations
Arrows of God, 171–84
Arsa D'Gadda, as Bed of Gad, 182–83, 220
Ascendant degree, 22–23, 48
the Ascendant (6:00 A.M.), 211–18
  basis for horoscope, 23–24, 48, 156
  for chart interpretation, 68, 215–16
  Cusp of first house, 24
  described, 22–23, 47–48
  favorable to righteous, 169
  orbital period, one year, 53
  rulership of, 203
  and variable planetary forces, 58
  and Vernal Equinox, 119
Ascendant twins, 212
Asher, son of Jacob, 34*t*, 40, 202*t*
Asher, tribe of, blessed by Moses, 40
aspects
  allowable distances (orbs) of, 53–54
  basis for horoscopes, 23
  for chart interpretation, 70
  described, 22, 50
  See also planet location
Assyria, 32
Astarte, Goddess, 115, 132
astrologers
  acceptance of, 189–90, 191
  biblical reference to, 114, 122
  compared to star gazers, 114–15
  Egyptian, 157–59
  "esoteric" school, 115, 157
  interpretive functions, 144–46
  "scientific" school, 115, 157
Astrology
  fatalistic, 190, 191, 198
  general principles of, 19–32
  mandate for, 185–200
  modern. *See* Sun Sign Astrology
  mundane, 217
  origins of, 19–21, 37, 88
  See also Biblical Astrology; Talmudic Astrology
Autumnal Equinox, 207*t*
  coincident with Descendant, 119
  hour of beginning, 204, 207*t*
  zero⁰ Libra, 25, 120*t*

269

BOOKS OF RELATED INTEREST

KABBALAH AND THE POWER OF DREAMING
Awakening the Visionary Life
by Catherine Shainberg

KABBALISTIC HEALING
A Path to an Awakened Soul
by Jason Shulman

KABBALISTIC TAROT
Hebraic Wisdom in the Major and Minor Arcana
by Dovid Krafchow

THE KABBALAH OF THE SOUL
The Transformative Psychology and Practices of Jewish Mysticism
by Leonora Leet, Ph.D.

THE SECRET DOCTRINE OF THE KABBALAH
Recovering the Key to Hebraic Sacred Science
by Leonora Leet, Ph.D.

THE ARABIC PARTS IN ASTROLOGY
A Lost Key to Prediction
by Robert Zoller

HOW TO PRACTICE VEDIC ASTROLOGY
*A Beginner's Guide to Casting Your Horoscope
and Predicting Your Future*
by Andrew Bloomfield

TAOIST ASTROLOGY
A Handbook of the Authentic Chinese Tradition
by Susan Levitt with Jean Tang

Inner Traditions • Bear & Company
P.O. Box 388
Rochester, VT 05767
1-800-246-8648
www.InnerTraditions.com

Or contact your local bookseller